WILLIAM OF MALMESBURY

MIRACLES OF THE BLESSED VIRGIN MARY

Boydell Medieval Texts

Boydell Medieval Texts is a new series of parallel text volumes (Latin/English) presenting major medieval works, which aims to meet both the requirement of scholarly editions to the highest standard and the need for readily available translations at an affordable price for libraries and students who need access to the content of the works.

The series volumes will be issued initially in hardback, followed by distribution in electronic form to a variety of platforms such as JSTOR. A year after publication, a paperback version of the translation only will be produced, with appropriately revised introduction and footnotes.

The editors of the series are Rodney Thomson and Michael Bennett, both Emeritus Professors of Medieval History at the University of Tasmania, and Dr Julie Barrau, Lecturer in Medieval British History at Cambridge University, and Fellow of Emmanuel College.

WILLIAM OF MALMESBURY

MIRACLES OF
THE BLESSED VIRGIN MARY

Edited and Translated by R. M. Thomson
and M. Winterbottom

THE BOYDELL PRESS

First published 2015
The Boydell Press, Woodbridge
Paperback edition 2017

ISBN 978 1 78327 016 3 hardback
ISBN 978 1 78327 196 2 paperback

The Boydell Press is an imprint of Boydell & Brewer Ltd
PO Box 9, Woodbridge, Suffolk IP12 3DF, UK
and of Boydell & Brewer Inc.
668 Mt Hope Avenue, Rochester, NY 14620–2731, USA
website: www.boydellandbrewer.com

A CIP catalogue record for this book is available
from the British Library

The publisher has no responsibility for the continued existence or accuracy
of URLs for external or third-party internet websites referred to in this book,
and does not guarantee that any content on such websites is,
or will remain, accurate or appropriate

Contents

Preface and Acknowledgements

In 1985 MW and RMT began collaborating on the Oxford Medieval Texts edition and translation of William of Malmesbury's *Gesta Regum Anglorum*, projected long before by Sir Richard Southern and Sir Roger Mynors. We had no plans, at the time, to do more than that, but in the event we have since then together produced editions and translations of all of William's historical, hagiographical and scriptural works (except for his *Historia Novella*, edited and translated with exemplary skill by Edmund King and K. R. Potter). This is the last, and with it we sign off, not without regret, on thirty years of collaboration, although our friendship continues. We believe that over the period we have come to know and understand William, with a degree of intimacy. That he was an impressive historian and classicist as well as a dedicated monk, though flawed just like us, we have no doubt. We hope that we have done him justice.

At an early stage in the present project we thought of producing a revised version of the Oxford DPhil thesis (1959) of Peter Carter, which consists of text, translation, and abundant introduction and commentary. We cannot speak with sufficient acclaim of Carter's work, which in certain respects ours does not seek to displace. Nonetheless, on closer inspection it seemed that the best course was to revisit the surviving manuscripts, to provide a more literal translation than Carter's, and to supply an introduction and commentary reflecting more than fifty years of scholarship since the completion of his thesis.

MW is entirely responsible for collating the MSS and establishing the text, and for the account of that process given in the Introduction. He is also primarily responsible for the translation. RMT is responsible for the Introduction down to and including the List of MSS, and for the account of the reception of *MBVM* later on. He is also primarily responsible for the notes which accompany the translation, though MW has made a major contribution to them also. Each editor has read and contributed to the work of the other. We hope that the result is an internally consistent whole.

For information on particular points we wish to thank Martin Brett, Roger Powell, Christopher Brooke, Nigel Morgan, Philip Shaw, and Laurel Broughton.

MW is grateful to all the libraries which have supplied reproductions of items in their collections, and in particular to Mohamed Graine (Lyon), Anna Sanders (Balliol College, Oxford), Edward Probert (Salisbury Cathedral) and Peter Thomas (Exeter Cathedral) for help well beyond the call of duty. We especially thank Kati Ihnat for her generosity in providing us with the text of her London DPhil thesis, and for reading drafts of our work and responding with helpful commentary and bibliographical references.

We have much pleasure in recording our debt to our publishers. Richard Barber encouraged the book from the start, and laid the foundation for its general appearance. Chris Reed set his meticulous mark on the format of the book; we owe a great deal to his taste and his eagle eye. It was a pleasure to work with Nick Bingham and Rohais Haughton. We thank them all, and others behind the scenes, most warmly. The errors that remain are not theirs but ours.

RMT
MW

Abbreviations

AASS	*Acta Sanctorum* (1st edn, Antwerp and Brussels, 1643–1894)
AB	*Analecta Bollandiana*
Barré 1953	H. Barré, 'Le "De quattuor uirtutibus Mariae" et son auteur', *Ephemerides Mariologicae* 3 (1953), 231–44
BHL	*Bibliotheca Hagiographia Latina*, ed. Bollandists (2 vols, Brussels, 1898–1901)
BHL Suppl.	*Novum Supplementum*, ed. H. Fros (1986)
BL	London, The British Library
BnF	Paris, Bibliothèque nationale de France
Bodl. Libr.	Oxford, The Bodleian Library
Canal	J. M. Canal, *El Libro De Laudibus et Miraculis Sanctae Mariae de Guillermo de Malmesbury* (Edizioni 'Ephem. Mariol.', Rome, 1968²)
Carter	P. N. Carter, 'An Edition of William of Malmesbury's Treatise on the Miracles of the Virgin', unpublished DPhil Diss., Oxford University, 2 vols (continuously paginated), 1959
Cat. Royal MSS	G. F. Warner and J. P. Gilson, *British Museum: Catalogue of Western Manuscripts in the old Royal and King's Collections* (4 vols, London, 1921)
CCCC	Cambridge, Corpus Christi College
CCCM	*Corpus Christianorum, Continuatio Medievalis*
CCSL	*Corpus Christianorum, Series Latina*

Comm. Lam.	*Willelmi Meldunensis Monachi Liber super Explanationem Lamentationum Ieremiae Prophetae*, ed. M. Winterbottom and R. M. Thomson (CCCM 244, 2011), cited by book and line-number
Cottineau	L. H. Cottineau, *Répertoire topo-bibliographique des abbayes et prieurés* (2 vols, Mâcon, 1935)
CPL	E. Dekkers and A. Gaar, *Clavis Patrum Latinorum* (Turnhout, 1995³)
Crane	T. F. Crane, *Liber de Miraculis Sanctae Dei Genitricis Mariae* (Ithaca, NY, 1925)
CSEL	*Corpus Scriptorum Ecclesiasticorum Latinorum*
Dexter	E. F. Dexter, *Miracula Sanctae Virginis Mariae* (Univ. of Wisconsin Studies in the Social Sciences and History, vol. 12, 1927)
Dominic	Dominic of Evesham, *De Miraculis Sanctae Mariae*, ed. J. M. Canal (Studium Legionense no. 39, León, 1998)
Early Lives	*Early Lives of St Dunstan*, ed. and tr. M. Winterbottom and M. Lapidge (Oxford, 2012)
EHR	*English Historical Review*
GP	William of Malmesbury, *Gesta Pontificum Anglorum*, ed. and trans. M. Winterbottom, commentary by R. M. Thomson (2 vols, Oxford, 2007)
GR	William of Malmesbury, *Gesta Regum Anglorum*, ed. and trans. R. A. B. Mynors, R. M. Thomson and M. Winterbottom, commentary by R. M. Thomson (2 vols, Oxford, 1998–99)
HE	Bede, *Historia Ecclesiastica Gentis Anglorum*, ed. C. H. Plummer, *Venerabilis Baedae Opera Historica* (2 vols, Oxford, 1896), I, pp. 5–360
Heads	D. Knowles, C. N. L. Brooke, and V. C. M. London, *Heads of Religious Houses, England and Wales, 940–1216* (Cambridge, 2001²)
Hesbert	R.-J. Hesbert, *Corpus Antiphonalium Officii* (6 vols, Rome, 1963–79)

HM-TS	The collection of miracles of the Virgin described below, p. xvii and n. 16
HN	William of Malmesbury, *Historia nouella*, ed. and trans. E. King and K. R. Potter (Oxford, 1998)
Ihnat, *Mary and the Jews*	K. Ihnat, 'Mary and the Jews in Anglo-Norman Monastic Culture', unpubl. PhD Diss., University of London, 2011
Jennings, 'Origins'	J. C. Jennings, 'The origins of the "Elements Series" of the Miracles of the Virgin', *Mediaeval and Renaissance Studies* 6 (1968), 84–93
Jennings, 'Writings'	J. C. Jennings, 'The writings of Prior Dominic of Evesham', *EHR* 77 (1962), 298–304
Knowles, *Monastic Order*	D. Knowles, *The Monastic Order in England* (Cambridge, 1963²)
MB	The collection of miracles of the Virgin described below at p. xviii n. 17
MBVM	William of Malmesbury, *De miraculis beatae uirginis Mariae*
Memorials of St Anselm	*Memorials of St Anselm*, ed. F. S. Schmitt and R. W. Southern (Oxford, 1969)
MGH	*Monumenta Germaniae Historica*
Mussafia, 'Studien', I–V	A. Mussafia, 'Studien zu den mittelalterlichen Marienlegenden', *Sitzungsberichte der Kaiserlichen Akademie der Wissenschaften zu Wien (Phil.-Hist. Klasse)* 113 (1886), 917–94; 115 (1888), 5–92; 119 (1889) Abh. ix, 1–66; 123 (1891) Abh. viii, 1–85; 139 (1898) Abh. viii, 1–74
ODML	*Oxford Dictionary of Medieval Latin from British Sources*, ed. R. E. Latham, D. Howlett *et al.* (1975–2013)
Oxford Dictionary of Saints	D. Farmer, *The Oxford Dictionary of Saints* (Oxford, 2004⁵)
PG	*Patrologia Graeca*
PL	*Patrologia Latina*

Polyhist.	William of Malmesbury, *Polyhistor Deflorationum*, ed. H. Testroet Ouelette (Binghamton, NY, 1982)
Poncelet	A. Poncelet, 'Miraculorum B. V. Mariae quae saec. VI–XV latine sunt conscripta index postea perficiendus', *AB* 21 (1902), 241–360
RB	*Revue Bénédictine*
RS	Rolls Series
RTAM	*Recherches de théologie ancienne et médiévale*
Saints' Lives	William of Malmesbury, *Saints' Lives*, ed. and trans. M. Winterbottom and R. M. Thomson (Oxford, 2002)
SAO	*Sancti Anselmi Opera Omnia*, ed. F. S. Schmitt (rev. edn, 6 vols in 2, Stuttgart and Bad Cannstadt, 1968)
Sharpe, *Handlist*	R. W. Sharpe, *A Handlist of the Latin Writers of Great Britain and Ireland before 1540* (Turnhout, 1997)
SK	D. Schaller and E. Könsgen, *Initia Carminum Latinorum Saeculo Undecimo Antiquiorum* (Göttingen, 1977)
Southern, 'The English origins'	R. W. Southern, 'The English origins of the miracles of the Virgin Mary', *Mediaeval and Renaissance Studies* 4 (1958), 176–216
Stubbs, *Memorials*	W. Stubbs, *Memorials of St Dunstan* (RS, 1874)
Thomson, *William of Malmesbury*	R. M. Thomson, *William of Malmesbury* (Woodbridge, 2003²)
VD	William of Malmesbury, *Vita Dunstani*, in *Saints' Lives*, pp. 166–303
VW	William of Malmesbury, *Vita Wulfstani*, in *Saints' Lives*, pp. 8–155
Walther, *Sprichwörter*	H. Walther, *Proverbia Sententiaeque Latinitatis Medii Aeui* (9 vols, Göttingen, 1963–86)

INTRODUCTION

The Making of the Miracula

Ascription and Date

William of Malmesbury's *Miracles of the Blessed Virgin Mary* (*MBVM*) belongs to that group of predominantly hagiographical works written by the Benedictine monk (c.1090–c.1143) late in his life.[1] By now, as he passed his fortieth year, he was professing regret for the time and effort spent on researching and writing his great historical works (prior to the end of 1125), and expressed the intention of composing works more in keeping with his profession as a monk and more conducive to the salvation of his soul.[2] The attribution to him of the work edited below is secure. First of all, there is no doubt that he wrote a work of this kind. It is mentioned admiringly by the Augustinian canon Robert of Cricklade, in his *De connubio Iacob*.[3] This reference also provides a good *terminus ante quem* for its composition. In the same work Robert says that he has just heard of the death of Godfrey abbot of Winchcombe, which occurred on 5 March 1137.[4] At the time Robert was at the abbey of Cirencester (12.5 miles/20 km from Malmesbury), so the *De connubio* was certainly written earlier than 1138/9, by which time he had become prior of St Frideswide, Oxford.[5]

That the work referred to by Robert is the one edited below is proved beyond doubt by two lines of evidence. First of all, it is attributed to William in two places. One is in Salisbury Cathedral MS 97, one of the two surviving copies. The prologue alone is quoted and attributed to him in an anonymous commentary

---

[1] On William's life and works, see Thomson, *William of Malmesbury*, with full bibliography of earlier literature. Relevant subsequent publications include *GP* (including addenda and corrigenda to *GR*, and additional bibliography) and *Comm. Lam.*

[2] Regret and intention are expressed in *Comm. Lam.*, prol. 7–18.

[3] R. W. Hunt, 'English learning in the late twelfth century', in *Essays in Medieval History*, ed. R. W. Southern (London, 1968), pp. 110–24, at 117–18. Robert's work is unprinted.

[4] Hunt, p. 117 n. 3, slightly corrected in *Heads*, p. 79. Hunt does not print Robert's actual words (Bodl. Libr., Laud. misc. 725, f. 152r): 'Ecce ille amator clericorum, honor monachorum, abbatum gloria, quem in praefatiuncula opusculi huius salutaueram, uix prima parte perarata, et secunda ad medium usque perducta, dum uiuum speramus, nuntiatur defunctus.' In other words, Robert had dedicated his work to Abbot Godfrey, when in the course of writing bk. 2 he heard of his death. In the event, the work was dedicated to the Winchcombe monks Laurence, Gervase (abbot from 1156) and Achard.

[5] *Heads*, p. 284.

on the early chapters of John's Gospel, found in a fifteenth-century MS from south-west England.[6] Secondly, William's authorship is supported by the work's elaborate latinity, by the array of sources for its stories, and by the writings used for historical context and embellishment, including material lifted from his own earlier historical and hagiographical works.[7] A *terminus post quem* is provided by William's miracle no. 12, recounting a series of events which took place in 1134, but which probably only became known to him in or after 1135–36. *MBVM*, then, was completed 1136–39, probably by early 1137.

Of course, it is one thing to establish the date by which the work was finished, another to ascertain when it was begun. Philip Shaw[8] has argued that some of the miracle stories must have been at least drafted much earlier than the 1130s, perhaps before 1125. We shall return to this point after a discussion of William's sources.

Inspiration and Purpose

William participated in a new wave of Marian devotion in England[9] which included the compilation of her miracles, but he was not its leader. However, given the imprecision of the dates that can be established for both his and the other collections of *miracula* known to him, it is hard to locate William's exact position in the movement, or indeed to map the development of the movement itself. The new expression of devotion, focusing on the doctrines of the Immaculate Conception and Assumption, though it may have owed something to pre-Conquest tradition, seems to have originated in writings of Anselm of Canterbury and rapidly spread through the Benedictine network in southern England.[10] It was expressed much more overtly in writings of Anselm's disciple Eadmer, of the German monk Honorius Augustodunensis, who spent time at Canterbury and Worcester, of Dominic prior of Evesham, of or commissioned by Anselm abbot of Bury, of Osbert of Clare, prior of Westminster, and of Nicholas,

---

[6] BL Royal 8 F. II, ff. 10–142v. The commentary (beg. 'Carissimi auctores et sanctarum literarum scriptores quilibet libro suo') consists of a series of sermons and extracts, of which those from *MBVM* prol. are attrib. to 'Will. Meldunensis de 4 uirtutibus cardinalibus beate Marie': *Cat. Royal MSS*, I, p. 261. For the circulation of the prol. alone, see below, pp. xliv–xlvii. The commentary also quotes Aquinas, so must be a product of the late thirteenth century or later still.

[7] Stories also told in his earlier works are nos 7 (in *GP* and *VD*), 8 (in *GR*), 23 (in *GP*), 31 (in *GR*), 33 (in *GR*), 45 (in *VD*). In addition, there are hundreds of instances of shorter passages, locutions and quotations shared by *MBVM* and William's other works, signalled in the notes to our translation.

[8] P. Shaw, 'The dating of William of Malmesbury's Miracles of the Virgin', *Leeds Studies in English*, n. s. 37 (2006), 391–405.

[9] For the phenomenon, see now Ihnat, *Mary and the Jews*, ch. 3. French collections dating from as early as the second half of the eleventh century, but not used by William, were all local, not general collections.

[10] The story is outlined by Knowles, *Monastic Order*, pp. 510–14.

monk of St Albans and perhaps abbot of Malmesbury.[11] Other important sponsors of Marian devotion, named in contemporary sources but not themselves writers, were Warin prior of Worcester and Benedict, prior then abbot of Tewkesbury (1125–37).[12] An important landmark in the development of this devotion, for once precisely datable, was the legatine council held at London in 1129, at which the doctrine and feast of the Immaculate Conception were proclaimed.[13]

Sources for the Stories

Of the individuals named above, William seems to have known in person Anselm of Canterbury, Eadmer, Warin and Dominic; he may also have known Honorius and Anselm of Bury.[14] This network of contacts presumably influenced him in his own devotion to Mary and his promotion of her cult. By the time he wrote *MBVM* he was able to make use of several pre-existing collections and other relevant writings by some of these same people. None of these writings could have been much more than a decade old by the time *MBVM* was finished. Eadmer of Canterbury wrote his *De conceptione sanctae Mariae* c.1125, the *De excellentia Virginis Mariae* earlier. Dominic of Evesham's *Miracula beatae Virginis Mariae*[15] is not closely datable, but was apparently influenced by the HM-TS collection, probably written or at least commissioned by Anselm, abbot of Bury 1121–48.[16] The English career of Honorius Augustodunensis, whose *Sigillum S. Mariae* and probably *Speculum Ecclesiae* were known to William, is now dated to the first two

---

[11] For Eadmer, Honorius, Dominic and Anselm, see below, pp. xvii–xviii, 97 n. 1. Osbert: J. A. Robinson in *The Letters of Osbert of Clare*, ed. E. W. Williamson (Oxford, 1929), pp. 11–14. Nicholas of St Albans: Knowles, *Monastic Order,* pp. 513–14; C. H. Talbot, 'Nicholas of St Albans and Saint Bernard', *RB* 64 (1954), 83–117; R. M. Thomson, *Manuscripts from St Albans Abbey 1066–1235* (2 vols, Woodbridge, 1985²), I, pp. 66–7. He may have been the same man who was abbot of Malmesbury 1183–87 (*Heads*, pp. 55–6).

[12] Their devotion is mentioned in *The Chronicle of John of Worcester*, ed. and trans. R. R. Darlington, P. McGurk and J. Bray (Oxford, 1995-), III, pp. 223–7.

[13] Ibid., pp. 186–9.

[14] Thomson, *William of Malmesbury*, pp. 5, 46–7, 72–3, 207–8; *VW* (*Saints' Lives*, pp. 8–11) was dedicated to Warin; cf. *GP* II, p. 15, for evidence that William may have recorded words of Anselm that he had heard directly.

[15] Ed. Canal, without reference to the earlier unprinted edition of J. C. Jennings, *Prior Dominic of Evesham and the Survival of English Tradition after the Conquest*, B. Litt. thesis, Oxford University 1958.

[16] This collection consists of a stable core of seventeen stories (HM), to which another seventeen additions were made, probably over time and by the original compiler (called in toto TS). The clearest exposition of this is Southern, 'English Origins', pp. 183–8, who also advanced plausible reasons for its compilation or commissioning by Anselm of Bury (ibid., pp. 198–200). Slight modifications to Southern's account were made by Carter, pp. 37–42, and Ihnat, *Mary and the Jews*, pp. 120–2. See also below, Appendix A. However, little has changed since Southern wrote (p. 187 n., after listing the HM-TS MSS known to him) 'I have been dependent on descriptions in which many details are left unclear, and almost all these manuscripts have puzzling features which I cannot pretend fully to understand. A more exact analysis of the manuscripts is badly needed ...'.

decades of the century. Another of William's sources, Carter's MB Collection, six stories in rhythmic Latin, is found in at least eight MSS, the earliest from the first half of the twelfth century; it cannot be associated with any particular person or locality.[17] The sum of the evidence, such at it is, suggests that the impulse to compile miracles of the Virgin began in the 1120s. *MBVM* marks the culmination of this first creative impulse, before its spread to the Continent and incorporation in much larger collections, from the late twelfth century onward.

If we consider these writers and promoters together, it seems significant that they were all Benedictine monks, most of them senior officeholders (abbots, priors, precentors), and that all the writers of *miracula* were involved in other hagiographical works, mainly of their local saints. Dominic wrote the Life and Miracles of abbots of Evesham, Ecgwine, Odulf and perhaps Wigstan, Eadmer of Archbishops Oda, Dunstan and Brecgwine.[18] Anselm of Bury probably commissioned a Life and Miracles of St Edmund.[19] William wrote, on commission, Lives of Wulfstan of Worcester, and of a series of Glastonbury saints (including Dunstan again), as well as of the patron of his own abbey, St Aldhelm.[20] In addition, his *Gesta Pontificum* includes Lives, extracted or digested, of most of the saints of England down to his own time.

It is possible that William found some of his sources already combined in the same manuscript. Oxford, Balliol Coll. 240 (English, s. xii ex.), contains, apart from a reworked version of *MBVM* itself, a selection of its sources: Dominic of Evesham, HM 15–16, TS 1–2, and Fulbert's sermon 4 on the Nativity *Approbatae consuetudinis*, used by William in *MBVM*'s Prologue and elsewhere. Even more interesting is BL Cotton Cleo. C. X (Glastonbury, s. xii med.), containing (as Book One) Dominic miracles 1–6, (as Book Two) HM 1–17 (i.e. the complete series), and (as Book Three) TS 1, 5–17 (a large part of that dossier), breaking off in the middle of the second of two independent miracles. The second manuscript in particular is just the kind of compilation that would have been of great convenience to William in writing *MBVM*; indeed, he might himself have originally assembled it.[21]

---

[17] Carter, pp. 44–5. The MSS known to him were CCCC 42, Chicago Univ. Libr. 147, BL Arundel 346 and Egerton 2947, Bodl. Libr. Laud. misc. 359 (a prose adaptation of four stories), and BnF lat. 2672, 13336, and 14463. Of these, CCCC 42 (see below, n. 21), which contains all of the stories preceded by a brief prologue, seems to be the most authentic witness. See also below, Appendix A.

[18] Sharpe, *Handlist*, pp. 104–5.

[19] *Letters of Osbert of Clare*, pp. 26–32; R. M. Thomson, 'Two versions of a saint's Life from St. Edmund's Abbey', *RB* 84 (1974), 383–408, at pp. 392–3.

[20] *VW*, *VD*, and, for Aldhelm, the fifth book of *GP*.

[21] Another example is CCCC 42 (s. xii, from Dover Priory), containing a collection of *miracula* drawn from Dominic, HM, TS and MB, mixed up together.

Other Sources

William reworked a few stories supplied in toto by other earlier writers: the ninth-century *Visio Wettini* (very little known in medieval England), the poem *Spiris locus est famosus*, and Cassiodorus' *Historia tripartita*. He mined many other sources to supply historical background (Jerome, Ferrandus, Bede, Paul the Deacon, Hugh of Fleury, a collection of decretals, Gregory's letters, Isidore), theological doctrine (Ambrose, Paschasius, ?Alcuin, Ildefonsus, Anselm, Fulbert of Chartres, Eadmer), or stylistic adornment (Lucan, Virgil, Ovid, Juvenal, Persius, Cicero, Horace, Seneca, Statius, Claudian, Sedulius, Sidonius, Ausonius, Hildebert). We draw particular attention to the remarkable use of Ausonius' *Ephemeris* 3, a passage from which was expanded by William and interlarded with his own prose, to supply part of the extended prayer that makes up *MBVM*'s Epilogue. William recalls short passages and recycles longer ones from some of his own historical and hagiographical works (*GR, GP, VD*).[22] A certain amount of information seems to have come to him by word of mouth, for instance the stories, or parts of stories, concerning foreign places: Clermont, Pavia, Fraga, and Constantinople.[23]

At this point we return to the question of when William actually began compiling the stories that went into the making of *MBVM*. The evidence for an early date, advanced by Philip Shaw, consists of the cases in which it can be shown that William used the sources already mined by Dominic of Evesham in particular.[24] These cases are undeniable; however, in every instance William seems to have used both Dominic's sources and Dominic himself. Prima facie then, it cannot be determined whether William used Dominic's source in the first instance, then Dominic himself at a later date, or Dominic in the first instance, having later recourse to Dominic's source when he became aware of or managed to locate it. To us, a procedure of recycling Dominic, then expanding the resulting account from Dominic's more detailed source, would seem more likely than one in which the thinner Dominic was grafted on to a fuller account which William already knew. The same is true of the two or three miracles for which William used both HM-TS and its sources. Such a procedure – adding details from an earlier source to a more recent one – would be entirely characteristic of William, who thought highly of ancient texts in general and liked to refer to them if he could.[25] But let us admit that we do not know how long he was engaged in the compilation of *MBVM*. Some individual stories may have been known to, and

[22] See above, n. 7, and the footnotes accompanying the translation below.
[23] 6, 11, 11a–b, 12, 51.
[24] *MBVM* 1–2, 19, 33, 40, used Dominic and his sources, 3, 31 and perhaps 41 HM and its sources.
[25] Thomson, *William of Malmesbury*, pp. 16–24.

copied by him early on; on the other hand, features of the complete work suggest that it was hastily planned and written, and perhaps never finished, in the sense of given a final polish.[26]

Characteristics

Historical content

It is important to stress, first, that despite the impression that might have been created by our earlier discussion, *MBVM* is no mere scissors-and-paste compilation. Although most of its stories depend upon an earlier written version, there are very few instances in which William merely reproduced that source with little alteration. In nearly all cases there are substantial differences, not just of language but of information. Sometimes this was because William was stitching together more than one pre-existing written account, at others it was because he was filling out the earlier account using his own imagination, or correcting it in the light of other information. Very commonly William, always the historian, supplied historical background and context from non-hagiographical writings, in order to place a particular story in time and space. Not all of this was successful, and the *MBVM* is littered with (mostly understandable but sometimes careless) factual errors. On the other hand, William was sometimes bored by, or apologetic about the stories found in his sources, and provided only bald summaries of them. In such cases his own versions were discarded by later compilers because William had added nothing to the alternatives except difficult language.

Internationalism

Earlier and contemporary collections of Marian miracles made on the Continent were invariably associated with a particular place; all of the English ones were independent of the Continental ones, and quite different in being cosmopolitan, none more so than William's.[27] This is perhaps because the original impulse to compile them began with a well-travelled foreigner, the Italian Anselm of Bury. If the HM-TS collection was commissioned or written by Anselm, then it is significant that none of its stories concerns Bury. Only one of Dominic's stories is situated at Evesham. Like Dominic,[28] William promoted the hagiography of his own monastery. As mentioned above, much of the fifth book of his *Gesta*

---

[26] See the discussion below, pp. xxx–lv. Shaw (pp. 398–9) argues that some wording in 8 suggests that it was written earlier than the version of the same story in GR. We do not find the argument convincing, but in any case an obvious error in the GR version was later corrected in the B redaction of the same work; it is avoided altogether in the *MBVM* version (see below, p. 36 n. 3).

[27] The difference is stated, trenchantly, by Southern, 'The English Origins', p. 178.

[28] Sharpe, *Handlist*, pp. 99–100, lists Dominic's writings, omitting Canal's edition of his *De miraculis*.

pontificum was a history of Malmesbury abbey, encapsulating a Life and Miracles of Aldhelm; most of the miracles recounted in it occurred locally. In *MBVM*, however, the Virgin performs no miracles at Malmesbury (despite the dedication to her of its great church), let alone any connected with William. Most of the *MBVM* miracles, in fact, did not even occur in England. The following table will make the point clear:

LOCATIONS OF MIRACLES IN *MBVM*

England	14
Bury	38
Canterbury	7, 13
Eynsham	23
Glastonbury	45
France/Normandy	15
Burgundy	24
Chartres	8–9, 25–6
Clermont	6, 31
Cluny	19–20
Mont St Michel	44, 49
Toulouse	5
Germany	18
Cologne	17
Italy	
Chiusa	21
Pavia	11, 11a–c, 22
Pisa	27, 33–4
Rome	31
Spain	
Fraga	12
Toledo	3–4
Eastern and Southern Mediterranean	
Adana	1
Alexandria	40
Constantinople	32, 51–3
Jerusalem	40, 50
Kayseri	2

Some of the internationalism of the *MBVM* stories was already present in William's sources, but his own additions considerably strengthened this characteristic.

He was, after all, keenly interested in the history and current affairs of places outside England, particularly in Germany, Italy and the eastern Mediterranean, though the information available to him was limited and often inaccurate. Book 4 of *GR* is in large part a major diversion from his main theme: a history of the first Crusade, with references to the topography of Rome, Constantinople and Jerusalem. What these places possessed by way of saints' shrines, dedications and relics was a particular focus of his attention.

William and Mary

William's explicit promotion of Mary's cult is contained in the *MBVM*'s long Prologue, his personal devotion to her in the Epilogue. The Prologue contains a strong statement of Mary's role in God's plan of incarnation and salvation, founded upon passages in the writings of Anselm and Eadmer in particular. It also includes a moment of ambivalence, typical of William, in which he acknowledges his disquiet at the absence of patristic authority for this elevation, and especially for the doctrine of Mary's Assumption. He proceeds to argue for this, nonetheless, on the basis of (Anselmian) dialectic. The Epilogue is a long and moving personal prayer in which William acknowledges his sinfulness and pleads for the Virgin's mercy and protection. And yet, *MBVM* contains stories that have nothing to do with Mary and are present for reasons that can at best be described as tangential.[29] This is particularly true of those miracles dealing with Jews.

William and the Jews

The prominent place occupied by the Jews can scarcely be overlooked. Jews appear in, or are the subject of, Miracles 1, 3–5, 32–3, and 51. While a few negative remarks about individual Jews or the Jewish community may be found in William's earlier works,[30] it is in his Commentary on Lamentations and *MBVM* that he gives full vent to what can only be described as violent anti-Semitism. He cannot forgive the Jews' original and continuing rejection of Christ, but also credits them with a variety of unpleasant racial characteristics.[31] In the Commentary on Lamentations William says that he had been reliably informed that when a Saracen wished to express complete contempt for some individual, he would exclaim 'He is a (real) Jew!'[32]

---

[29] 4–5, 11a–b, 34–5, 40 (where the brief mention of Mary is marginal to the main action).
[30] *GR* 135. 4, 170. 6, 286. 2, 317; *GP* 55. 3β2, 276. 3.
[31] E.g. *Comm. Lam.* I, 79–81, 477–9, 697–9, III, 2140–73, IV, 181–206, 304–21, 511–25, 648–52.
[32] *Comm. Lam.* I, 2623–6.

Manuscripts

Complete copies

Salisbury, Cathedral Library, 97 (S).

S. XIII in. Modern binding, no endleaves. 117 leaves, 290 × 215 (written space 210 × 160) mm, written in early Gothic bookhand by a single scribe in 2 cols of 42 lines. Written above top line. Quired in 8s.

CONTENTS

1. Alexander Neckam *et al.*, *Sermones de tempore.*[33] ff. 1–40; 40v blank.
   As forty-seven numbered chapters. Alexander Neckam (103), 1, Geoffrey Babio 34–5, Neckam 3, Babio 2–3, 6, Neckam 11, 14, Babio 4, 8, Garnier de Langres 5 (*PL* 205. 599–608), Neckam (104), 22, Babio 11–13, 'Os quod est hostium corporis debet esse apertum ad confessionem', Ps.-Augustine, *Serm.* 393, Babio 59, 62, 15, 5, 22, Neckam 24, 30, Babio 25, 'Clementissimus omnipotens Deus pietate et misericordia semper largissimus', Augustine, *Serm.* 105, Haimo of Halberstadt, *Hom.* 92 (*PL* 118. 530–4), '*Ascendit Dominus super nubem*. Vt ait apostolus Sapientiam loquimur inter perfectos', Babio 31–2, '*Veni Sancte Spiritus*. Vtinam calculo igneo sumpto de altari labia mea mundarentur', 33, Neckam 41, Babio 48–9, 'Hodie f. k. natiuitatem beati Iohannis celebramus qui Christum prophetauit', Peter Comestor 97, Guilelmus de Merula 164, 'Quomodo poterunt labia tam uanis tam pudendis tam nociuis tociens polluta sermonem explicare', Neckam 32, Babio 28, '*Puluis sum ego*. Erubesco inquam quia nostra conuersatio in celis est', 'Maria comparatur mirre et hoc mirabiliter dicitur'.
2. Geoffrey Babio *et al.*, *Sermones*. ff. 41–73v.
   Forty-two pieces, numbered as far as 40. 'Diligenter adtenditis f. k. ad omnes sacerdotes Domini', Babio 9, 14, 17–18, '*Magnus Dominus noster.*

---

[33] The sermon-numbers are derived from J. B. Schneyer, *Repertorium der lateinischen Sermones de Mittelalters* (11 vols, Münster in Westfalen, 1969–90), for Neckam corrected and supplemented (the numbers in brackets) by R. W. Hunt, *The Schools and the Cloister: The Life and Writings of Alexander Nequam (1157–1217)*, ed. M. Gibson (Oxford, 1984), pp. 150–3.

Magnus quia loco incomprehensibilis magnitudinis eius', Babio 20, '*Pluuia terram irrorat*. Sit splendor in letitia sit pluuia in dolore', Neckam 39, 37, '*Operamini opus uestrum*. Vt sciretis et intelligeretis quod sit opus uestrum', 40, 31, '*Inclina cor meum in testimonia tua et non in auariciam*. Inclina per humilitatem cor meum ut plus uelim in testimonia tua', 'Est archa saluacionis s. archa Noe', Babio 52–3, 60–1, 36–8, 50–1, 67, 55, 57, 56, '*Super muros tuos Ierusalem constitui custodes*. Ierusalem f. super cuius muros Dominus custodes posuisse per prophetam testatur', 58, 66, 24, Ps.-Augustine, *Serm. 58 fr. er.*, 'Misericordia f. peccatorum sunt remedia', Ps.-Augustine, *De Obedientia et Humilitate* (PL 40. 1221–4), Serlo of Wilton, Commentary on the *Pater noster* (Sharpe, *Handlist*, p. 605), '*Leua oculos tuos et uide*. Verba sunt Abrahe ad Loth filium fratris sui', '*Separauit Moyses in ciuitates refugii*. Moyses legislator doctor et ductor', '*Descende sede in puluere uirgo*. Recte de Babilonis specie dicitur', 'Anno secundo regni sui uidit Nabugodonosor sompnium … uere Deus uester Deus deorum', '*Herodii domus dux est eorum*. In psalmo cuius hic uersus est pars monet Dauid', '*Vox clamoris a porta*. Verba sunt Sophonie prophete'.

3. Ambrosius Autpertus, *De conflictu uitiorum et uirtutum*. ff. 74–8.

4. Anon. *De contemptu mundi*. ff. 78v–85v.

   Beg. 'Si predicator uult inuitare auditores', apparently the unique copy. The first thirteen chapters each deal with a particular vice then virtue. Followed by sermons continuing the numbering from 14. '*Clama ne cesses*. Hec est admonitio Ysaye ad ecclesiastes', 'Dominus dicit in euangelio Omnem decimationem uestram distribuite pro propheta', 'Sicut a stella differt stella in claritate sic sacerdos differt a sacerdote in sua conuersacione', '*Letatus sum in hiis que dicta sunt mihi*. Domus est Ierusalem', '*Descendi in ortum*. In campo diuini eloquii tres descensus legimus', '*Sapientia edificauit sibi domum*. Audite f. quid per os Salomonis Spiritus Sanctus pronunciat'. ff. 85v–89v.

5. 'Versus continentes miracula S. Marie'. ff. 89v–90; 90v blank.

   A series of distichs each summarising a miracle story as found in B (Oxford, Balliol College, 240; see below, pp. xxviii–xxix) and in the same order: 'Virgo Dei ueri natum peperit; inspice mirum. / Huius eo maius; nescio scire uirum. / Virgo Byturice puerum seruauit Hebreum / Ne patris irati flamma uoraret eum'.

6. *MBVM*. ff. 91–114v.

7. Anon. sermons and notes. ff. 114v–117v.

   Note on the Saviour's parentage, beg. 'Sancta Maria, mater Domini', ending with the commonly found verses 'Nupta fuit Ioachim mater prius

Anna Marie' ff. 114v–115. Anon. sermon on the Holy Cross 'Conuenite populi nacionum ad stupendum diuine uirtutis spectaculum' ff. 115–17. Another of the same, 'Audistis quomodo per crucis mysterium mors uitatur … redimens a morte maligna' f. 117rv.

The contents of this book reflect a late twelfth-century English milieu. While it could have been made at Salisbury Cathedral, it is more likely to have come from elsewhere, a high probability being a nearby house of Augustinian canons.

(H. M. Thompson in) S. M. Lakin, *Catalogue of the Manuscripts and Books in the Cathedral Library of Salisbury* (London, 1880), p. 20; H. Schenkl, *Bibliotheca Patrum Latinorum Britannica* (3 vols in 10 separately paginated parts, Vienna, 1891–1907), 3/1. 24–5; Mussafia, 'Studien', IV, pp. 18–30; Carter, pp. 17–31, 72; Canal, pp. 36–40. None of these provides a complete or accurate account of the contents.

BnF, lat. 2769, ff. 55–84v (P).

S. XIII in., in the lower margin of f. 55 the fourteenth- and fifteenth-century shelfmarks of the Benedictine abbey of Saint-Denis, Paris. The fact that it lacks the thirteenth-century abbey shelfmark may mean that it was acquired after that date. The whole MS consists of seven fragments of different dates and provenances, brought together apparently by Pierre Pithou between 1567 and his death in 1596, certainly by the time of Colbert's binding (before 1683). 220 × 145mm, heavily retrimmed; written in early gothic bookhand by a single scribe in 30 long lines; red or blue initials. Originally six quires of 8, of which the first two are intact, the third and sixth lost, the fourth and fifth bound in reverse order, the outermost bifolium of the original fourth quire lost.

BMVM alone, ending impf.
Bibliothèque nationale, Catalogue général des manuscrits latins 2 (Paris, 1952), pp. 63–5 (attributing *MBVM* to Eadmer); Carter, pp. 32–6; Canal, pp. 40–2; D. Nebbiai-Dalla Guarda, *La Bibliothèque de l'abbaye de Saint-Denis en France du IXe au XVIIIe siècle* (Paris, 1985), pp. 88, 106, 132, 212.[34]

---

[34] The account of the MS in this study is thoroughly confused. At p. 88 (not indexed) we learn that ff. 55–84v have the fourteenth-century St Denis library shelfmark. At p. 132 the various fragments of the MS are said to have been acquired by Pierre Pithou, separately and unbound, the first one at Basel in 1563 (inscription on f. 1). ff. 55–84v, described as ninth-century and containing Eadmer's *Miracula Marie* (!) are said, without supporting evidence, to have been acquired by Pithou in 1567, apparently also in Basel. It is implied that it was he who bound the fragments together. At p. 212, ff. 55–84v are dated to the twelfth century, and the whole book is said to have been acquired, already bound, by Pithou at Basel in 1563.

Prologue only

Brussels, Bibliothèque royale, 1927–44 (Br).

S. XV (1460), from the Augustinian house of Corsendonk. Patristica &c.

J. Van den Gheyn, *Catalogue des manuscrits de la Bibliothèque royale de Belgie*, vol. 2 (Brussels, 1902), pp. 198–200 (no. 1187); Canal, p. 34.

Cambridge, Trinity College, B. 11. 16 (255)

S. XIV–XV, English. 'Lecciones proprie in commemoracionibus beate Marie per totum annum pro illis septimanis in quibus plenum seruicium semel fit de eadem in ecclesia Exoniensi iuxta ordinale episcopi Iohannis de Grandissono'; Gerald of Wales, *Vita Ethelberti*; miracles of Thomas Cantelupe of Hereford.

M. R. James, *The Western Manuscripts in the Library of Trinity College, Cambridge: A Descriptive Catalogue* (4 vols, Cambridge, 1900–04), I, pp. 357–8; J. N. Dalton, *Ordinale Exoniense* 2 (Henry Bradshaw Soc. 38: 1909), pp. 506–8; Canal, p. 34.

Exeter, Cathedral Library, 3504, 3505 (E_2, E_1).

S. XIV med. Lectionary of Bishop John Grandisson for Exeter Cathedral, presented by him on 25 Mar. 1366.

J. N. Dalton, *Ordinale Exoniense* 3 (Henry Bradshaw Soc. 63: 1926), pp. 1–8; Canal, p. 33; N. R. Ker, *Medieval Manuscripts in British Libraries* (6 vols, Oxford, 1969–2002), II, pp. 809–10.

Lyon, Bibliothèque municipale, 622 (Ly).

S. XIV, from the cathedral of St Sernin, Toulouse.

Catalogue général des manuscrits des bibliothèques publiques de France, 30 (Paris, 1900), pp. 166–7; Canal, p. 34.

Marseille, Bibliothèque municipale, 230.

S. XIV, from the Carthusians of Marseille.

Catalogue général des manuscrits des bibliothèques publiques de France, 25 (Paris, 1892), pp. 87–8; Canal, p. 34.

Miracles

Aberdeen, University Library, 137.

S. XIII, English, at St Paul's London by s. xv². Gregory, *Homiliae in Evangelia*, a collection of miracles of the Virgin, Fulbert, *Serm.* 'Approbate consuetudinis'.

M. R. James, *A Catalogue of the Medieval Manuscripts in the University Library Aberdeen* (Cambridge, 1932), pp. 40–6; Carter, p. 73; Canal, p. 36.

Cambridge, Sidney Sussex College, 95 (Z).

S. XV, from the Cistercian house of Wardon (co. Beds.). An enormous collection of miracles of the Virgin Mary, 499 stories in 5 books.

M. R. James, *A Descriptive Catalogue of the Manuscripts in the Library of Sidney Sussex College, Cambridge* (Cambridge, 1895), pp. 76–109; Carter, p. 66; Canal, p. 35.

Cambridge, University Library, Mm. 6. 15 (C).

S. XIV, English. Several booklets or fragments, containing works of pastoral theology (confession, penance, virtues and vices, &c.), bound together at an unknown date.

H. R. Luard *et al.*, *A Catalogue of the Manuscripts preserved in the Library of the University of Cambridge* (Cambridge, 6 vols, 1856–67), IV, pp. 388–92; Mussafia, 'Studien', II, pp. 19–33, IV, pp. 18–28; Carter, pp. 77–8; Canal, p. 35 (as MS 2474).

Dublin, Trinity College, B. 1. 10 (167) (D).

S. XIV–XV, from the Cistercian abbey of Fountains (co. Yorks.). An enormous collection of miracles of the Virgin Mary, 485 stories in 5 books.

Carter, p. 66; M. Colker, *Descriptive Catalogue of the Mediaeval and Renaissance Manuscripts in the Library of Trinity College Dublin* (2 vols, Aldershot, 1991), I, pp. 284–304; Canal, p. 35.

London, British Library, Add. 57533 (formerly owned by Francis Wormald).

S. XII ex., from Burton Abbey. A collection of miracles of the Virgin Mary.

Catalogue of Additions to the Manuscripts, n.s. 1971–75, part 1 (The British Library, 2001), pp. 107–8; Carter, p. 71.

London, British Library, Royal 5 A. VIII (Ra).

S. XIII, from the abbey of Bury St Edmunds. Patristic and medieval theology, twenty-nine miracles of the Virgin Mary.

Cat. Royal MSS, I, p. 97; Carter, p. 76; R. M. Thomson, 'The Library and Archives of Bury St Edmunds Abbey', unpublished PhD diss., University of Sydney (2 vols, 1973), II, pp. 214–15.

London, British Library, Royal 6 B. X, ff. 1–41v (part 1) (Rc).

S. XIII. The complete MS consists of five originally separate books or fragments, from the abbey of Bury St Edmunds. Part 1 contains works on the life and miracles of the Virgin Mary.

Mussafia, 'Studien', IV, pp. 10–11; H. L. D. Ward and J. A. Herbert, Catalogue of Romances in the Department of MSS in the British Museum (3 vols, London, 1883-), II, pp. 642–5; Cat. Royal MSS, I, pp. 137–9; Carter, p. 67; Thomson, 'The Library and Archives of Bury St Edmunds Abbey', II, pp. 215–17.

London, British Library, Royal 6 B. XIV (Rb).

c.1200, from Battle Abbey. Pseudo-Clementine Recognitions, twenty-eight miracles of the Virgin Mary.

Ward, Cat. of Romances, II, pp. 637–42; Cat. Royal MSS, I, p. 142; Carter, p. 77.

London, Lambeth Palace Library, 51 (L).

c.1200. Peter of Cornwall, Liber reuelationum, from the Augustinian Priory of Holy Trinity, Aldgate, London.

M. R. James, A Descriptive Catalogue of the Manuscripts in the Library of Lambeth Palace (Cambridge, 1932), pp. 71–85; Carter, p. 61.

Oxford, All Souls College, 22.

S. XVI med., English, probably Oxford. A collection of eighty-nine miracles of the Virgin.

A. G. Watson, A Descriptive Catalogue of the Medieval Manuscripts of All Souls College Oxford (Oxford, 1997), pp. 46–8.

Oxford, Balliol College, 240, ff. 137–89 (part III) (B).

S. XII^2. The complete MS consists of four originally independent parts, bound together at an unknown date in or after s. xiv, the date of part 4. I Chronicles,

Ecclesiastes, Songs, glossed. II anon. homilies. III Miracles of the Virgin, followed by sermons and excerpts. IV Acts, glossed. Parts I, III–IV, and probably part II, from the alien priory of Monks Kirby (co. Warwick). Given to Balliol College by Richard Bole, archdeacon of Ely (d.1477).

Mussafia, 'Studien', II, pp. 19–37; R. A. B. Mynors, *Catalogue of the Manuscripts of Balliol College Oxford* (Oxford, 1963), pp. 260–3; Carter, pp. 70–1; Canal, pp. 35–6.

Oxford, Corpus Christi College 42, ff. 1–31 (part I).

S. XIV in., from the Augustinian priory of Lanthony, Gloucester. Four physically distinct books, I perhaps independent for a time, the rest together early if not from the beginning. A collection of 115 miracles of the Virgin ('Compilatio de libello qui dicitur Mariale et de miraculis beate Virginis'). The other parts contain *Barlaam et Josaphat*; Isidore, *De ortu et obitu patrum*, the Latin Aesop and stories about the eucharist.

Carter, p. 64; R. M. Thomson, *A Descriptive Catalogue of the Medieval Manuscripts of Corpus Christi College Oxford* (Cambridge, 2011), pp. 22–3.

BnF, lat. 3177 (Pr).

S. XII ex. A collection of miracles of the Virgin Mary, in two parts, from the Cistercian abbey of Beaupré (dioc. Beauvais).

Bibliothèque nationale: Catalogue général des manuscrits latins 4 (Paris, 1958), pp. 292–7; Carter, p. 68.

BnF, lat. 14463 (Pv).

S. XII, from the Augustinian house of Saint-Victor, Paris. A collection of miracles of the Virgin, originally put together at the abbey of Capelle (Pas-de-Calais).

Mussafia, 'Studien', I, pp. 953–9; E. F. Wilson, *The Stella Maris of John of Garland* (Cambridge, MA, 1946), *passim* but esp. pp. 12–16; Carter, p. 67.

Toulouse, Bibliothèque municipale, 482.

S. XII², French, later owned by the Jesuits of Toulouse. A collection of miracles of the Virgin in three books, followed by patristic and medieval tracts and sermons on the Assumption &c.; the latest work is Eadmer, *De excellentia uirginis Mariae*.

Catalogue général des manuscrits des bibliothèques publiques de France, 7 (1885), pp. 288–91; Mussafia, 'Studien', II, pp. 19–33; IV, pp. 18–28; Carter, pp. 74–5; Canal, p. 36.

Structure and Transmission

Only two manuscripts contain the *MBVM* as a whole. One, Salisbury Cathedral 97 (S), is complete. The other, BnF lat. 2769 (P), is only partly preserved. And the work has only twice been edited: once in an unpublished Oxford D. Phil. thesis by P. N. Carter (presented in 1959, and examined in the following year), and a second time by J. M. Canal, in two identical editions appearing in 1968 (we cite from the differently paginated second edition, in which, however, the line numbers remain the same as in the first).

The Salisbury MS was brought to the attention of Mariologists in one of a series of remarkable articles by Adolf Mussafia,[35] who analysed its contents in detail. It was left to H. Barré to rediscover the Paris MS.[36] The hard labour of ordering the miracle stories as William intended was done by Carter, building on the perceptions of Mussafia. Canal either did that labour himself without showing his working, or took it over from Carter without acknowledgement.[37] In either case, his ordering of the stories is virtually the same as Carter's. We present our own analysis, which reaches Carter's conclusions by a different route.

---

[35] Mussafia, 'Studien' IV, pp. 18–26.

[36] Barré 1953. Carter, who did not know Barré's work, found it for himself (p. 32).

[37] The story of the relations between the two is told in Canal, p. 43 n. 59 (largely printed on p. 44). Canal had started work on an edition of the *MBVM* at least as early as 1958, but had let it drop. In 1961 he heard from R. W. Hunt that his pupil Peter Carter had presented a thesis on the topic. Hunt suggested a joint edition, an idea that Canal took up only in 1962. He failed to make contact with Carter (who lived till 1983). He wrote that 'la obra del Dr. Carter nos es desconocida', though he could have consulted a copy of it in the Bodleian Library.

The ordering of the stories[38]

We take for granted Carter's demonstration that S reflects a primitive state of the ordering of the miracle stories, P a state revised by William himself.[39] This indeed is the inescapable basis of the discussion that follows, which aims to show that S, besides having suffered (in the dossier from which it was copied) a major dislocation of a block of stories, presents only a fitful and incomplete ordering by hierarchy of status of the persons treated, together with a 'pending file' of stories not yet assigned to their proper places: not to speak of several repeated passages and other flaws. All this was presumably remedied in P. But as P is only preserved in part, we have to try to work out an overall picture from S and from what is left of P. We cannot be sure of all the details, especially towards the end of the book. 'The best we can do' is summarised on pp. xl–xliii.

The Salisbury MS (S)

That the order of stories in S is not as William intended it is made quite clear by the fact that, though what is signalled[40] as the first item (*Theophilus*)[41] does indeed immediately follow the lengthy prologue (**1**), the story no less clearly signalled as the second (*Julian the Apostate*) does not make an appearance until much later in the manuscript (**25**).

What is more, that second story starts with a short paragraph that tells us what William's method of arrangement is to be: 'Et quia iam dicendi primitias libaui, ita in posterum seriem narrationis attexam ut ostendam beatam Virginem omni hominum gradui, omni conditioni, utrique sexui, pietatis suae uiscera effudisse. Apponenturque res temporibus diuersae, locis discretae, generibus promiscuae, quasi flores in sertum reginae caeli contexti.' The Virgin is to be shown as pitying every rank and condition of mankind, men and women alike. The material will differ in time, place and *genus*. The result will be like a garland[42]

---

[38] In this discussion (in which numbers in bold signal the ordering of the stories in S, or, where appropriate, P), readers would be well advised to refer to the Concordance (pp. lx–lxii). The numbering of the stories in S and P is our own. S numbers the stories consecutively with sections of the Prologue, and also has a Contents list (f. 91r); P does not number them at all. References to our own system are given only when subsections need to be specified.

[39] Mussafia had laid the foundations: 'eine Umarbeitung' 'entweder durch [Wilhelm] selbst oder durch einen Anderen' ('Studien' IV, p. 26).

[40] '… quod primum de Theophilo suggerit mens ponere' (1. 1).

[41] The naming of the stories has never been properly standardised (Carter, p. 9). We have normally employed those used in the Oxford *Cantigas de Santa Maria* database (http://csm.mml.ox.ac.uk), though sometimes abbreviating them.

[42] Cf. Gildas 73. 1 (plucking a few flowers from the meadows of the New Testament; cf. Jerome, *Epist.* 122. 4). The idea is extended to poetic collections in Alcuin, but it seems independent of the Greek *anthologia* (*florilegium* is a very late coinage). Generally, see *Oxford Classical Dictionary* (4th edn) *sub* anthologies, Latin.

woven for the Queen of Heaven: the flowers, in the simile, will not all grow in spring, or all be native to one country, or all belong to a single variety.

That 'genus' refers not to the type of story but to the *rank* of those involved becomes clear at once, when William goes on to say: 'De episcopis igitur, quod est summum genus hominum, facturus pollicitum,[43] primum ponam Basilium ...'. 'De episcopis' is a conscious heading, and it will prove to introduce a succession of dignitaries who follow Basil in S. William alludes to his hierarchical order[44] when he starts *Jerome of Pavia* (34): 'Ibis et tu in has paginas, *ampliabisque numerum episcoporum*, Ieronime ...' (11. 1), and he only turns[45] from bishops to lesser mortals in *Devil in three beast-shapes* (35), the tale of a sacristan.[46] Another sacristan consciously follows in 36 ('eiusdem offitii' [16. 1]), before a group of ordinary monks carries us to the end of Book One (at 41).

The section on bishops, however, requires further examination. This will well illustrate both William's impulse to variety and his technique in linking stories. After *Ildefonsus*, archbishop of Toledo (26), follows more on that city (27). 'Iudeorum' is the first word of this new story, and 'Hispanias' the fourth. And though an archbishop will play a part in the story, it is Jews in Spain who are the focus of attention (see the transitional 4. 5). And it will be a Jew who dominates the next tale (*Jews of Toulouse*: 28), this time set in Gascony, though we are at once told that that province borders on Spain; a count, not a bishop, is the leading figure. William has gone off on a tangent that takes him away from his ordering by rank, but it is a tangent that works by association of ideas.

It may not be by chance that when William comes back to bishops in *St Bonitus* (29)[47] he mentions that Clermont was on the old border between Goths and Gauls, as Gascony bordered on Spain. But there is no link between this story and that of Dunstan (30); he is an archbishop, and that is enough to qualify him for entry, though William, by making 'Britannia' the first word and describing the position of the island, shows that he is perfectly aware of the move overseas. We come back to France in *Chartres saved* (31), William here commenting openly on the geographical move: 'Hinc extra Angliam pergat ... oratio' (8. 1). We should not regard this section as a proper part of the series, for its hero is (again) a count, not a bishop; William, while taking the opportunity to tell a tale that does the Virgin credit, is (one presumes), mainly setting the scene for the next story. This

---

[43] His 'promise' is the layout of material sketched in the previous sentence.

[44] Contrast Carter, p. 25.

[45] The turn is not overtly signalled. But a reference back to 1 (34c 'predictum regem Theodericum' [11c. 1]) gives some sense of ring composition.

[46] There is no explicit transition to monks, but 35 begins 'Non parui momenti apud monachos ille estimatur cui thesaurorum aecclesiae cura delegatur' (15. 1), and 'apud monachos' may serve as a heading. There is a third sacristan in 6 (see pp. xxxv–xxxvi).

[47] There is a reference back to Siagrius in 26 (6. 8 ~ 3. 5).

is *Milk: Fulbert* (**32**); the link with what precedes is signalled ('in eadem urbe' [9. 1]), and the hero is, properly, a bishop. The story concerns Mary's milk, and this leads on to the otherwise out of place *Milk: monk with quinsy*, for the monk also benefits from her breast (**33**).[48]

We return to bishops with *Jerome of Pavia* (**34**), already commented on. Pavia links the next tales (**34a–34c**: *Syrus, Augustine, Boethius*); only two of these concern bishops,[49] but the geographical link is emphasised ('ibi [11a. 1] ... ibi [11b. 1] ... ibi et' [11c. 1]).

William now comes (see above, p. xxxii) to the two sacristans (**35–36**), before completing his Book One with a series of other monks. These too have their links. *Monk of Cologne* and *Vision of Wettin* (**37–38**) are signalled as a pair dated to the time of Louis the Pious ('duo miracula ... primum in Colonia, secundum in Alemannia' ~ 'simile huic alterum quod Alemanniae dixi contigisse'). *St Odo and the thief monk* (**39**) retails a vision as did *Vision of Wettin*, and the remarks on Cluny (19. 2) lead on to *Pilgrim of St James* (**40**: 'eiusdem loci' [20. 1]). *Stained corporal* (**41**), set in Italy, will need attention below (p. xxxviii).

To sum up so far: the tale signalled as second (**25**), which contains the *divisio* for the whole book, is followed in S by a series of tales structured overall by a ranking order, first of bishops, then of monks (**26–41**). Where the ranking is neglected, it is because William is happy to follow associations of ideas and places. The few references back work smoothly. There seems no doubt that this all reflects William's intended ordering. This block forms the core of what will prove to be Book I.

✠

We come now to another group. Here again the starting point is clear enough. S, immediately after *Stained corporal*, gives a lengthy Prologue to a second book (**41a**). All that is relevant here is the start (2 pr. 1): 'Recens narrandi in laudibus Dominae assumpsimus exordium, duplici consideratione illecti, ut et admissis interim dictandi feriis meae teneritudinis mederer incommodo et lectorum, si qui erunt, prouiderem fastidio. Sed iam utriusque intuitum leniuit aliquanti temporis spatium. Nam et amor Dominae torpentem in laudes suas suscitat et ego iam pene persuasum habeo quod istius modi scriptum nullum alicui importabit tedium.' William, that is, had paused in his work because of illness and a worry

---

[48] William remarks on the *similitudo* of the stories, and uses it to excuse his diverging from the set order (10. 1): 'Quod nunc hic pre similitudine per anticipationem [i.e. before the section on monks has started] dicam, licet preuaricare personarum ordinem uidear.'

[49] The Virgin is not mentioned in 11a–11b, and in 11c only in the pious addendum on Jerome of Pavia. The intimate connection of **34, 34a, 34b** and **34c** is made quite clear in **34c** by 'Haec omnia eo spectant ut animaduertatur quantam clemens Dei Mater cancellario suo [i.e. Jerome] exhibuit dulcedinem' and what follows (11. 2), looking back to **34**.

that he might be boring his readers. He is now making a fresh start, as his health has improved and he has come to be convinced that no one could find the topic of the Virgin uninteresting. There is no hint as to the content of the succeeding Book.

There follow in S three *pairs* of stories:

1. Two tales about clerks, **42–43**. They are linked by the first words of the second (28. 1 'eiusdem austeritatis suauitatem pro commissis *alter* habuit *clericus*, immanius quam iste scelus ausus').[50]
2. Two tales about priests, **44–45**. The first follows on well from **43**, as it concerns a priest harassed by clerks. The second is linked to the first by its opening words (30. 1 'et *hic* quidem bonae uitae per dominam Mariam tulit pretium; sed *alter* quidam per *eandem* sempiternum euasit exitium'); the hero proves to be someone 'secta scholasticus, gradu[51] sacerdos'.
3. Two tales (**46–47**) linked by the opening words of the first (31. 1), which promise a pair set in the most important Christian cities. They prove to be Rome[52] and Constantinople.[53] The second (**47**) alludes to the pairing (32. 1).

After these pairs, comes a singleton. *Dying rich man* (**48**), introduced by the words 'nec illa putentur friuola quae procedens sermo percurret' (35. 1), which might seem, but do not need, to refer back to some other remark on the importance of a story. It is followed (**48a**) by an assurance that Mary's miracles do not need any brilliance of style in their narrator (*Multa quidem ...*). But then there comes a somewhat mysterious transition (44a. 3): 'Hucusque omnium quasi proemium uirginis Mariae scribitur miraculorum. Exhinc speciale quoddam et a seculis inauditum non faleratis sermonibus, non eloquentiae fuco, sed simplici stilo referre conabimur miraculum, iustis pariter et peccatoribus †per necm†.'[54] All the previous miracles have been as nothing compared with the one to come. This build-up is not answered by anything especially remarkable in the tale that follows, *Mead* (**49**). William seems to share this judgement, for he ends it with the admission that anyone might think this story 'paruum ... et pene *friuolum*' (45. 4), and implies that it is one of the *minima miracula* with which Mary disports herself when she has nothing better to do (the passage will be quoted just below). And the introductory words of **50** (46. 1), 'sunt illa quoque leuia et ad incentiuum amoris eius rigida [*leg.* frigida]', hardly suggest that what had come

---

[50] For *res est amentiae* (**43a** = 11) see below, p. xliii.
[51] Perhaps consciously alluding to the hierarchical order.
[52] In **46** there is a reference back to **29** (31. 6 'in superiori libro' ~ 6. 1).
[53] This story had been recopied to fulfil this new function: see below, p. xxxvi.
[54] Good sense would be given by reading *proficuum* or *profuturum*, though (*per*)*necessarium* is more probable palaeographically.

before was of great import. William says he will run through these *leuia* briefly. They are the next short tales (**50–52**), deprecated in **52a** (*uilis*).

We thus have a group of stories (**49–52**) whose only unity lies in William thinking them unremarkable. And the end of the group is signalled by the ring composition that links the transitional paragraph **52a** (*Talibus dicendis*) to the coda of **49** mentioned above. The words there 'nisi quis *mirandum et laudabile* dixerit quod illa maiestatis sullimitas, per quam totus in suo statu constat orbis, ad haec humiliora famulis suis impertienda se inclinat, ut quasi ludat in minimis quae principatur in maximis' (45. 4) seem to be picked up in **52a** by 'ideo si amatores suos patitur Domini mater mundanorum gaudiorum mutilari dispendio, *non mirandum sed laudandum* omnino pronuntio' (48a. 2). As an introduction to this well-marked group of minor tales nothing could be less appropriate than the grandiose phrasing of **48a**, which William cannot have intended to place here.

52a ends 'Facit ergo [sc. Virgo] cuncta ut uidet animabus expedire', and *denique* (49. 1) at the start of **53**, *Fire at Mont St Michel*, shows that an instance of this not very demanding dictum is meant to follow. William does not underline the point, but the final tales in S, **53–57**, all concern images.[55] The last four relate to one image at Constantinople, whose protection of the city is exemplified in **55** ('denique [52. 1] … quoque [52. 2] … hanc imaginem [52. 3]'); and in **57** William remarks (53. 1) that he should have placed it earlier among the Constantinopolitan stories.[56] Here then is another block.

To sum up Book II, we have three paired stories, with three themes (clerks, priests, cities); then a singleton (*Dying rich man*) preceding a block of unremarkable minor tales; then finally a group of image stories. Only right at the start is there any overt interest in status. But it is true that the book is largely concerned with laymen, some of high status, and some women. There is some linking, but **48a** sticks out like a sore thumb.

✠

We come finally to tales **2–24**.

The second tale in S (**2**), *Guy of Lescar*, concerns a bishop. It is followed by *Ælfsige* (**3**), where an abbot is hero (though a bishop also appears), and by *Guimund and Drogo* (**4**), added, William says (14. 1), because the miracle is similar to that in **3**, 'quanuis diuerso tempore et in diuersa persona factum' (Carter, 21 remarks that they are both seafaring stories). *Stained corporal* (**5**) concerns a monk (in fact a deacon), while **6** concerns a monk (sacristan), though

---

[55] For **55** see also below, p. xxxvi.
[56] Misunderstood, we think, by Carter, p. 29. It should be observed that the story ends on a closural note that is entirely appropriate to its position.

also a prior. Both **5** and **6** are set in northern Italy. Monks are the topic of **7–8**, which are set in England and France respectively.[57]

8 ends 'si de monachis satis diximus, ad alium accedamus gradum', and we now have stories about a clerk of Chartres (**9**), then a canon (**10**) 'of the same church' (26. 1; indeed the one incident is said to have sparked off the other).[58]

Jewish boy follows as **12**, and **13** is signalled as 'conterminum et pene simile' (34. 1) to it as well as being set in the same city. The following tales (**14–17**) are equally about *laymen*; **14** is linked to **13** only by *item* (36. 1), but in **16** 'illud quoque … uulgo tritum' alludes to the start of the preceding **15** (38. 1 ~ 37. 1 'celeberrimae relationis studio … frequentatur').[59]

18 starts 'quoniam uero suffitienter, ut mea fert opinio, in principali sexu facta texuimus miracula, nunc de inferiori dicendum' (40. 1). A group of tales about women accordingly follows (**18–22**). The first, *St Mary of Egypt*, is appropriately the longest. This exotic creature is followed by *Musa*, from Gregory's *Dialogues*, but the next tales show some sign of hierarchy (abbess-nun-laywoman).

Image insulted, concerning the icon of Mary at Blacherna (**23**), at first came next. Later it was recopied as S **55**, where it forms part of the group on images and heads the subgroup on Constantinople. In its original position there was a reference forward to the immediately following story of Theodorus (**24**); in its new one a reference back had to be substituted.[60] What is more, William decided to change the position of the Theodorus story too. As **24**, it had begun 'Huius ciuitatis erat Theodorus', signalling the juxtaposition of two stories concerning Constantinople. In its new position, as **47**, it begins with a sentence establishing it as the second of the pair of tales about Rome and Constantinople (above, p. xxxiv); this is followed by one sentence, beginning 'Huius erat ciuis Theodorus' (32. 1–2).[61] In all this, we have a foretaste of the sort of changes that William would later make wholesale to produce his 'second edition'.

---

[57] The transitional passage on Mary's help to her devotees (**7a**) explicitly (23. 2) mentions the monastery that will be the scene of the following **8**.

[58] For *res est amentiae* (**11** = **43a**) see below, p. xliii.

[59] The opening sentence of **17** (39. 1) remarks that this story is smuggled into an alien context because it for a change gives an instance of Mary's severity (that, it seems, is what makes it 'alien' here). The point is repeated in §5 (*clandestinum* picking up *furtiuum*), and a renewed assertion of Mary's kindness, together with the impressive quotation from Lucan, gives closure to the whole group.

[60] 51. 3. On the recopying see Carter, p. 600 with n. 1, who suggests that the rearrangement in B (also found in D and Z), by which the summarising remark that there were two *imagines* of Mary in Constantinople was (helpfully) made into the prologue to the item, may go back to William. This is one illustration of the truth that we cannot be sure of William's final thoughts where P is deficient (see also p. xxxi).

[61] The sentence starting with these words and ending 'ueritatis' is the only part of the tale that was copied in this new position in S. P has 32. 1, 32. 2 'Huius erat ciuis Theodorus … ueritatis', and then the rest of the story, no doubt ultimately from (the parent of) S **24**. For all this see (excellently) Carter, p. 27.

In **19** William remarks that he is doing no more than cite Gregory's actual words, rather than recast them, as he normally would do: 'nolo enim hoc breuiarium de laudibus dominicae matris preter metam extendere, ne stili noui necessitas uoluntatem claudendi opusculi moretur' (41. 1). He is in a hurry to close his *opusculum*.

In this not very coherent batch (**2–24**) we have seen three notable hints as to what William is doing.

1. At the end of **8**, he announces an end to tales of monks and a move to another *gradus*. **5–8** have indeed concerned monks. And **9** and **10a** do concern men of 'another grade', a clerk and a canon. Then there is a turn to an assortment of laymen.
2. At the start of **18** William announces a move from men to women. This promise is clearly fulfilled in **18–22**.
3. Early on (**19**) in the section on women he shows signs of wishing to hasten towards the end of the *opusculum*.

✠

We can therefore form some idea of the principles governing the arrangement of Book II (**41a–57**), in which William takes up his theme after a period of illness and disillusion. It is not a book concerned over much with hierarchy, but, as we have seen (p. xxxv), it has a good deal of internal linking, three noticeable pairings, and a block of image stories. It is not tightly organised, but it is not a mess. It reaches a modest climax at the end of **57**, and it is followed by a substantial and in the end prayerful Epilogue. And when William came to the revision seen in P, he did not do much to change the order of what he found in S. P, after a lacuna, gives us the latter part of S **41a**, then **42–47** in the same order, then **48**, after inserting two earlier stories (once S **12–13**; see below, pp. xxxix–xl).

What we are to make of Book I is less straightforward. As has been seen (p. xxxiii), we have, in **1** + **25–41**, an intelligible and more or less coherent sequence of stories, with a rank order announced and fulfilled in the sense that stories about (arch)bishops (with some tangential diversions) are succeeded from **35** onward by stories about sacristans and monks. The crunch comes when we need to fit into this same book the remaining tales, **2–22** (above, pp. xxxv–xxxvi; as we saw, William had already in S reordered **23** and **24**).

There is no difficulty about the section on women (**18–22**). William announces in **19** that he is hastening towards the end of the opuscule, which will mean the present book, Book I alone. It may be that he was in a hurry just because of the illness that he looks back on in the prologue to Book II.

But what of **2–17**? They could not be *appended* as a block to the core determined above (**1** + **25–41**); for that core concludes with a series of tales about monks, and William could not have proceeded with a group of assorted religious, beginning with a bishop. Moreover, he at this stage intended the book to *finish* with **41**. This story, *Stained corporal*, appears twice in S. As **5**, it starts with the non-committal 'Mirum contigit de monacho'. Later, William copied it again (in full) at the end of the group of monks, so that it became **41**,[62] gave it a new start 'Quale est[63] illud de monacho' (21. 1), and provided it with a sudden Explicit to the first book (see app. to 21. 2); the prologue to Book II follows. Eventually, however, as we shall soon see, he found a more satisfactory ending for Book I.

One can only deduce from all this that **2–17** represent material that William did not at this stage succeed in incorporating in his book. It will be convenient to list the tales in question, giving the status of the persons involved. Their eventual destination in P is given in brackets where applicable:

2	Bishop
3	Abbot
4	Royal chaplains (one of whom was in fact a prior, though William does not say so)
5	Monk (transferred as we have just seen)
6	Monk (sacristan)
7–8	Monks, ending with a move at the end of **8** to another *gradus* (24. 6). This properly organised ending for Book I (contrast the unexpected *explicit* in S **41**: see above) will have been the one later employed in P.[64] Carter (p. 36) may well be right to suppose that C's 'noua narratio secundi libri nouabitur initio' (or some such formula) derives from P (lost at this point).
9	Clerk [P **15**]
10a	Canon (in effect clerk) [P **16**]
11	*Res est amentiae* [P **18**]; see below, p. xliii.
12–17	Laymen [P **23–24, 26–29**]

There is order here, reinforced by the internal links noted earlier (pp. xxxv–xxxvi). The whole batch could be the result of William filing, on

---

[62] Carter remarks (p. 25) that 'The story is rewritten here to remind him (or his copyists) that the series of stories following S **5** should be transferred to this new position in some later recasting of the text'. For that transference see below, p. xl.

[63] This links the story, in its new position, to the remarks at the end of **40a**: this is one of those miracles that Mary herself would have thought 'everyday'. 'Quale et illud' at the start of **6** makes that story too (*Prior of St Saviour's*) one of the everyday miracles. The same *may* be true of 'Illud quoque' (23. 1) at the start of **7** (*Monk of Eynsham*).

[64] Note too the closural tone of the penultimate paragraph (24. 5 'Talia per Dominae …').

separate sheets and in hierarchical order, stories for which he had not yet found a place (though he by now knew that **8** would be placed last in Book I): a 'pending file'. When he came to the major reshaping that led to the P version, he (so far as we can see) kept them in the same order. In the Salisbury MS the whole 'file' was wrongly inserted after **1**.[65]

The Paris MS (P)

P has lost a good deal of the text,[66] but it preserves enough to confirm what has been deduced so far about the originally intended order and to show how William revised that order for a second shot at his book.

P gives, after the Prologue, S **1** + **25–34c** as P **1–14**, keeping the same order exactly. There follows a lacuna, starting after 'indigena haut' (11c. 2) in *Boethius* (S **34c**), and the text does not resume till 'eius enim' in the prologue to the second book (24a. 2). In what is left of Book I, therefore, we have only the *bishops* (together with the assorted tangential material already analysed: above, p. xxxii). When the stories resume, we have come, as we should expect from S, to those concerning *clerks*.

These now number P **15–18**, corresponding respectively to S **9–10a** and **42–43**. That is, William has removed two clerkly items from his 'pending' material,[67] and placed them before the pair of clerk stories that in S stood after the prologue of Book II.

There follow in P, as in S, the pair of stories concerning priests (P **19–20** = S **44–45**) and the pair set in Rome and Constantinople (P **21–22** = S **46–47**).[68] We have now moved to laymen. P therefore adds all the other laymen from S (P **23–29**),[69] before finally expiring during *Three knights* after 'quod est legis' (39. 2). These all come from S's pending file (S **12–17**) and in the same order; but among them is inserted *Dying rich man* (S **48** = P **25**). This had not been well integrated

---

[65] An item headed 'Miraculum de sancto Laurentio' appears in S on ff. 102v–103r, that is, between S 24 (*Jew lends*) and S 25 (*Julian*). This is the place where the wrongly inserted material ends, and the Laurence story will have travelled with it, perhaps by accident. Presumably it did not appear in P. It bears none of the hallmarks of William's style and interests, and has nothing to do with the Virgin Mary; it appears indeed to be taken from a sermon (the last sentence is addressed to 'dilectissimi'). We, like Carter (see his p. 24) have not printed it. It can be read in Canal, pp. 145–7.

[66] The folios are also disarranged (discussion in Carter, pp. 33–4), but we ignore this complication here.

[67] P **15**, but not the corresponding S **9**, has a reference back concerning Fulbert (P **9** = S **32**): 'ut dixi' (25. 1).

[68] In P a final paragraph (32. 16) is added to S **47** = P **22**, linking the story to *Jewish boy* (P **23**, formerly S **12**). We cannot agree with Carter, pp. 35–6, that 'omnium superius dictarum sententiarum' refers back to the opening lines of *Julian the apostate* (S **25** = P **2**) rather than to the preceding (wide-ranging) sentiments in 32. 14–15.

[69] P **23** (formerly S **12**) adds 'de qua superius dixi' (33. 1), a reference back to P **17** = S **42**.

in S (see p. xxxiv). But now, it would seem, William was attracted by the idea of a piquant juxtaposition of the luxurious rich man and the generous poor man.

It has to be assumed that P continued with (at least) the lay persons, and other items, now available to us only in the later part of S (49–57), together with the Epilogue. But of course rewriting, deletion and addition is by no means ruled out. Indeed William might well have taken the opportunity to improve on the rather sketchy treatment of some of these later tales.

We return to the pending file posited above (pp. xxxviii–xxxix). S 9–17 have just been accounted for; they found their due place in the revised book. So too, we must assume, did the other items. That is, S 2 will have been added to the bishops; S 3 (the only abbot in the whole collection) will have been placed after the bishops. S 3 carries with it S 4 (see p. xxxv). S 5 had become S 41 (above, p. xxxviii), and S 6–8 will have gone with it to join the monks (above, pp. xxxv–xxxvi).[70] All this will have found a home in P, but it is lost to us there because (as we saw) P's lacuna, which starts in the course of the last bishop story (*Boethius*), means that we pass from bishops to clerks with no intervening religious.

The primary purpose of the revision seen in P, therefore, was to tidy up the hierarchical order (that had always been envisaged) by the redistribution of the 'pending file' seen in S 2–17, which had probably been a separate batch of folios copied into S (or some earlier MS) at a time when someone, very prematurely, copied William's material on the Virgin under a single cover. The circumstances are difficult to reconstruct, but William himself can hardly have been responsible for such a botched job, in which, quite apart from the undigested pending file, a whole group of items (S 25–41) was so conspicuously misplaced.

The best we can do

Naturally we must follow the order of stories in P so far as we can. But its lacunas mean that the evidence of S (as to ordering as well as wording) has perforce to be brought to bear where P is absent,[71] even though we may strongly suspect that what S gives will not have been what William finally intended, in order or wording.

The principles just sketched lead to an order identical to that adopted by Carter, though he does not argue for it in the detail brought forward here. The summary below (where an asterisk signals presence in William's 'pending file') also contains, in the right-hand column, the sigla of the subsidiary manuscripts employed in this edition, to be discussed later (pp. xlviii–liv).

---

[70] For the order 5 6 7 8 see above, pp. xxxv–xxxvi and xxxvii. S 6 is placed among the monks, for, though it concerns the soul of a prior, the focus of attention is a sacristan.

[71] For the evidence of the Balliol MS see p. xlviii.

BOOK ONE

Bishops[72]

1	Theophilus	S 1; P 1	
2	Julian the Apostate	S 25; P 2	C
3	Ildefonsus	S 26; P 3	
4	Toledo	S 27; P 4	C
5	Jews of Toulouse	S 28; P 5	BDZ
6	St Bonitus	S 29; P 6	BCL
7	St Dunstan	S 30; P 7	BCL
8	Chartres saved	S 31; P 8	C
9	Milk: Fulbert	S 32; P 9	BCLPr
10	Milk: monk	S 33; P 10	BCL
11	Jerome of Pavia	S 34; P 11	
11a	Syrus	S 34a; P 12	
11b	Augustine	S 34b; P 13	
11c	Boethius	S 34c; P 14 (in part)	
12	Guy of Lescar	S 2*	RcZ

Abbots

13	Abbot Ælfsige	S 3*	BCL
14	Guimund	S 4*	BC

Sacristans[73]

15	Devil in three shapes	S 35	BC
16	Drowned sacristan	S 36	

Monks

17	Monk of Cologne	S 37	
18	Vision of Wettin	S 38	BCL
19	St Odo	S 39	CL
20	Pilgrim of St James	S 40	
21	Stained corporal	S 5 = 41*	
22	Prior of St Saviour's	S 6*	
23	Monk of Eynsham	S 7*	BCL
24	Sudden death	S 8*	BCL

---

[72] In this list various stories that come in tangentially (see the earlier analysis of S) are not distinguished from the rest.

[73] For this group (if William meant it to be one), see p. xxxii.

BOOK TWO

	Prologue	S **41a**; P **14a** (in part)	

Clerks

25	Clerk of Chartres	S **9***; P **15**	
26	Five *Gaudes*	S **10***; P **16**	Z
27	Clerk of Pisa	S **42**; P **17**	
28	Love by black arts	S **43**; P **18**	BCLPr

Priests

29	Priest of one mass	S **44**; P **19**	
30	Prayers of a friend	S **45**; P **20**	BCLPr

Laymen

31	Two brothers at Rome	S **46**; P **21** (in part)	
32	Jew lends	S **24** = **47**; P **22**	BCL
33	Jewish boy	S **12***; P **23**	
34	Bread offered	S **13***; P **24**	CDL
35	Dying rich man	S **48**; P **25**	CDLZ
36	Charitable almsman	S **14***; P **26**	
37	Ebbo the thief	S **15***; P **27**	
38	Rustic church	S **16***; P **28**	BCL
39	Three knights	S **17***; P **29** (in part)	BC

Women

40	St Mary of Egypt	S **18**	(B)C
41	Musa	S **19**	C
42	Abbess delivered	S **20**	
43	Nun's penance	S **21**	B[74] CL
44	Childbirth in the sea	S **22**	

Trivia

45	Mead	S **49**	BC
46	Wife and mistress	S **50**	B
47	Woman cured	S **51**	
48	Foot cut off	S **52**	

Images

49	Fire	S **53**	
50	Saracens	S **54**	BDZPr
51	Image insulted	S **23** = **55**	BDZ

[74] B (163r) prefaces this with the first sentence of 40, which moves from men to women.

| 52 | Constantinople | S 56 | BDZ |
| 53 | Purification | S 57 | BC |

Interludes

We comment briefly here on what may be called Interludes, paragraphs of general reflection written to break up, and give further variety to, the series of narratives. They are omitted in the list above; in the Concordance they are registered by the italicised Latin of their opening words.

Res est amentiae (28. 8–11) S **11**. This was part of the pending file in S. After the revision it was transferred to form a part of S **43** = P **18**. It is found in C.

Haec profecto (20a) S **40a**. This follows a Monk story only found in S, whose evidence determines its position in Book I.

Multa quidem (44a) S **48a**. For the problems raised by this section (which Carter does not seem to feel), see above (pp. xxxiv–xxxv). As we have seen, it is in S placed after **48** (*Dying rich man*) and before **49** (*Mead*). When S **48** was transferred to become P **25**, it did not carry *Multa quidem* with it, which suggests that William was not happy with this position. We can only guess where he eventually placed it. It would fit tolerably well before S **22** (*Childbirth in the sea*), which is an extraordinary enough miracle for William to rhapsodise about it in the last section (44. 5 'O uirgo decora nimis …') and to claim that it 'iam predicatur per orbem terrarum'. Furthermore, 'miraculum iustis pariter et peccatoribus profuturum [or the like]' would pick up 'i nunc, peccator, …' (43. 7) at the end of S **21**.

Talibus dicendis (48a) S **52a**. See above (p. xxxv) for the way in which it seems to pick up the coda of S **49**.

The subsidiary manuscripts

It is fortunate that though S and (the now incomplete) P are the only manuscripts containing the complete text of *MBVM*, there is a good deal of evidence to support their testimony, some of it relevant only to the Prologue, some only to the main body of the text, that is the miracle stories themselves.

The Prologue[75]

The Salisbury and Paris MSS (S and P) are as crucial for the transmission of the prologue[76] as for that of the main body of the text. We have seen that P represents a later version of William's book, in which not only was the order of the stories fundamentally revised but some rewriting was done. It is natural to assume that the latter holds good of the Prologue also. Indeed the very first words of the book, where one can hardly imagine scribal error could be in question, appear in different forms in the two MSS:

S   Multi *miracula Dei genitricis et perpetue uirginis Marie* stilo formare conati ....

P   Multi *Domine sancte Marie laudes* stilo formare conati ....[77]

As we go on, however, it is a matter of weighing up probabilities as each variation appears.

Fortunately, as in the main body of the work, further evidence comes to our aid, this time in a more manageable form. Two separate strands need to be distinguished.

1) At some stage, the Prologue was quarried to construct a free-standing treatise on the four virtues of Mary. This is attributed in the manuscripts that carry it to Anselm. It is found in its purest state in Lyon, Bibl. mun. 622 (Ly), ff. 104v–111r, which contains everything down to the end of 31. The two further witnesses are less full.[78] Exeter, Cathedral Library 3505 (E$_1$), ff. 132r–136r, proceeds like Ly up to the end of 31, but it is subject to abbreviation and rewriting of the original wording, not to speak of the interposition of extraneous pious material. Brussels, Bibl. royale 1927–44 (Br), ff. 147v–149v is more sincere, but it breaks off at the end of 18 ('circumplectebatur spiritualiter').[79]

---

[75] The Latin text signals (in small Roman numerals, within square brackets) the rather arbitrary chapter numbers as seen in *PL*, but subsections have been added, numbered throughout the Prologue (as throughout the Epilogue). S and P do not agree on the paragraphing of the Prologue, and only S assigns chapter numbers (not those seen in *PL*).

[76] At one point a block of text is given only in P: 'Vnde michi uidentur ... ab angelo salutatur' (19–20). There is no obvious mechanical reason for the omission of these words in S, but William can hardly have added them when revising his book. They reflect a different source (Anselm's *Cur Deus homo*) from what immediately precedes (which is based on a sermon of Fulbert); but that source is still being used in 21, which starts 'Amplius'.

[77] Discussion by Barré 1953, p. 241, who rightly points out that the S version fits well with the general thrust of the whole book (*miracula*), the P version with the purport of the Prologue (*laudes*: cf. 40 *de laudibus*): and indeed it is the version found in the MSS giving the Prologue only (Ly and E$_1$: see below). But Barré seems wrong to throw doubts for this reason on the fidelity of the scribe of S.

[78] Another witness adduced by Barré 1953 (p. 233), Marseille, Bibl. mun. 230 (s. xiv), was not accessible to us.

[79] In fact just before where the words not found in S (see n. 76) begin.

How were these manuscripts related to each other? We may be certain that Br is copied, or at least descended, from Ly, which it consistently follows,[80] adding further errors of its own. Leaving Br out of account, we list agreements of LyE₁ against SP.

	SP	LyE₁
	SP	LyE₁
2	namque	nam
4	careret	carebat
	salutes	salutationem
5	uotum (*P uncertain*)	et uotum
6	in ea coaceruarant	coaceruauerant in ea
9	comitantur	comitatur
11	seruatum	obseruatum
	incomparabilem sibi et aliis	sibi et aliis incomparabilem
	nullus	nullus ea Ly, nullus etiam ea E₁
	et (*after* natiuitate)	*om.*
13	meditatur	*om.*[81]
	tolerantur	tollerat
	confidenter	quod conf. Ly, et quod conf. E₁
15	domini matre	matre domini
18	est (*after* ipse)	est etiam
	secreuit	sacrauit
	pridem plenam	plenam pridem
	suprascriptis	supradictis
19[82]	sit omnipotens	omnipotens sit
	sed (*before* peccatum)	sed est
	eo	deo
	debuit	decuit
	debuisse nec potuisse	potuisse nec debuisse
20	aduertit	animaduertit
22	erit irrita	irrita erit
	non uoluit (*after* et quia)	noluit
23	antiquorum	antiquorum patrum
31	et (*after* saluantur)	*om.*[83]

[80] But it has *affectum* in 15, correctly (with SE₁), against *effectum* (PLy). In the same section BrE₁ agree on *ambigit* (replacing *ibit in infitias*), but in Br the word has been added by a second hand in a gap.
[81] Instead, Ly has *conatur*, E₁ has *cogitat*, both after *magnificum*.
[82] S is not available in 19–20.
[83] Apparently erased in Ly.

Some of these readings are wrong; some might be right, but none is certainly so.[84] We almost never cite them in the apparatus, where readings of Ly and E_1 are given only when an entry is needed for other reasons, normally where S and P differ from each other. (Where E_1 is not mentioned, it is because it is defective at that point.)

The relationship of Ly and E_1 to S and P will be discussed shortly (below, p. xlvii), and some individual readings will be provided from them in a footnote (n. 90). Ly, as we have seen, is fairly sincere. As for E_1 it normally follows Ly, when it is not adapting the text for its own purposes. Occasionally it diverges from it in following SP, or S rather than P.[85] It is not, we think, quite out of the question that E_1, like Br, descends ultimately from Ly.

2) Exeter, Cathedral Library MS 3504 (E_2), ff. 239v–240v, part of the same compilation as 3505, carries the continuation of the Prologue, 32–9 (40–2 contain William's reflections on his own book, and were not suitable for inclusion in the treatise).[86] Here again, William's original wording has been a good deal tampered with. Both these Exeter texts will descend from the same doctored manuscript (see also n. 87).

The heading of E_2 is of great interest. The extract from William is stated to be taken 'de libello beati anselmi de uirtutibus et miraculis beate marie que [*leg.* qui] incipit: Multi domine sancte marie. et accipit raciones beati augustini in quodam sermone qui incipit: Ad interrogata'. We learn from this a) that the original from which it was taken contained not just the Prologue (starting in its P form, as we knew from Ly, E_1 and Br) but the miracle stories too, William's whole book indeed;[87] but that the entire book was regarded as being the work of Anselm. Further b) some learned person had conjectured that 32–9 take over the reasonings of a work attributed to Augustine and beginning *Ad interrogata*. This work is not in fact a sermon, nor by Augustine himself. It is the ps.-Augustinian

---

[84] E.g. 4 *salutationem*; but that might be a conjecture (cf. e.g. 43. 1).

[85] Thus it follows S at 4 *in ea*, 15 *effectum*, 16 om. est (*after* ipsa), 22 nec] non. For agreements of E_1 with SP against Ly, see below, n. 90. At 31 E_1 uniquely has the correct *fratribus* for *filiis*, with Anselm.

[86] A copy of this part of E_2, found in Cambridge, Trinity College B. 11. 16 (255) (s. xiv–xv), and printed by Dalton 2. 506–8 (there is no cross-reference to the same material when it appears in summary at 3. 153), can be disregarded, though Canal gives readings from it (under the siglum Y).

[87] E_2 contains, besides this part of the Prologue, some of the Miracle stories, e.g. 7 on Dunstan (Dalton, 3. 342), much tampered with (the scene is set in Glastonbury) but recognisably in a B version (*increpacionem* is added in §5). We need to reckon with the possibility that E_2 combined with E_1 goes back to a manuscript that contained a B type text of the miracles together with a doctored version of the Prologue.

De assumptione (PL 40, 1141–8), cited by both Carter and Canal as a source of these chapters.[88]

In 32–9, E_2 (Ly now being absent) provides a welcome means of discriminating between S and P variants,[89] though its usefulness is much reduced by the numerous omissions in the text caused by the desire to abbreviate. We have normally cited it (like E_1) only when variations between S and P necessitate an entry in the apparatus. We do mention in the apparatus one intriguing unique reading (38 *trutinata*, where SP's *cumulata* seems inappropriate); for a selection of other variants see n. 90.

SPLYE

There remains the crucial matter of the relationship of the Prologue tradition represented by Ly and E (= E_1 and E_2) to S and P. Experience seems to show that LE can safely be used as a criterion for deciding between S and P where they differ. But we still need to ask whether we have a tripartite stemma, S, P and LyE, or a bipartite one, S and P deriving from a hyparchetype (call it π) on the same level as LyE. Answering this question involves careful weighing of the readings of LyE. If they were found to include a fair number of good readings not known to S and P, then S and P would be linked by common errors proving the existence of π. It is here that the list of LyE_1 agreements given above (p. xlv) comes into play, for as we have seen E_2 does not present any patent truth. The same may in fact be said of the list above (see p. xlvi with n. 84). A tripartite picture, then, seems to be the correct one. And as all the important variants of S and P are registered (in the apparatus), it seems improper to suppress those of Ly and E. It is true that LyE readings will be formally eliminable by the agreement of S and P; but they will themselves eliminate individual S and P variants. And the reader needs to be able to decide whether the editor has judged the stemma correctly. It is on this basis that agreements of Ly and E_1 against SP are either cited in the apparatus to 1–31 or listed above. Individual readings of Ly and (selectively) E_1 are listed in a footnote here, together with some readings of E_2 in 32–9.[90] If any of them are right, it will doubtless be by conjecture.

---

[88] For all this see Barré 1953, p. 244 n. 34 (added in proof), who commented: 'Le compilateur avait sous les yeux le *De Miraculis* de Guillaume de Malmesbury.' Barré thought (rightly) that the Ps.-Augustine work is not really a source.

[89] But at pr. 37 'sancti' (S) is correct, even though P and E_2 agree on the inclusion of 'spiritus'.

[90] **Ly** (but not E_1): 3 illa[1]] ita (*perhaps in a gap*) (*om.* E_1); 7 perseuerauerit; 12 memoria; 13 permagnifice; <et> perseueranter; 22 potissimam. For 13 (*conatur*) see above, p. xlv n. 81.

Ly where E_1 is defective (any or all of these could go back to the common source of LyE): 15 illo] illi; 17 itemque (*before* in)] idemque (*after correction?*); per prophetam] propheta, 21 uero] enim; haec (*after* sit)] hoc; 24 decidit] defecit; parente] parenti; 25 hic] hinc; ergo ei] ei ergo; 26 nonne eum amarat; 28 uiderunt; fruerentur. [It seems from this and the preceding list that Ly was the main source

The miracle stories

THE SELECTION

The picture here is far more complex than in the Prologue. We begin with Oxford, Balliol College, 240 (B), a miscellany that includes a block of miracle stories concerning the Virgin Mary, first (ff. 137r–152v) the collection of Dominic of Evesham (one of William's sources: see above, p. xvii), then (ff. 155r–164r)[91] twenty-four stories based on William's own book. These stories follow almost exactly[92] the order proposed by Carter and confirmed above. Nothing could demonstrate more clearly the ultimate dependence of this part of B on William's book,[93] and the correctness of Carter's order. But, as we shall see, the usefulness of B is limited by its general nature: someone has set himself to abbreviate and adapt William's stories, and William's own wording is only fitfully preserved.[94]

The popularity of this reduced and adapted redaction of *MBVM* is apparent from B's relations, of which we do not have full enough information to organise them into a stemma. The three known to us are a MS formerly owned by

(though sometimes corrected) of the printed editions on which Carter relied in editing §§1–31: the more accessible is *PL* 159, 579C-586D.]

E$_1$ (but not **Ly**): The text has been much tampered with, as a result of abbreviation, adaptation and scribal error. We list here the more plausible or interesting readings not appearing in the apparatus criticus: 1 singularis <et>; 3 *om.* illa[1] (see above on Ly); 8 hae] quatuor cardinales; disposuere <sancti patres>; 10 angeli <ita>; 11 acta uel dicta integre colligit de preterito; 31 fratres] confratres.

E$_2$: Again the text has been tampered with and much shortened. In the absence of Ly, however, E$_2$ would be a primary witness if the stemma were bipartite (see above), and its individual readings would then be of consequence. The following selection, however, is not impressive: 33 percipiat] accipiant; dotatam; 35 <quomodo> sufficere; 39 mari (*after* enim)] in mari [*contrast* in mari esse *below*]; autem <fore>; fulgore.

[91] The intervening material (ff. 152r-154v) consists of four stories from other collections: HM 15–16 and TS 1–2. It is of interest that among the material following 164r we find Fulbert's sermon on the Nativity *Approbatae consuetudinis* (f. 165r), used by William in the Prologue to *MBVM* (above, p. xviii). Mynors' catalogue alludes to the parallel collection seen in BL Cotton Cleo. C. X. That manuscript, which Stubbs (in his edition of William's *Gesta Regum Anglorum* [RS, 2 vols, 1887], I, pp. cxxiii-cxxviii) wrongly thought to contain William's own copy of his *MBVM*, may be of some significance for our story nonetheless; see above, p. xviii. There is a detailed description in Ward, *Cat. of Romances* II, pp. 600–18.

[92] The stories are (our) 5, 6, 7, 9, 10, 13, 14, 15, 18, 24, 23, 28, 30, 32, 38, 39, 40 (§1 only), 43, 45, 46, 51, 50, 52, 53. There is no question of William having placed 24 before 23, because the latter has a reference forward to the former (above, n. 57; omitted in B), and the order 23 24 is confirmed by C and L (nn. 100, 101). As to 51 and 50, B's order (confirmed by D and Z) might be William's own second thought (cf. n. 60). What is said here about the order of stories in B, C and L builds on the observations of Carter (p. 18), though he did not make explicit use of B's order to confirm his own. Mussafia did not know of L, but B's order is central to his own ordering.

[93] The explicit speaks of 'liber tertius miraculorum' (f. 164r); that presumably counts Dominic's one book (his collection as we have it ends 'Explicit primus liber miraculorum': so Canal's edition, though not in B) along with William's two.

[94] 'All the Stories from William are more or less abbreviated and also amended in vocabulary, where William's language seems unduly difficult' (Carter, p. 70).

Francis Wormald, now BL Add. 57533;[95] Aberdeen, University Library, 137;[96] and Toulouse, Bibl. mun. 482, used (like the Aberdeen MS) by Canal for his edition of Dominic.[97] Further, the elegiacs found in S (ff. 89v–90r) were based on a text of this kind.[98] As we shall see, the influence of the B version spreads even wider than this (below, p. lii).

We come now to two collections that, unlike that in the Balliol MS, aimed, in some degree, to preserve William's wording.

One is Cambridge University Library, Mm. 6. 15 (C).[99] The order of those (twenty-six in number) of William's stories that it includes is again of interest, for it carries clear traces of William's original: ff. 134r–137r contain the stories in the range 2–8 in the same order; those in the range 10–28 are in that order on ff. 137r–141v; those in the range 34–39 are in that order on ff. 143v–144v; 41, 43 and 45 follow each other on ff. 145v–146v.[100] The stories have not been much reworded, but the text is sadly corrupt. At 6. 2 C adds *de presentibus tutelam* to the text found in SPBL. The words sound authentic, but a parallel passage at Epil. 6 suggests they are not; and it is hard to imagine how they could have come to be preserved in this manuscript alone.

Hardly less useful is London, Lambeth Palace, 51, first exploited by Carter. This contains sixteen stories.[101] Again the ordering is of interest (see Carter, p. 61). Eleven appear in William's order on ff. 324v–329r; four (18, 23, 24, 30) appear in William's order on ff. 116v–118r; the odd one out (32) appears on f. 337r. L is much less corrupt than C. It has some good unique readings, presumably the result of conjecture.

Carter knew of B, C and L, Canal of B and C only (and he used them little). Neither scholar stopped to enquire how these witnesses relate to each other, or to the main manuscripts, S and P.

[95] This has exactly the same stories as B, in the same order, except that it adds 'Non est silendum ...' (41. 2), *Musa*, before 5. Fulbert's 'Approbatae consuetudinis' follows the stories from William.

[96] Carter, p. 73. According to Carter (pp. 5, 62) it includes a single story (34) taken direct from William's book.

[97] Carter, p. 74. Some readings are given by H. Kjellman, *La deuxième collection anglo-normande des miracles de la sainte Vierge et son original latin* (Uppsala, 1922); soundings suggest that it might be a little closer to William's text than B is.

[98] Carter, p. 72. See p. xxiv.

[99] First discussed by Mussafia, 'Studien' II, pp. 35–42.

[100] The stories are: 2, 4, 6–10, 13–15, 18–19, 23–24, 28, 30, 32, 34–35, 38–41, 43, 45, and 53. C also includes HM 1–4, 6–10, 13–15, 17 (in that order) and Dominic 7–8, 12, 1–2 (in that order), both interspersed with other material. For the positioning of stories 9, 30, 32 and 53 see n. 105.

[101] 6–7, 9–10, 13, 18–19, 23–24, 28, 30, 32, 34–35, 38, 43.

If we do enquire, we find, first, that the three between them cover only a little more than a half of the stories available, with many overlaps. The total number is thirty-one.[102]

It is remarkable that these are made up of representatives of all the groups identified above (pp. xli–xliii): Bishops 2, 4–10; Abbots 13–14; Sacristans 15; Monks 18–19, 23–24; Clerks 28; Priests 30; Laymen 32, 34–35, 38–39; Women 40–41, 43; Trivia 45–46; Images 50–53. It is hard to believe that this is a coincidence. Rather, it points to a conscious selection having been made from the whole book: some representative highlights, perhaps meant to give a foretaste of a bigger book to come. It must also be significant that no fewer than sixteen of the thirty-one are stories not found in the Marian collections known to William (Dominic, HM, TS, MB).[103] These are just the sort of eye-catching novelties that William (if it was he who was responsible) might have put into a selection.[104]

B, C AND L

It remains to discuss the interrelationships of B, C and L.[105]

We have seen that, while B is an adapted abbreviation of some of William's stories, C and L both aim, at least in some degree, to reproduce William's text. It does not seem possible to show that all three derive from a single MS copied from William's autograph incorporating the Thirty-one ('the Selection'). We have

---

[102] BCL contain 13 stories: 6–7, 9–10, 13, 18, 23–24, 28, 30, 32, 38, 43; BC contain 6 stories: 14–15, 39–40, 45, 53; CL contain three stories: 19, 34–35; B alone contains five stories: 5, 46, 50–52; C alone contains four stories: 2, 4, 8, 41. Total thirty-one (out of fifty-three). The more significant number thirty could perhaps be obtained by a different articulation of the stories.

[103] The sixteen are 5, 7, 9, 14, 18, 23–4, 28, 30, 32, 34–35, 38, 50, 52–53. The only 'exotica' omitted in the selection are 12 (*Guy of Lescar*) and the mixed bag 11a–11c. This account builds on Carter's perception (p. 70) that the compiler of the B abridgement 'only took from William of Malmesbury's Stories those which were not already transcribed, in different words, in Dominic's collection ..., HM ... and TS' (similarly already Mussafia, 'Studien' IV, p. 26). Cf. Carter, p. 18 n. 5, on the way in which S 'some later writer' has marked off ('scriptum est' as opposed to 'scribe') stories already known to him from others that were needed for some new collection.

[104] There is an unwelcome consequence: the stories not found in any subsidiary MS are those that are based on the major collections (overwhelmingly Dominic and HM). We may hope (perhaps vainly) to find these stories somewhere in the unexamined remainder of the Marian tradition. But that means looking (as Carter did) at each MS in detail. Even where a catalogue gives titles, they may well mislead: e.g. 'Theophilus' is more likely to mean Dominic's story than William's. Stubbs' list of titles from BL, Cotton Cleo. C. X makes it look as though it contains many William stories; in fact it contains none (see n. 91).

[105] A complication is hived off to this footnote. In a number of stories (9, 30, 32, 53) the usual picture is upset: C sides with B (complete with new openings) against L in 9 and 30, while BC share similar new openings in 32 (where L is independently aberrant) and 53 (not in L). As Carter knew (p. 77), these are the only four stories preserved from William's book in Rb (BL, Royal 6 B. xiv, interspersed with other material in ff. 82v–99r; the order there is 9, 30, 53, 32); and their text is close to that in C. It is noticeable (Carter, p. 77) that in C the four found in Rb appear on ff. 114v (9), 116v (53), 117r (30) and 120r (32), whereas the bulk of the stories from William come on ff. 134r–146v (see above, p. xlix). These four stories, then, found their way as a group into C and Rb, in a B version.

1

identified only two 'errors' conjoining B, C and L against SP:[106] 6. 2 *excibat* SP, *excitabat* BCL; 28. 5 *Mariae* SP, *sanctae Mariae* BCL.[107] Both may be the result of coincidence, and they have been excluded from the apparatus criticus.[108] This is a meagre haul indeed,[109] compared with the abundance of good readings given by BCL in support of SP.[110] We have rejected three readings of BCL against S alone: 13. 2 *beatae* S, *beatissimae* BCL;[111] 18. 5 *de* (before *misericordia*) S, *pro* BCL; 43. 4 *proxima* S, *proximo* BCL. None is impossible (though William's usage does support S in the last case). But they have to be discounted as proof of a common independent source of the three, for if we had P at these points it might prove to agree with them.

On the other hand, in a number of stories C and L regularly share errors and innovations against BS (or BSP), as well as displaying errors that separate them from each other;[112] they thus go back to a common ancestor (call it β), copied or descended from William's working text.

What can be said about the state of that working text at the point or points when it gave birth to (the ancestor of) the B version and to β? Perhaps one thing only, but a vital one: its order of stories was that found (at least in part) in P and deduced by Carter from indications in S. As for the wording: from the evidence of B, C and L, as it comes and goes, we can see a course being steered between the text of S and that of P. In our edition, it is used, where possible, as a criterion for deciding between variants between S and P (just as Ly and E could between S and P in the Prologue). This procedure can perhaps be defended only from its results: it is almost always possible to use it to produce a reading that either can be or must be true. We shall discuss below (p. lv) the consequences of this for attempting to come to the important judgement as to how far P is a second edition of the book

---

[106] Errors common to BCL can, of course, only be looked for in the thirteen stories (see n. 102) where they are all available to us. And even here the adaptation and abbreviation to which B has been subject reduces the scope for comparison. Worse still, only eight of the thirteen stories are carried by both S and P; and we ideally need agreements in error against both.

[107] In the stemmatically unconnected Pr (for which see below, p. liii) piety has similarly added *beate*.

[108] For *excibat* cf. *Comm. Lam.* III, 1703, for *excitabat Comm. Lam.* I, 1008. But the former is more choice.

[109] It might be added to if we had the evidence of L and of P in a number of stories where agreements in innovation of BC against S are available: 14 (1 *om.* sui; 2 multo post] post multum), 15 (4 quae (*before* iusserit)] quaecumque; and four variations in order), 23 (2 diligens) and 45 (3 supereffluere). These agreements of BC are in any case equipollent to S (see below, p. lix).

[110] See the apparatus *passim*. It will be seen there that one or two of BCL quite often accompany either S or P in error. No single explanation will account for these phenomena.

[111] Note also 13. 4 *liberari a periculo* S, *liberari de periculo* CL, *deliberari periculo* B.

[112] The only trustworthy evidence can come from passages where all of SPBCL are to hand. Examples of CL against SPB (cited first): 6. 5 *palam extulit: extulit palam*; 7. 5 *hac terra: terra*; 10. 2 *medullis resolui: resolui medullis*; 10. 4 *huiusmodi: huiuscemodi*; 28. 6 *cum ille: cumque ille*. It is hardly necessary to give examples of readings peculiar to C (an exciting one at 6. 2 was mentioned on p. xlix) and L. C and L agree against SP in the absence of B at 34. 1 *inuitare*; this would be added to the evidence for a common ancestor of BCL if B were present and in agreement.

in any other respect than its ordering of the stories. Meanwhile we need to turn to other, less important subsidiary manuscripts.

TWO MAJOR COLLECTIONS

One manuscript raised hopes that were later to be dashed. Cambridge, Sidney Sussex College, 95[113] had since M. R. James' Catalogue been known to contain what James described as 'a large collection, the largest I have seen, of Miracles of the Virgin'; and inspection of the table of contents supplied by James shows many items that might be taken from William. Canal gave it the siglum Z, and provided references to various items in it that corresponded to ten of William's stories;[114] but he did not cite any readings. Carter knew the collection but did not exploit it.[115]

The most tempting story turning up in Z is no. 12 (*Guy of Lescar*), where S, but not P, is available; but Canal did not use it to edit that story, or any other (he proclaimed its relevance to the Prologue to Book II, which it does not appear to contain). Collation shows that Z is indeed an independent witness to 12, of which it has a full and sincere text. As Carter knew,[116] the story is found also in BL Royal 6 B. x (Rc),[117] and BnF lat. 14463 (Pv); it is the only story from William that these MSS carry. This 'exoticum' might have been in the Selection (see n. 103), but failed for some reason to find a place in B or β. Alternatively, it could have been added to the book after the selection was made. In editing it we have used Z and Rc[118] to supplement the evidence of S.

Z in fact is dependent on William's book in many more stories than Canal realised, but unfortunately its usefulness for the editor of *MBVM* does not go very far. Often Z is demonstrably no more than a further witness to the B version (see n. 119). But it performs some service in 26, where fragments of William gleam through the dross of a verbose retelling, and where we do not have the help of B, C or L (or D). We also use it in five other stories where it is joined by the testimony of another major collection.

This is found in Dublin, Trinity College B. 1. 10 (167) (D). The book was meticulously catalogued by M. R. Colker, though he so differs from James in his method of identifying the stories that it is a tiresome task to work out where

---

[113] MW gratefully acknowledges the many kindnesses he received from Laurel Broughton in his early dealings with this MS.

[114] Pp. 175–6.

[115] Carter, p. 66.

[116] The MSS had been discussed by Mussafia, 'Studien' IV, pp. 10–11, and I, pp. 953–9 respectively.

[117] It may be noted here that Carter also used another thirteenth-century Royal MS, which he called Ra (5 A. VIII). It carries 53, but contributes nothing.

[118] Our information on Pv is incomplete. Carter's apparatus suggests that it is closely related to Rc, and he remarks (p. 67) on their similar ordering of the surrounding stories.

D overlaps with Z. The two often in fact give the same stories, whether from William[119] or not, and their texts are at times close to each other.[120] They seemed worth citing in five stories:

5   Z and D give independent adaptions of a B type source.
35   Z and D have the same adapted text ultimately derived from William (B is absent).
50–52   Z and D are related, but not B type. (There is no point in going here into the complications attending their treatment of these stories.)

D is used in 34 (it corresponds to Z v. 106),[121] but has little to contribute.

OTHER SUBSIDIARY MANUSCRIPTS

BnF, lat. 3177 (Pr), uncovered by Carter,[122] is employed by us in stories 9, 28, 30 and 50. The first three of these stories are found in B, C and L, the last only in B. But Pr does not show decisive signs of affiliation to any one of these.[123] Indeed it seems to offer a tantalising glimpse of the state of William's working copy before the copying of B and of β. The selection has, it seems, been made, but Pr shows a number of primitive readings that do not make their way into B and β. For though Pr normally supports the truth, it preserves S readings at 28. 4 om. *factum*; 28. 5 *erat proxima*; 30. 2 *sit omni*. It also has the correct form of the dative at 28. 3 *pruritui*, and the (more) correct *dissulcatas* at 50. 1. It is indeed of especial importance in 50, where P is absent.

  Carter also knew of Oxford, Corpus Christi College 42, ff. 1r–31r. This contains very abbreviated versions of more than a hundred stories, over thirty of them from William. Its readings do not help us, even though it knows stories beyond those familiar from the Selection. It has the primitive error *citharum* (S) for *Scitharum* (B) at 52. 1. Like BC it has *ad reddendam pecuniam constitutus* at 32. 10; like L it has *cistulam* (for *statuam*) in the same section. At 7. 4 it has *leti*

---

[119] The stories derived from William, so far as we have identified them, are (we give here the references to Z and D where they are not given in the Latin text): 5, 6 (Z iii. 20, D 47r: both B type), 7 (Z iii. 8, D 45r: both B type), 9 (Z iii. 22, D 47v: Z is B type, D much adapted), 12 (see main text; D 47v may be independent of Z, but it has been much tampered with), 14 (Z iii. 45, D 52v: both B type), 18 (Z iv. 22, D 76r: both B type), 23 (Z iv. 59, B type; D 67r), 30 (Z iii. 40, B type; D 51v is very abbreviated), 32 (Z ii. 10, D 37r: both B type), 35 (see main text), 38 (Z iii. 43, D 52r: both B type), 50–52 (see main text), 53 (Z i. 66, D 18v: related, but not B type). The texts of Z and D are often very different, usually because D is more adapted and shortened than Z. Stories found in Z (but not D) are: 10 (iv. 32: B type), 15 (iv. 27, B type), 26 (see text above), 28 (iii. 58: B type), 43 (iv. 103, largely B type). Stories found in D (but not Z) are: 34 (see Latin text), 41 (Z v. 98 = TS 3; D 107v does derive from William, but is much adapted), 45 (Z v. 88, now lost; D 103v is B type).

[120] But they are not 'twins', despite Carter (p. 66).

[121] Lost with missing leaves.

[122] Carter, p. 68.

[123] That is not to say that it is free of error and rewriting, especially in 28.

(with *VD* 2. 28. 2). At 24. 5 it, like B, clarifies the end of the story, but in different words from B's. At 33. 3 its *quo extracto* might show that someone recognised what lies behind the corrupt *expellitur*; but a debt to Paschasius (or his source Gregory of Tours) is possible.

We cannot praise Carter's discoveries of subsidiary manuscripts too highly. Canal did not do as well as he; and we have only been able to add a single novelty, Oxford, All Souls 22. Only one story (it seems) comes from William; this is 35 (§§2–3 only: at ff. 17v–18r), a passage already well served by witnesses. In this short passage, the MS follows DZ at the four entries in our apparatus ad loc.

That does not mean that there are no more discoveries to make, in particular (judging by Pr) in France.[124] But we suspect that any new find would not materially alter the picture we have drawn.

The primary witnesses again

What light does this investigation of the subsidiary witnesses throw on the development of William's work on the *MBVM*? As we have seen, from a primitive and not finally ordered state, providentially preserved for us by being copied into a relatively late manuscript (S), grew a reordered version seen in an early thirteenth-century copy, the (unfortunately defective) P. If these were the only witnesses to the book, we should have some difficulty in deciding between variants where S and P differ. Sometimes of course one will be obviously wrong, the other obviously right. But often we cannot be sure which (if either) is right, not least where word order is concerned. A plausible variant in S may be *either* what William wrote, *or* an error in copying from his working version, *or* a conscious change by a scribe. Equally, a plausible variant in P may be *either* the result of William's reworking of the primitive version *or* a scribal error *or* a scribe's conscious change. In these circumstances, we cannot lightly *assume* that P is at any given point superior to S (or S, for that matter, to P). It may be, but it must make its own case each time. P represents the later version, but that does not make it automatically better in any particular passage. As a result, we do not really know what we should very much like to know, how far William reworded as he went along. It is clear from the stories of *GR* and *GP* that William was prone to constant tinkering with his books. There is no reason to suppose that he behaved differently in writing the *MBVM*. If its editor decides to print his final version, he needs to know what that final version is. And it is not enough to say that it is P. It might be a sensible

---

[124] Carter looked at most of those in Paris. But no one has done for France (or Germany) what was done for Italy with exemplary patience by M. V. Gripkey (see *Mediaeval Studies* 14 (1952), 9–47 and 15 (1953), 14–46); it looks unlikely from her findings that the influence of William's book spread so far.

rule of thumb to print the variant of P if it is better than, or as good as, that of S. But some further criterion would be helpful.

Such a criterion is to some extent supplied by the subsidiary witnesses. As already stated (pp. xlvii and li), practice (in the Prologue as well as in the Stories) suggests the soundness of the rule of thumb that the editor should favour a variant supported by the subsidiary MSS plus S (or P) against P (or S).[125] Often, of course, the subsidiary manuscripts are not available. Even when they are, what they have to tell us is limited in scope. If a reading is found only by S, it may mean that, by the time the Selection was made, that reading had given way in William's working version to a rival. Alternatively, though, the S reading may never have been in William's text at all, but was merely a scribal error in S. In either case, however, we can confidently reject the S reading. But if a variant is supported only by P, that might be the result of scribal error in P; or it might be the result of William's having changed his mind since the making of the Selection. In some cases we can see that error must be the reason: thus when P omits a word essential to the sense (e.g. 32. 12 *arbitratus*) or contradicts outside evidence (e.g. 7. 3 *Domin(a)e*). But often we cannot be sure. Interested readers are therefore asked to keep their eye on the apparatus, and judge for themselves if we have been right to reject (or in some cases approve) the P reading.[126]

In this connection, it is worth noting that, where S, P, and subsidiary manuscripts are available, the subsidiary MSS support P against S in roughly 75% of the instances registered in the apparatus. This superiority is even greater (80%) when we look only at variations of word order. It follows from this that in stories where S and P are both available, but subsidiary manuscripts are absent, we may take it as a rule of thumb that where they vary P is appreciably more likely to be right than S, and especially so where word order is in question. Naturally, this is of little or no help in judging any particular variant, but it may show if an editor is proceeding on more or less the right lines.[127]

---

[125] For three (arguable) exceptions see app. crit. on pr. 18 *Dei fortitudo*, 28. 6 *cetera* and 38. 4 *omni familia* (the first two especially are candidates for late improvements in P). At 5. 3 S (despite everything) seems right to keep *unum* away from *palatium*. At 26. 1 the agreement in error of PZ (om. *pertinent*) might reflect the lateness on the scene of at least some stories in Z; but their agreement in error at 5. 3 (*adoremus*) seems coincidental.

[126] For some enticing rejected readings see pp. 6 (app. n. 51), 21 (n. 2), 32 (n. 27), 40 (n. 13), 105 (n. 13).

[127] Our own apparatus gives a ratio of 72% to 28% in favour of P (about right). If only word order variations are counted, P is favoured 60% to 40% (suggesting some bias in favour of S). We have made no adjustments in the text in the light of these figures.

Influence

William's work was and was not influential. On the one hand knowledge of it spread quickly through southern England, and before the end of the century it was known on the Continent as well. But knowledge of the *complete* text, let alone the attribution to its author, was soon dissipated, and thereafter its influence, though extending beyond these shores, was confined to individual stories subsumed into larger collections. Part of the story is told by the provenances and contents of the manuscripts listed and discussed above; the rest, as far as we can know it, derives from a variety of sources. As mentioned earlier, the work was known and correctly attributed by the Augustinian Robert of Cricklade, in William's lifetime. By the mid-century it was known in London: at St Paul's the canon Adgar (c.1150–1250) mined at least twenty-two stories for his own larger collection, and dean Ralph of Diss (d.1199/1200) drew on *MBVM* 53 in his *Abbreuiationes chronicorum*. Peter of Cornwall, prior of the Augustinian canonry of Aldgate (d.1221), drew upon fifteen stories in his enormous compilation, the *Pantheologus*.[128] It was known at Canterbury by the late twelfth century, where the monk Nigel Witeker (*d.* after 1206) drew fifteen of the seventeen stories in his *Miracula S. Virginis Mariae metrice* from William.[129] Our MS S, whenever it arrived at Salisbury, is clearly a west-country production which tells us that a primitive version of William's work was known and correctly attributed in the area, unsurprisingly, by c.1200. After that we have little more information from within England until the sixteenth century. The most important exception is the use of the prologue, explicitly attributed, in the anonymous biblical commentary mentioned above.[130] This seems to reflect the same local knowledge as the attributed early draft that survives in the Salisbury manuscript. Of the Tudor antiquarians, John Bale did not know of it, but John Leland saw copies, which must have carried explicit attributions, at places not too far from Malmesbury: the Augustinian house at

---

[128] Carter, p. 62.

[129] The unique copy is BL Cotton Vesp. D. XIX; ed. J. Ziolkowski, Toronto Medieval Latin Texts 17 (Toronto, 1986); Sharpe, *Handlist*, p. 401.

[130] See above, n. 6.

Keynsham (Somerset, nr. Bristol) and Wells Cathedral.[131] Overseas, it was known at Chartres Cathedral by c.1200,[132] and at the abbey of St Denis in Paris (the provenance of MS P) about the same time. Parts of it were known throughout France by the late thirteenth century. So far we know of no evidence for its spread further afield.[133] The Prologue assumed a life of its own, and circulated under the name of Anselm. Although *MBVM* as a whole was the product of a traditional Benedictine environment, it seems that many of its stories rapidly captured and held the attention of the Augustinians and the Cistercians.

---

[131] J. Leland, *Collectanea*, ed. T. Hearne (6 vols, 2nd edn, London, 1774), IV, pp. 68, 155, the latter said to be in four books.
[132] Carter, p. 69.
[133] Gripkey's studies (above, n. 124) seem to rule out the likelihood that *MBVM* was ever known in Italy. Germany is largely *terra incognita*, though Mussafia found nothing there.

Concordance

	S	P	This ed.	Canal
Theophilus	1	1	1	1
Guy of Lescar	2		12	12
Abbot Ælfsige	3		13	13
Guimund and Drogo	4		14	14
Stained corporal	5 = 41 q.v.			
Prior of St Saviour's	6		22	22
Monk of Eynsham	7		23. 1	23
Transition	7a		23. 2	(23)
Sudden death	8		24	24
Clerk of Chartres	9	15	25	25
Five *Gaudes*	10	16	26	26
Res est amentiae	11 = 43a q.v.			
Jewish boy	12	23	33	33
Bread offered to Christ-child	13	24	34	34
Charitable almsman	14	26	36	36
Ebbo the thief	15	27	37	37
Rustic church enlarged	16	28	38	38
Three knights	17	29	39	39*
St Mary of Egypt	18		40	41
Musa	19		41	42
Abbess delivered	20		42	43
Nun's penance incomplete	21		43	44
Childbirth in the sea	22		44	45
Image insulted	23 = 55 q.v.			
Jew lends to Christian	24 = 47 q.v.			

	S	P	This ed.	Canal
Julian the Apostate	25	2	2	2
Ildefonsus	26	3	3	3
Toledo	27	4	4	4
(Transition)			4. 5	(4)
Jews of Toulouse	28	5	5	5
St Bonitus	29	6	6	6
St Dunstan	30	7	7	7
Chartres saved	31	8	8	8
Milk: Fulbert	32	9	9	9
Milk: monk with quinsy	33	10	10	10
Jerome of Pavia	34	11	11	11
Syrus	34a	12	11a	(11)
Augustine	34b	13	11b	(11)
Boethius	34c	14	11c	(11)
Devil in three beast-shapes	35		15	15
Drowned sacristan	36		16	16
Monk of Cologne	37		17	17
Vision of Wettin	38		18	18
St Odo and the thief monk	39		19	19
Pilgrim of St James	40		20	20
Haec profecto ...	40a		20a	(21)
Stained corporal	41		21	21
Prologue to Book II	41a	14a	not numbered	not numbered
Clerk of Pisa	42	17	27	27
Love by black arts	43	18	28. 1–8	28
Res est amentiae	43a	18	28. 8–11	(28)
Priest of one mass	44	19	29	29
Prayers of a friend	45	20	30	30
Two brothers at Rome	46	21	31	31
Jew lends to Christian	47	22	32	32
Dying rich man	48	25	35	35
Multa quidem	48a		44a	(46)
Mead	49		45	46

	S	P	This ed.	Canal
Wife and mistress	50		46	(47)
Woman cured	51		47	(47)
Foot cut off	52		48	(47)
Talibus dicendis	52a		48a	(48)
Fire at Mont St Michel	53		49	48
Saracens	54		50	49
Image insulted	55		51	50
Constantinople	56		52	(50)
Purification	57		53	51

*Canal 40 = St Laurence (above, n. 65).

MIRACLES OF THE BLESSED VIRGIN MARY

Prologue

1. Many, in attempting to give written expression to the praises of Our Lady Saint Mary, have been glad to lay before the human race (so far as they could) what a store of virtues *once* flowed into her, and with what readiness she *now* aids mortals in their need; with what grace of gifts she was *then* lofty and wonderful, with what compassion she is *now* powerfully unique and uniquely sweet.

2. Philosophers have asserted that there are four virtues, Justice, Prudence, Courage and Temperance, from which, as from a square,[1] the whole troop of virtues might dart forth. Our forebears[2] taught that the four primary virtues reigned in Mary.[3] So it was a very light task for them to show that the other appended virtues fitted squarely in her mind.

3. As for her Justice, their claim was that she clung so tenaciously to God's precepts as contained in the Law that she did not think that even those should be ignored that are known to be alien to her chastity: for example, purification after childbirth, sacrifice on behalf of her child, the ascent to the Temple each year.[4] For who of the faithful would doubt that she did these things over and above the call of duty?

---

[1] Carter thought of a crossroads, but the idea is rather of a square, each side of which represents a main virtue, but can take on 'appended' ones. William seems to be varying the idea of 'cardinal' virtues (the term first used by Ambrose, *In Luc.* 5. 62), without achieving lucidity. That idea was widely taken up in western hagiography, especially during the eleventh and twelfth centuries, is demonstrated by I. P. Bejczy, 'Les vertus cardinales dans l'hagiographie latine du moyen âge', *AB* 122 (2004), 312–60, not mentioning this text. The metaphor is military: for 'agmen emicet' cf. Orosius 2. 13. 5; note also Cicero, *Phil.* 13. 18 'agmine quadrato' and esp. Seneca, *Epist.* 59. 7 'ire quadrato agmine exercitum, ubi hostis ab omni parte suspectus est' (in the context of a philosophical simile about virtues).

[2] To whom (or to the *antiqui*) William appeals at §§23, 32 and 40 below (cf. also §8), though he clearly found their testimony (or rather lack of it) disconcerting. See the discussion in Carter, p. 300.

[3] Probably a reference to Fulbert of Chartres' widely known and influential sermon 'Approbatae consuetudinis', for the Virgin's Nativity (*PL* 141. 320B-324B); ed. J. M. Canal, 'Texto crítico de algunas sermones marianos de San Fulberto de Chartres o a él atribuibles', *RTAM* 30 (1963), 6–87, at p. 59 lines 99–116. Canal lists surviving copies in 'Los sermones marianos de San Fulberto de Chartres († 1028)', *RTAM* 29 (1962), 33–51, at pp. 36–7, and 'Los sermones marianos de San Fulberto de Chartres. Adición', in *RTAM* 30 (1963), 329–33, at p. 330. Early English copies are Cambridge, Pembroke Coll. 84 (s. xi ex., Bury St Edmunds), ff. 140–5, Trinity Coll. B. 14. 30 (315), ff. 48–51 (s. xii), Corpus Christi Coll. 451, ff. 189–94 (s. xii), and Worcester Cath. F. 94 (s. xii in., Worcester), ff. 77v–78v, 219–220v. It is also in the much later Exeter Cath., MS 3505 (see above, pp. xxvi, xliv). Fulbert, however, has 'fides' instead of 'iustitia'. Commentary on the content and influence of this text is provided by M. Fassler, *The Virgin of Chartres: Making History through Liturgy and the Arts* (New Haven, CONN, 2009), pp. 81–9, 122–6.

[4] Levit. 12, Luc. 2: 22 and 24 (purification and sacrifice), 2: 41–2 (annual ascent to the Temple at Passover). Cf. Fulbert, *Serm.* 'Approbatae consuetudinis', ed. Canal, p. 59 lines 108–12 (*PL* 141. 322C-D): 'Quis enim non uideat ac uidendo miretur iustitiam eius, qua sic uniuersa praecepta diuinae legis satagebat implere, ut nec ad se <non> pertinentia inexpleta relinqueret? Verbi gratia, post partum enim purificatione legali quam agebat, non egebat, quia uirum in concipiendo non nouerat.'

4. Prudence, enabling the first of women to take note of something unparalleled: how pleasing to God was the sacrifice of her chastity, which she had herself vowed[5] to God, disregarding[6] the curse of the Law. Further, after being greeted by the angel, how prudently she spoke, how easily she believed.[7] For to furnish forth her prudence she had faith and belief, for she was confident that the Holy Spirit could enable her to bring forth a son without intercourse with a man, with no danger to her modesty, and in the absence of the sting of lust.

5. Courage, enabling her unhesitatingly to vow and steadfastly to fulfil what she in her prudence recognised should take place in accordance with justice. Now it is just that you should, when He asks it, offer to God, giver of all good things, the most pleasing and beautiful thing you possess.[8] The Virgin in her prudence wisely took this point, and courageously vowed to God, and most courageously preserved, her own virginity, which she regarded as more to be cherished, more beautiful than anything else.

6. Temperance, in that to the aforesaid virtues she linked zeal for humility, which enabled her to guard whatever good the devotion of her straightforward mind and the grace of Heaven had piled up in her.

7. It was therefore a mark of Justice that she did good, of Prudence that she understood how to do it, of Courage that she persevered, of Temperance that though placed on such a height she had the humility to take care not to fall.

8. Now these virtues, as I said, have others attached to accompany them, as followers and attendants. Their application to the Mother of the Lord <our forebears>, if I remember rightly, laid out in the following scheme.

9. Justice, they say, is accompanied by Religion, which is cleanliness of life, enabling God to be pleased thereby; Piety, by which one loves one's neighbour; Gratitude, which is the recollection of a benefit received; Service, which serves Him whom it is right to obey; Truth, which teaches one to live in accordance with nature and to speak in accordance with the facts. These virtues the blessed

---

[5] Cf. Fulbert, *Serm.* 'Approbatae consuetudinis', ed. Canal, p. 57 ll. 29–30 (*PL* 141. 320D): 'uirginitatem simul et humilitatem Deo sacrificauit'; Honorius Augustodunensis (Ps.-Augustine), *De cognitione uerae uitae*: 'haec prima inter mulieres uouit Deo uirginitatem' (*PL* 172. 1001). The vow is first mentioned in the West by Augustine, *De sancta uirginitate* 4. 4 (*PL* 40. 398), and appears in the Latin *Gospel of Pseudo-Matthew* (12. 4; ed. J. Gijsel, *Corpus Christianorum, Series Apocryphorum* 9 [Turnhout, 1997], pp. 405, 407).

[6] Cf. Deut. 7: 14, not as the Vulgate but as cited in e.g. Honorius below. Cf. §25: 'uirginitatis amor et legalis maledictionis timor'. For the notion of God's pleasure at Mary's breach of the law cf. Honorius Augustodunensis, *In annuntiatione S. Mariae*: 'Lex omnes uirgines maledictioni addixerat, sicut scriptum est: Maledictus qui non fert fructum in Israel. Hanc maledictionem Deus a uirginibus per Mariam uirginem detersit, dum ipse auctor benedictionis ab intemerato utero ut sponsus de thalamo processit' (*PL* 172. 904A); also Eadmer, *De excellentia beatae Mariae*, 4 (*PL* 159. 563).

[7] Luc. 1: 34, 45–55; Fulbert, *Serm.* 'Approbatae consuetudinis', ed. Canal, p. 59 lines 107–8 (*PL* 141. 322C): 'in colloquio angelico, ubi tam constanter eloquitur, tam prudenter interrogat, tam facile credit'.

[8] See *Comm. Lam.*, p. 321 (note on I, 1745–8).

2

Mother of the Lord practised in such a way that with *religious* cleanliness of life she built a temple to the Lord God in her own body;[9] that she cultivated her neighbour in *piety*; that she was *grateful* to God for the benefits conferred on her, and in return herself made an offering of her body and soul to Him as a living sacrifice.[10] 10. She was sedulous in *serving* her elders and the deserving, so much so that, when she had heard from the angel that she was to be the Mother of God, she went up in haste to the hill country, in order to comfort an old relation when she gave birth.[11] The Mother of the Truth,[12] she leaned on *truth*. She was accustomed to live in accordance with *nature*, for she carried in her untouched womb the Architect of nature Himself; and fully knowing how to speak in accordance with the *facts*, she carefully weighed up the angel's promise in the balance of reason, so as to learn fully how what she had no doubt could and should be done was <in fact> to be done.

11. Prudence is escorted by Foresight, which sees in advance what may usefully be done in the future; by Intelligence, which understands what may usefully be done in the present; by Memory, which faithfully stores good and bad actions and past sayings.[13] No one had more *foresight* than this Lady, who, before she vowed her virginity to God, clearly foresaw what profit the making and strict keeping of that vow would bring to herself and the whole world. For she would not have made so unusual a vow if she had not foreseen that glory[14] beyond compare was thereby being heaped up for her and others. No one had more *understanding* than her: for so clear was her mind, and so aware was she of God, that she fully understood all the good for the present that was involved in the birth, Passion and Resurrection of the Lord, and the incomparable fruit that would follow in the future. 12. She had a singularly tenacious *memory*: she knew without help from others all that concerned her son, in her inner counsel heaping together things known to herself alone before pressing them upon the awareness of mankind. Hence is said of her: 'But Mary kept all these words, pondering them in her heart'.[15] It is for this reason that the whole world owes to her the full knowledge of its salvation; for she did not begrudge the apostles the knowledge she so fully commanded. As a result, since the Gospel would have made only tiny progress if the purport of its beginning had not been known, she is rightly called the apostle of apostles and evangelist of

---

[9] Cf. 1 Cor. 3: 16.

[10] Cf. Rom. 12: 1.

[11] Luc. 1: 39–56. However, Mary left her kinswoman, Elizabeth, before the latter gave birth (to John the Baptist).

[12] Ioh. 14: 6.

[13] From 'Prudence' much from Cicero, *De inv*. 2. 160, with overlap of wording.

[14] P's *gratiam* ('grace') may be preferable.

[15] Luc. 2: 19.

evangelists;[16] for it was thanks to her that the foundational doctrine shone forth on the very founders of the faith.[17]

13. To Courage are attached Greatheartedness, which plans to embark upon something great; Confidence, which takes on with assurance what has been gloriously conceived; Perseverance, which steadfastly drives forward what has been well begun; Patience, through which difficulties are borne for the sake of the expedient.[18] Now the expedient, which I have spoken of here and above,[19] I mean to be understood in the sense employed by Ambrose in his *On Duties*:[20] the useful is what is honourable and the honourable is what is expedient (though there is a different definition in the secular schools).[21] In fact, the fortunate young woman acted with Greatheartedness, so that she searched about for a good thing to begin; she began it with Confidence, and completed it with Perseverance. She maintained Patience both when she and when her son were insulted. It was a mark of Greatheartedness that she said: 'My soul doth magnify the Lord, and my spirit hath rejoiced in God my Saviour'.[22] Of Confidence: 'For behold from henceforth all generations shall call me blessed'.[23] Of Perseverance: 'Because he that is mighty hath done great things to me, and holy is his name. And his mercy is from generation unto generations, to them that fear him'.[24] And of her Patience was said: 'And thy own soul a sword shall pierce'.[25]

14. On Temperance border: Continence, through which the evil greed of the mind is ruled by the steering of counsel; Mercy, by which the mind is reined back

[16] The title 'apostola apostolorum' had been applied, not to the Virgin, but to Mary Magdalen, from the turn of the second and third centuries, though it was no longer commonly used in William's day: S. Haskins, *Mary Magdalen: Myth and Metaphor* (London, 1993), ch. 3, esp. pp. 65–7, 88–90, 134, 220–2. Remarkably, this role, if not the exact title, is given to Mary in her earliest Life, by Maximus the Confessor (d.662): Maximus the Confessor, *Life of the Virgin*, 95–9, tr. S. J. Shoemaker (New Haven, CONN, 2012), pp. 122–6 at p. 126 'a leader and a teacher to the holy apostles'. One notes also the strongly anti-Jewish tone of 96–8, 100–1. Now this Life survives only in a Georgian translation and can hardly be held to have influenced Western thought. Nonetheless, it makes one wonder whether William was acquainted with Byzantine theology, and whether for instance the Greek prelate who spent his final days at Malmesbury (*GP* 260) might have been his source of information.
[17] There is play (hard to translate) on *principii, principalis, principibus*.
[18] The passage from 'To Courage' ultimately draws on Cicero, *De inv.* 2. 163–4, but the wording rarely coincides.
[19] At the start of §11 above.
[20] Ambrose, *De offic.* 2. 25.
[21] Cf. Cicero, *De inv.* 2. 158, a standard text on rhetoric used in the non-monastic schools of William's day.
[22] Luc. 1: 46–7.
[23] Luc. 1: 48.
[24] Luc. 1: 50.
[25] Luc. 2: 35. In this period this text became central to the conception of Mary's role at the foot of the Cross: cf. Eadmer, *De excellentia beatae Mariae*, 5 (PL 159. 566–7), and Honorius Augustodunensis, *In purificatione S. Mariae* (PL 172. 850). For Anselm of Canterbury's key role in this, see R. Fulton, *From Judgment to Passion: Devotion to Christ and the Virgin Mary, 800–1200* (Columbia, NY, 2002), pp. 195–203, 232–43.

when it is thoughtlessly roused to hate someone; Modesty, from which results a careful and cautious cutting back of excess in either direction.[26] These virtues the Lady obviously practised, for she was certainly not incontinent when goaded by some pleasure, or hasty to feel hatred, or immodest in mind. How could she do what is unlawful when she was temperate in doing what is lawful?[27] 15. In addition to the precepts of Continence, she had the character that a virgin should have; as Ambrose teaches, in his customary honeyed language[28] that others cannot imitate, a virgin is one who 'defiles her sincere feelings by no desire to trick: humble of heart, serious in speech, prudent in mind. If she takes any pleasure, at least in food, she satisfies it on a little. She altogether suppresses the vices of the flesh. She is parsimonious in speaking, keen to read. Her gestures are not affected, nor her gait free and easy, nor her voice immodest. As a result, the outward appearance of her body reflects her mind and figures her uprightness'.[29] No one will deny that the Mother of the Lord had these characteristics, for her glorious life, as is sung,[30] gives light and beauty to all churches.[31]

16. Into this young woman, decked like this with a diadem of virtues, the Son of God poured all of Himself, especially by His own coming protecting the good qualities characteristic of her virginal mind.

For not only is He just: He is Justice itself, to whom is said in the psalm: 'Thou hast loved justice and hated iniquity.'[32] Therefore the justice of God penetrated His mother, who was already just, and anointed her with the oil of gladness, that is, the Holy Spirit,[33] above all her fellows, that is, all virgins, conferring fruitfulness on His mother without taking away her virginity.[34]

17. Not only is He wise: He is the Wisdom of God itself, and in Him rest all the treasures of wisdom, yea corporeally.[35] Finding a young woman possessed of

---

[26] I.e. a keeping to the middle, neither too much excess nor too much parsimony. From 'On Temperance' cf. Cicero, *De inv.* 2. 164.

[27] For *licita/illicita* cf. *GP* 75. 29: 'fructum dignum penitentie esse si qui multa illicita commiseris etiam licitis abstineas.'

[28] Cf. *GP* 77. 3: 'familiari illo et dulci stilo', wrongly translated by us. See also §41 n.

[29] *De virginibus* 2. 2; transcribed by Augustine, *De doctr. Christ.* 4. 129. 'Voluptatem … compescens', however, is not in Ambrose.

[30] This suggests a sung part of the liturgy such as an antiphon, but we have not succeeded in identifying it.

[31] Cf. Paschasius, *De partu virginis* 1 (CCCM 56C, p. 47 ll. 1–5): 'Quamuis omnium ecclesiarum uirginitas beatae et gloriosae genetricis Dei Mariae sit decus, honor et forma uirtutis, maxime tamen sanctimonialium ac uirginum, quarum castitas eius specialius illustratur uirtutibus, informatur exemplis, corroboratur et meritis.'

[32] Ps. 44: 8.

[33] Ibid. For the gloss, cf. Isidore, *Etym.* 7. 3. 29: 'Dominus oleo exultationis, hoc est Spiritu sancto, legitur fuisse unctus.'

[34] Cf. Ps.-Jerome (Paschasius), *De assumptione beatae Mariae uirginis (Cogitis me)*, 3. 16: CCSL, *Clavis Patristica Pseudepigraphorum* (Turnhout, 1990–), 2. 858; *PL* 30. 122–42, at 125; ed. CCCM 56C, pp. 109–62, at 116.

[35] Cf. Col. 2: 3, 9. With 'Not only … subject to sins' cf. Fulbert, *Serm.* 'Approbatae consuetudinis', ed. Canal, p. 59 ll. 95–8 (*PL* 141. 322B-C): 'Hoc ergo in primis astruere fas est, quod anima ipsius et caro

wisdom, the wisdom of God preserved her in that state, that is, kept her safe and pure in heart and body. For it is written: 'Wisdom will not enter into a malicious soul, nor dwell in a body subject to sins'.[36]

He is temperate, and Temperance itself, as He says in the Song of Songs: 'I am the lily of the valleys',[37] that is, the flower of the humble,[38] and also in the Gospel: 'Learn of me, because I am meek and humble of heart'.[39] Deigning to receive the Virgin's humility, he flowed into her bosom with full divinity, as he says through the prophet: 'On whom shall I rest but on him that is humble and quiet?';[40] and Mary herself says in the Gospel: 'Because he hath regarded the humility of his handmaid'.[41]

18. Not only is He strong, but He is also the Strength of God, through whom God the Father made all things from nothing.[42] Coming upon Him in His strength as the stronger, He despoiled the courts of the Devil and distributed the spoils.[43] He did not thereby enfeeble the strength of His mother, but raised it high by His power, to make her the imperial mistress of all creation, conciliating and soothing those on high and upturning and terrifying the low. God who searches the hearts and reins[44] chose her alone from all the virgins in the world, setting her apart in order to live corporeally in her whom long since, full as she was of the virtues of which I have written, He had been cherishing and embracing in the spirit.

19. Hence it seems to me that those who say that God could have saved man either through another virgin or by other means than through a virgin are very far from the truth.[45] As for those who think that God could have been embodied in some other virgin, I make a summary reply: On the contrary, He could not have because He did not wish to, and vice versa: He did not wish to because He could not. Omnipotent He may be, but there are many things which He is said not to be able to do, like lie or die, because He does not wish to. For if He wished to lie or die, He would not be omnipotent, because to lie is not a power but a sin, that is a lack of power to do good, and to die is to run short of power.[46] And it is said of Him: 'He hath done all things whatsoever He would'[47] just because He wished

---

quam elegit et habitaculum sibi fecit Sapientia Dei Patris, ab omni malitia et immunditia purissimae fuerunt, affirmante Scriptura "Quoniam in maleuolam animam ... subdito peccatis".'

[36] Sap. 1: 4.
[37] Cant. 2: 1.
[38] Cf. Ambrose, *De virginitate* 9. 51: 'lilium conuallium: flos enim humilitatis est Christus'.
[39] Matt. 11: 29.
[40] Is. 66: 2 (*Vetus Latina* version, as in e.g. Ambrose, *Exameron* 6. 10. 75 [CSEL 32. 1, p. 261]).
[41] Luc. 1: 48.
[42] Cf. Ioh. 1: 3, though not mentioning *fortitudo*. Note also §30 below.
[43] Luc. 11: 21–2 (cf. Is. 53: 12).
[44] Ps. 7: 10.
[45] Cf. Anselm, *Cur Deus homo*, 2. 8 (SAO II, p. 104).
[46] Cf. Anselm, *Proslogion*, 7 (SAO I, pp. 105–6).
[47] Ps. 113: 3.

<to do> nothing except what he ought. In the same way, I say that He neither should nor could have been born from another virgin, and (as I said) He could not just because He did not wish to.

20. Further, He did not wish because there was no reason. It is obvious that God, the Author of reason, wishes to do nothing, and what is more can do nothing, that is contrary to reason. But who could fail to see that God would have been recoiling from reason if, when He saw that absolutely all women were inferior in sanctity to the blessed Mary, He had spurned her and chosen some other to be His mother? Now I imagine that anyone who takes note of what has come earlier understands that she was superior in sanctity to all women. For other women merited *parts* of graces,[48] but she is greeted by the angel as 'full of grace'.[49]

21. What is more, to say that God should or could have repaired the sin of Adam otherwise than by a virgin birth is the same as to say that He should have done better or that He could have done equally well in another way. But if He should have done better or could have done equally well in another way, yet did not do so, He either did not wish to or did not know how to. If He did not wish to do better when He could have done, He was either grudging or slothful. If He did not know how to do better when He should have done, He was ignorant. But how alien to the nature of God are grudge-bearing, sloth and ignorance is acknowledged by anyone who sees how shameful it is to ascribe these vices to any good man. 22. It remains then that anyone who blushes to attribute these things to God, and accepts this chain of reasoning, must agree that God could not have repaired the world except by a virgin, and by this virgin in particular. He could not have because He did not wish to. He did not wish to because there was no reason. And because there was no reason, He had no obligation to. If you reverse this chain it will still be valid, thus: He ought not to have saved the human race in another way, because there was no reason to do so; and because there was no reason, He did not wish to; and because He did not wish to, He could not have, because He was neither able nor willing to act contrary to reason.

23. Now that I have briefly excerpted and brought together the views of the ancients on the virtues of the Blessed Mary, I shall wakefully speak in praise of her lofty position, which she won because of the grace of those virtues. In order to explain this the more lucidly, I shall set forth the love of Son for Mother and of Mother for Son.

24. God the Son, consubstantial and coeternal and co-omnipotent with the Father, who issued from the Father without a mother before time, wished to be born in time from a mother with no father; and He chose this young woman, for

---

[48] Cf. Ps.-Jerome (Paschasius), *De assumptione S. Mariae*, 5. 28 (CCCM 56C, p. 121).
[49] Luc. 1: 28.

the love He felt for her, to receive all His divinity flowing into her, and to become Mother of God and man. He loved her, therefore, before He was born of her, so that she might be one from whom He could worthily be born. Is this a small love, to make a mother of a girl,[50] and the Mother of the Creator from a creature? Nor did His love fall away after she gave birth; no, it increased immeasurably. For all men, born from two parents, share their love between both; but Lord Jesus, born from a mother with no father, owed and paid to His mother alone the love due to both father and mother.[51]

25. Also, there were two factors fighting it out[52] in the Virgin's mind in a mighty though unseen conflict: love of virginity and fear of the curse of the Law.[53] But after she had weighed up the issue for a long while, love proved of superior weight and fear turned tail.[54] Here God came to her rescue, snatching away from her what she feared and not removing what she loved, for her seal[55] was not broken. So He granted to her that she should be both fruitful in offspring and immune from losing her virginity.

26. As for her, did she not answer with fitting love to all she received from her son? Full she was of the Holy Spirit, which is love of father and progeny, a kind love, one that is sweet and pleasant, not fleeting but eternal. Was she not to love Him who made her mistress of all creation, queen of heaven and earth, conferring fruitfulness on her (as I said) without diminishing her chastity? No, she hung on His love with all her inmost strength; and the love that father and mother owe to their offspring she alone, that sweet and tender mother, lavished on her lord and son.[56] 27. There is no knowledge that can fathom, no eloquence that can express in words, with what sweet attention she fostered Him as a boy; with what care and attention she brought Him up as a youth on the way to manhood; with what joy she heard and saw the young man performing miracles and becoming celebrated for them; with what sadness she sighed at His Passion and death. Even these things are almost beyond our understanding, so unaccustomed are we to them. But at His resurrection and ascension, how happy were the eyes with which the lucky Virgin looked on at Him, with what joy did the blessed woman leap inwardly, not least because she could now see that what had been so long in the

---

[50] We take it that *filia* here means 'unmarried girl' (Carter translates 'maiden'); she changes her status by becoming a mother.

[51] Cf. Eadmer, *De excellentia beatae Mariae*, 4 (*PL* 159. 562C-D).

[52] For similar uses of *contendere* cf. *Comm. Lam.* I, 2158, and n. in Appendix (p. 332).

[53] Cf. above, on §4.

[54] Cf. *GP* 163. 5: 'Probeque iam conualuerat, et uictus furor terga dederat'.

[55] I.e. of her virginity. Cf. Ambrose, *Epist. extra collectionem traditae* 14. 33 (*CSEL* 82, p. 252, ll. 332–4): 'Qui cum ex Mariae nasceretur utero, genitalis tamen saeptum pudoris et intemerata uirginitatis conseruauit signacula'.

[56] Eadmer, *De excellentia beatae Mariae*, 4 (*PL* 159. 562D): 'Cum autem amorem, quem pater et mater singuli debent filio suo, debet haec felicissima matrum sola filio suo'.

fruition was being brought into effect. She saw the human race being called to salvation through the apostles, already aware as she was that it was for this reason that the Son of God had taken on His body through her and had suffered on the Cross.

28. Wherefore she rejoiced that the hope she had conceived before, and what she had hoped would prove the salvation of the whole world as a result of her vow of virginity, was now coming true. The angels rejoiced too, seeing the number of their citizens, previously diminished by sin,[57] being made up now by her blessed parturition. Men rejoiced and still rejoice that thanks to Mary they receive with a hundredfold interest what they lost thanks to the first woman. They fell as slaves, they rise as brothers and sons: brothers of the Lord, sons of Mary. This joy will grow to an incomparable degree when they enjoy present happiness in heaven in the presence of those who enabled them to attain such joys. All creation rejoiced and still rejoices. At the beginning of the world it was made by God to serve man; when man had removed himself from the knowledge and service of God, creation grieved to be subjected in foul slavery to a rebel against his Creator. But when man was saved by the blessed Mary, creation came into its old glory, grew green again in its original splendour; now it serves him[58] who serves his Creator in faith and in works.

29. So, just as God is Father and Creator of everything, so this virgin is mother and re-creator of everything, because just as nothing exists except what God made, so nothing is re-created except what the son of Holy Mary redeems.[59]

30. Let therefore the faithful soul ascend to the lookout place of the mind,[60] and see, so far as it can, how lofty is Lady Mary's position. All nature was made by God, and God was made from Mary. God, maker of everything, made Himself from Mary, and so re-made everything. He had the power to make everything from nothing, but, once everything had been violated, He did not wish to re-create it without Mary. God then is father of created things, and Mary is mother of re-created things. God begat Him through whom everything was made, and Mary bore Him through whom everything was re-made and saved.

31. On this line of reasoning it is impossible for a man to be damned if he turns to her and is looked upon by her. For because she bore Him through whom dead things live again, through whom men are saved from sin, and because there

---

[57] Referring to the doctrine (already enunciated by e.g. Augustine and Gregory) that the number of saved faithful entering Heaven made up for the number of angels who fell along with Lucifer: see Peter Lombard, *Sent.* 2. 9. 6–7 (ed. Brady, I, pp. 375–6).

[58] I.e. mankind.

[59] From 'God the Son' (§24) much from Eadmer, *De excellentia beatae Mariae*, 3–6, 11 (PL 159. 561–3, 565, 569, 577–8), with overlap of wording.

[60] An expression used by Ambrose and Bede, e.g. Ambrose, *Explanatio psalmorum xii*, Ps. 47, 1. 1 (*CSEL* 64, p. 346), Bede, *In I Sam.* 1. 1 (*CCSL* 119, p. 12).

is no justification except the one she cherished in her womb, no salvation except the one she brought forth, she is accordingly herself the mother of the Justifier and the justified, mother of the Saviour and the saved. Therefore the Mother of the God who alone condemns, who alone saves, whom alone we fear, in whom alone we hope, is our Mother. Our Judge and Saviour is our Brother. How then should we despair when our salvation or condemnation lies in the hands of a good Brother and a merciful Mother? Will a good Brother tolerate the punishment of his brothers, whom He redeemed, or a good Mother the condemnation of her sons whose Redeemer she herself bore? So the sweet Mother will ask her sweet Son, our merciful Brother, her Son on behalf of her sons, her only-begotten Son on behalf of His adopted sons. The merciful Son will gladly listen to His mother interceding for His brothers, the only-begotten for those He adopted, the Lord for those He freed.[61]

32. A further inference may be made as to the loftiness of this virgin: a matter not of affirmation but of argumentation. I speak without prejudice either to the caution of the ancients, who made no definite statement about her assumption or ascension,[62] or to any more probable opinion that may have occurred to moderns.[63] For some – and I am of their company – are not a little worried as to why our writers have either deliberately passed the matter over or hesitatingly kept silence, failing to assert roundly that the Lady, the Mother of the Lord, has already risen, and ascended to heaven with her virgin body; for this can, it seems, be proved by probable and perhaps true arguments, thus:

33. There is no doubt that the merits of the blessed Mary were in God's eyes uniquely distinguished: no single saint, or even all of them together, can be thought equal to her alone. Now it is only just that since her merits are greater in the eyes of God she should receive more excellent rewards from Him. It is

[61] From 're-creator' (§29) echoing Anselm, *Orat. 7 ad Mariam* (*SAO* III, pp. 18–25, esp. 22–4), 'All nature ... saved' (§30) as 22 ll. 97–105, almost verbatim. On this, generally regarded as the greatest of Anselm's prayers, see A. Wilmart, 'Les propres corrections de S. Anselme dans sa grande prière à la Vierge Marie', *RTAM* 2 (1930), 189–204.

[62] Cf. Ps.-Jerome (Paschasius), *Cogitis me*, 2. 12 (*CCCM* 56C, pp. 114–15): 'Quod, quia Deo nihil est inpossibile, nec nos de beata Maria factum abnuimus, quamquam *propter cautelam*, salua fide, pio magis desiderio opinari oporteat quam inconsulte *definire*, quod sine periculo nescitur'. For the development of the doctrine, see M. Jugie, *La mort et l'assomption de la Sainte Vierge: Étude historico-doctrinale* (Studi e Testi 114: Vatican, 1944), parts I–II, ch. 3. 1.

[63] Some of the subsequent discussion, as far as §40, resembles that of Ps.-Augustine (?Alcuin), *De assumptione beatae Mariae* (*PL* 40. 1141–8): copies listed by G. Quadri, *Il trattato 'De assumptione B. V. M.' de pseudo-Agostino e il suo influsso nella teologia assunzionistica latine* (Rome, 1951), pp. 6–18, H. Barré, 'La croyance à l'Assomption corporelle en Occident de 750 à 1150 environ', *Etudes Mariales* 7 (1949), 65–123, at pp. 80–100, and J. M. Canal, 'Guillermo de Malmesbury y el pseudo-Agustin', *Ephemerides Mariologicae* 9 (1959), 479–89. Early twelfth-century copies survive from Christ Church Canterbury (CCCC 332) and Worcester Cathedral Priory (Worcester Cath. F. 94). There are also reminiscences of Eadmer, *De excellentia beatae Mariae*, 7–8 (PL 159. 570C–573C).

agreed that God neglects to do nothing that is just. Wherefore we can presume to believe that the blessed Mary has by now been granted the glory of resurrection and clothed in perpetual immortality. His justice is too great, the grace given her too bountiful, for her body, the temple of God Himself, still to be waiting in the hope of rising again – a hope that stirs the ashes of all the saints with happy anticipation. But it is not presumptuous if we believe that she surpassed all the saints in her reward when we know her to have surpassed them all in merit. It is surely consistent with the just judgement of God that the greatness of the reward should be increased by the speed of its giving, especially as the liberality of the gift takes nothing away from the abundant stores of the giver: rather the Virgin's justice is shown in a good light,[64] her merits are heightened, and our faith is accordingly kindled.

34. Again: after the ascension of the Lord, though she rejoiced that the gentiles believed,[65] she was not completely happy, because she lacked the presence of her son. If I opine that the mother missed her son's presence, I am not at fault. But it is certain that she missed him not feebly but completely,[66] so that not only her soul but her body, that had known godhead and contained it, stood by her son, and certain too that her dutiful son fulfilled His mother's holy wish. For as (in the words of the apostle) 'no man ever hated his own body',[67] she loved her own flesh much more than another could: she knew that from its 'room' had issued the Saviour of the world, as a bridegroom coming out of the bride chamber.[68] The blessed Lady therefore wished that her flesh, that had done everything it could to serve the Lord, should be, together with her soul, as close as possible to her son. But who could believe that the Son resisted the wish of His mother, for in the Law He requires obedience to parents,[69] and in the most uncivilised corner of the earth child honours parent – unless there is someone so devoid of human attributes that he has passed into being as savage as a beast: though I should not think that even beasts lack love for their parents. 35. Did not He, then, the Author of pity and the Lord of nature, show to His parent what He himself commanded, and what anyone would do naturally, merely at the prompting

[64] I.e. the magnitude of God's reward *shows* how just she was.
[65] Similarly Maximus the Confessor, *Life of the Virgin*, 97–9 (transl. Shoemaker, pp. 124–6), though William must have had a different source (see p. 4 n. 16).
[66] William apparently revised this passage (see app. crit. nn. 104–5), but the outcome is still not elegant (note the three instances of *autem*).
[67] Eph. 5: 29 (where the Vulgate has 'his own flesh').
[68] Ps. 18: 6.
[69] Matt. 19: 19.

of instinct? Rather, He showed the most perfect honour to His sweet mother, honour that He understood she greatly wished. Now it would not have been perfect honour if He had not resurrected that virginal body, so that she might be completely[70] at the side of her son, whom she had completely laboured to serve.

It must be believed, then, that He placed His mother's body, His own abode, in heaven. The other saints, who, so to say, only dream of God's sweetness in their imaginations, do not think they will only be made perfectly blessed when they put on a second robe[71] in that glorious resurrection. Would then this Lady, who had tasted to the full how sweet is the Lord,[72] believe it was sufficient for her perfect blessedness if her body rotted away and she showed her presence to her son only in the spirit?

36. Nor should we imagine that He brought His mother into heaven with felicity half-mutilated and in some manner crippled; rather, we must believe that He showed her all the honour He could (and who may express how much He can?), and showed it her because He was obliged to, so as not by His own authority in turn to make void the law on honouring parents that He Himself had laid down on His own authority, and that He impresses upon the heart of men by nature.

37. More: it is written that 'The soul of the just is the seat of wisdom'.[73] Now the flesh of this virgin is the container of wisdom, and so her flesh was rich in a greater and more excellent sanctity than that of just any saint. Further, our faith is quite clear that the souls of the saints already reign in heaven. Since therefore those souls of the saints which are less in the eyes of God see God face to face, it seems unjust that one conscious of superior saintliness has not merited at least the same reward. However much this sojourning of the saints is prolonged,[74] they have bodies that are at war with their spirits, so that they each can only say: 'Unhappy man that I am, who shall deliver me from the body of this death?'[75] 38. And so, when the frame of the flesh is dissolved,[76] it is right that their bodies, which had weighed down their soul and dragged it into sin, should pay the penalty for this disobedience by rotting, and depart into earth, lapped in the quiet bosom of nature,[77] while their souls are meanwhile cleansed, by a distant hope of resurrection, from the filth accumulated through contact with their bodies. But

[70] I.e. body and soul.
[71] Cf. Ecclus. 45: 9.
[72] Ps. 33: 9.
[73] Ultimately Prov. 12: 23, but not in the Vulgate; quoted in this form by e.g. Augustine, *Serm.* 200 (*PL* 38. 1029), *Enarr. in Psalmos*, 46. 10. See Canal, p. 60 n. 45.
[74] Cf. Ps. 119: 5.
[75] Rom. 7: 24.
[76] Cf. *GP* 246. 5 (verse).
[77] Cf. Lucan 7. 810–11 (used by William elsewhere; see *GR* 49. 7 and n.).

the body of the blessed Mary did not rebel against her spirit like that, and she never experienced any discord between body and soul, for (as I said above)[78] she preserved the harmony of the virtues in such perfect balance.[79] Hence it is unjust that her body should turn to dust, for it had never brought its blandishments to bear on her soul in any wicked action.

39. What of the following point? Since we believe, as is proper, that the body of the Lord is in heaven and rules the whole universe, shall we not believe that the material of that body, which (so to say) crafted it, that is the flesh of the Virgin, is in the same place? But so as not to deal in guesswork, listen to a brief dilemma,[80] and draw the conclusion. The body of the holy Mary is either in heaven or in the earth. (Only a madman, I think, will say that it is deep in the sea or whirling through empty space.) So it is either in heaven or in the earth. It is not to be believed that it is in the earth. For her Son, who makes famous the bodies of certain saints with such a blaze of miracles, would much less permit the body of His own mother, in which He dwelt agreeably for nine months, to lie without honour if she were anywhere on earth. The glory of miracles would not be silent there; every country would hasten thither, emptying whole cities.[81] So since it is likely that her body is not in the earth or in the air or in the sea, it remains to believe that it is in heaven.[82]

40. This, more or less, is what comes to mind of what our forebears said in praise of the blessed Mary. They poured it out in fuller words and sentences; I have made a digest. But if the saints will allow me to say it, much is still lacking from this important task. By chance or on purpose, they altogether suppressed what I think is an apter means of kindling love for this Lady in the souls of the simple: I mean examples of her pity, and miracles, which are displayed to the world in no insignificant quantity. Reasonings may awaken the faith of the perfected, but it is the narration of miracles that awakens the hope and charity of the simple,[83] just

---

[78] Presumably above, §§3–15, though only by implication.

[79] For the harmony of virtues cf. *Comm. Lam.* I, 776. The intended meaning of *cumulata* is uncertain.

[80] Cf. *GP* 276. 3 ('pulcherrima disiuncta') and n.

[81] Cf. *GR* 348. 2: 'totis … migrabatur urbibus'.

[82] Cf. a part of Paul the Deacon, *In Assumptionem hom.* 2, omitted in the standard text (*PL* 95. 1569–74), but printed by G. Marocco from a Vatican manuscript (see 'Nuovi documenti sull'Assunzione del Medio Evo Latino', *Marianum* 12 [1950], 399–409, at pp. 402–3; also Canal, p. 62 n. 48, using another witness). Paul, like William, argues that Mary's body must have been treated at least as well as those of other saints. The crucial passage (reconstructed) is 'Neque fieri aliter potuit, quia, si usquam in terris esset positum, [non] crebris effulgentibus miraculis proderetur. Restat ergo ut, cum non inuenitur (inueniatur Canal) in terris, non incongrue fortasse credatur, non tamen sine anima, delatum in caelis' ('It [sc. Mary having no known tomb] could not be otherwise, for if her body were anywhere on earth it would be manifested by many brilliant miracles. The only remaining conclusion then is that, as it is not found on earth, it may appropriately be supposed to have been borne to heaven, though together with her soul.'

[83] Cf. Gregory, *Hom. in Ezech.* 2. 7. 3 (*CCSL* 142, p. 317): 'Plus enim plerumque exempla quam ratiocinationis uerba compungunt'.

as a sluggish fire revives when oil is thrown on it.[84] Reasonings teach that she *can* pity the pitiable, but it is examples of miracles that teach that she *wishes* to do what she is able to do.

41. So it is with an eye to being of use to others, as well as to serving my own interest, that I have decided to set down things I have learned, not from fleeting opinion but from reliable eyewitness or written record. I ought not to be judged to be doing harm if I repeat in my own language[85] what has been handed down in writing from the past, for maybe someone who has not come across those old accounts will by some accident dip into these new ones. But anyone who *has* read previous versions should not scorn mine, but should draw on both together to help form his mind to the service of the blessed Mary. But neither shall I make a laughing stock of myself if I write down things not written before, for I have been led to this act of daring not by a prejudice in favour of my own wit but by love for the empress of the angels. And it should certainly have been counted a fault if her particular servant had kept silent on the virtues of his Mistress. But I call the Lady herself to witness upon my soul,[86] that I have introduced absolutely nothing except what I have read in books or heard from the most respectable men.

42. Of course, if some unsought distinction of expression happens to attend the truthful telling of the facts, no fair judge should think them any the less true for that.[87] Mary does not go a-begging for men's praises. She needs no help from us, that we should try to extol her with false acclaims and muster lies to prove her piety.[88]

So, it being my intention to write something that (I hope) will be of the greatest benefit to my soul, I shall start my narrative like this.

[84] Cf. Hildebert of Lavardin, *Vita beate Marie Egiptiace*, 26–7: 'sacros ita creuit in actus / ut stagnum riuo uel torpens ignis oliuo' (ed. CCCM 209, p. 232). The poem is used later in the story of Mary of Egypt (40. 9 n.).
[85] This seems to be the meaning here (contrast §15 with n.), as also apparently in *GR* 132 (' in my own manner' rather than, as we translated, 'in ordinary language').
[86] Cf. II Cor. 1: 23.
[87] William hopes (with tongue in cheek) that any stylistic elaboration his work may accidentally take on (for he is in general aiming at ordinary language: see above) should not make it less worthy of credence.
[88] Cf. *GP* 230. 5, on Aldhelm.

BOOK ONE

1. Theophilus[1]

1. In my enthusiasm to start writing, many topics compete to press themselves upon me; but I am minded to speak first of Theophilus,[2] following a quite old source. He was a Cilician, who appeared to be living a pious life; he acted as deputy to a provincial bishop. In this post, he so deceived men's eyes, and so captured their hearts, that when the bishop was laid with his fathers the citizenry took sides with him and tried to honour him with the bishopric, despite his reluctance. It may have been the thought of the burden involved, or just pretence, that made him refuse; but by no prayers from his friends, no urgings from his metropolitan, could he be brought to give his consent. Perhaps his hope was that the next bishop would do nothing to reduce his past power.

2. As he had gone to all lengths to reject the bishopric, they looked for another man whose record made him suitable for so important a see, found him and gave him the post. New lords like having new subordinates, and prefer to employ people beholden to them and not passed on by others. So after a few days the bishop removed Theophilus from his post. He took it well for some time, happy to live a home life. But eventually he saw that the deputy who had replaced him had many attendants and flatterers, while *he* sat solitary,[3] with no one to escort him when he walked abroad. Little by little he came to feel the pain of it, gradually he began to sigh. In the end he fell sick of care:[4] he was tortured by

[1] Poncelet 74 (1634); Ihnat, *Mary and the Jews*, pp. 159–60. William's 'scriptura antiquior' is Paul the Deacon's translation of Ps.-Eutychianus, *De Theophilo poenitente* (*AASS Feb.* 1. 483–7; critical edn G. G. Meersseman, *Kritische Glossen op de griekse Theophilus-Legende* (Mededelingen van de kon. Vl. Akad. voor Wetensch., Letteren en schone Kunsten, Kl. der lett., 25, no. 4, Brussels, 1963), pp. 17–32; B. Dutton, *Gonzalo de Berceo, Obras completas*, 2 [Collección Támesis, ser. A. Monografías, 15, London, 1971], pp. 235–42), with some added anti-Jewish detail and curtailment of the end. Dominic 2 (ed. Canal, pp. 17–23), is a summary of this. A copy is found e.g. in the late eleventh-century Worcester Passional, BL Cotton Nero E. I, ff. 157–60: Jennings, 'Origins', p. 86; P. Shaw, 'The dating of William of Malmesbury's Miracles of the Virgin', *Leeds Studies in English*, n.s. 37 (2006), 391–405, at pp. 392–3. Both Dominic and Ps.-Eutychianus say that before his sacking Theophilus' piety was genuine; Dominic does not mention the execution of the Jew (this is in Ps.-Eutychianus 6: 484F); both say that the repentant Theophilus handed the charter over to the bishop, then later asked him to have it burnt.
[2] *Vicarius* of the church of Adana (southern Turkey), in the sixth century: see *BHL* 8121–6. Fulbert, in his *serm.* 'Approbatae consuetudinis' (ed. Canal, pp. 60–1; *PL* 141. 323B), mentions the miracle stories concerning Julian and Theophilus, in the reverse order, then proceeds to a summary version of the *De Theophilo poenitente* (323B-4A).
[3] Cf. Lam. 3: 28.
[4] Cf. Statius, *Theb.* 1. 400: 'aegrescit cura parenti'.

15

envy on the one hand and poverty on the other. So he looked around for remedies, drastic and wicked.

3. In the same city there lived a Jew. A widespread rumour had it that he, being skilled in the black arts, and with command over spells, could contrive anything he liked. To his house Theophilus went at dead of night, with no companion, for he was afraid of being found out – and wickedness is always fearful. He was let in at once through those cruel doors: the porter knew no one would have come there at such a frightful hour[5] if he had not been prompted by dire necessity. He obtained a private interview, and explained to the Jew why he had come, begging for his help and promising money, positive mountains of gold. The Jew, an old hand at hunting down innocent souls, was glad to promise services that would answer his need: there was nothing to prevent all he wanted happening, in fact it was in his power. Theophilus should feel no doubts, but, falling in with his advice in all confidence, he was to swear allegiance to the Devil. Theophilus could not wait to promise,[6] and made no objection to any of the Jew's instructions: such now was his lust for office.

4. For the moment he went away, filled full of promises and stuffed with hope. But the next night, at the hour appointed by the master, he came back. Hand in hand they proceeded to the town theatre. It was now in ruins, its stones scattered, but it still gave an impression of the evil that had gone on there of old. Theophilus was told that whatever he saw he should keep his head, and not be startled by any disturbance into crossing himself. In the conviction that demons do not fear that sign but abominate it,[7] he awaited the outcome of his prayers, trembling with hope. He could not help being afraid; he stood there, his blood running ice-cold with terror. Quite apart from the darkness of the night, he was harassed by awareness of his wicked actions. But his boundless desire for power suppressed and drove away all his fears.

5. And now here comes the Devil, casting before him a frightful blinding light. Surrounded by an array of henchmen, he took his place on a high platform. Then, leaning back,[8] as it seemed in his pride, he fixed the Jew with a kindly eye. He approached without a qualm, and displayed his prey. 'Look, my lord,' he said, 'how diligent I have been in serving you. As you see, I have caught this man in the toils of our arts, someone not without influence among the Christians. He is asking for your help, for he has been unjustly deprived of his office, and

---

[5] Cf. Sulpicius Severus, *Dial.* 3. 4. 4: 'in illo noctis horrore', *GR* 178. 2: 'in tali noctis horrore'; also below 31. 7: 'in ceco noctis horrore' (cf. Jerome, *Vita Pauli* 9. 4: 'per caecae noctis horrorem'; *VW* 1. 4. 2: 'in tam opacae horrore noctis').

[6] Illogically expressed: William means *citius* not *segnius*.

[7] And so would punish him for making it.

[8] Cf. *GR* 290. 1: 'dum resupinatis ceruicibus in conuiuio resideret'.

has no hope left.[9] It is of concern to your Greatness to see he does not go away empty-handed with his prayer unanswered.' 6. The Devil, 'darting his eyes, all shot with blood and gall',[10] said: 'Then let him swear homage to me, let him abjure his Christ and Mary His mother: I loathe them both equally, in hatred to the death.[11] No one can be mine if he has not rejected love and loyalty to them. And these Christians are certainly not to be trusted. When they need it, they beg for my help above all; but once their prayers are granted and they get their way they play the ingrate and run back to their Christ. To make sure there is no doubt about what he has done, let him confirm the arrangement in writing, and certify the document with an image of his face imprinted on wax.' Theophilus was not abashed[12] by these stern words. He fell at the monster's feet and plastered them with kisses; he promised the world, and did no less than he promised. The bargain once struck, all that lust for power faded away into smoke and cloud.

7. That night passed uneasily for the bishop, disturbed as he was by furies and dreams from hell. So when dawn was scarcely breaking, he leapt from his bed, summoned a meeting of the clergy, and restored Theophilus to his post, turning the other man out. He was not ashamed to confess openly that it had been the Devil's doing to have driven away a man of sound belief and upright behaviour in favour of that worthless character.

This swelled Theophilus' head. Delighted at getting what he wanted, he began to behave arrogantly, doing down the other's supporters and showing no moderation in word or action. From the Jew there came the pinpricks of almost daily reminders: Look how far the speed of the Devil outstripped the tardiness of Christ! His mere nod had given Theophilus back his position! But the Jew was shortly afterwards detected in his illicit ways. He was convicted and beheaded, learning to his discomfiture how severe the laws of the state are. As for Theophilus, he saw the error of his ways, and cursed the devilish practices which, when exposed, resulted here on earth in the public rejection of the devotee and cast him for the future into everlasting fires.

8. To cut a long story short, Theophilus for some time pondered the aid he might ask for from all the saints, before preferring to turn to the holy Lady, the Virgin and Mother, to mediate for him with her son. He went into her church in the city, narrow enough in area,[13] but distinguished by many miracles performed there. Inside, he stamped on the ground, his breast shaking with sobs; he shed

---

[9] Cf. *Comm. Lam.* III, 756: 'omnis spei naufragam', and *GR* 196. 6: 'qui nunc uitae naufragus, exul spei, alterius opem implorat.'

[10] Prudentius, *Psychom.* 114 (transl. H. J. Thomson).

[11] For 'digladiabili odio' cf. *VW* 2. 16. 2 and n.

[12] For 'nichilo refractior' cf. 32. 3 and elsewhere, e.g. *GP* 74. 28.

[13] Cf. *GP* 92. 2: 'aecclesiam, situ quidem pro angustia spatii modicam'. But in our passage *sinu* seems to go rather better with *parietum*.

floods of tears, he sent up groans to burden the stars; he called on Christ with wails of lamentation and drew Mary forth from heaven. He was heard instantly on high, and his words came through to the very throne <of judgement>. But the joy of having his prayer answered was for the moment delayed, so that the guilt of his hideous offence might be reduced by the passage of time. But when, forty days later, he settled his tired limbs to sleep, there appeared in his dreams the glory of the universe, the Lady of heaven, commanding reverence by her starry radiance and the wonder of her countenance. She rebuffed the wretch with well-meant sharpness, asking him how he had the face to call upon her when he well knew that he had denied both her and her son: 'It is folly to pile audacity on top of dire faithlessness. 9. Injuring a son is an insult to the mother, and conversely abusing the mother is a reproach to the son. My son is generous to grant a favour, but terrible in revenge.[14] Well, so far as I am concerned, I should give you what you ask.[15] For I fold all Christians in my sweet and tender embrace, especially those who never forget my church and continually cross its threshold. Them I cannot bear to make sad even in a small matter. It is they whom I reconcile with my son if He is angry, they whom I cherish as a mother. How though shall I appeal to my son? If you had offended only one of us two, you might have hoped for forgiveness: one would try to lighten the offence of the other, and beg for forgiveness, but since you have offended us both, you wretched manikin, what room will there be for asking pardon?'

10. With words to this effect the Lady Mary terrified Theophilus, shaking his bones and melting his marrow with their artful sweetness.[16] What delightful threats! What pity! If only you would find me, yes if only, worthy of the same anger, so that, even though I have not deserved to experience the sweetness of your chiding, I might undergo your menaces and cease from wrongdoing! Wounds inflicted by a friend in a rage are of more profit than the kisses of a flattering enemy. But Theophilus, confident in the constancy of the faith that filled him, replied along these lines (I pass over the exact words so as not to bore my readers): 'I do not deny that I am a sinner; I confess it, with groans. But I have not gone more astray than others whom I have read to have repented and been saved. 11. Rahab had once sold her body for gain in a brothel, making free of herself to the populace;[17] yet later she became ancestor of patriarchs and kings. David, from whose happy stock you yourself are descended,[18] committed a cruel

[14] Cf. *VD* 2. 22 (of St Andrew).
[15] This seems to be the sense.
[16] I.e. their sweetness was disguised beneath their sharpness.
[17] Cf. Ios. 6: 17.
[18] Cf. 44. 5. From early on it was claimed that Mary was descended from David through one or both of her parents, Ioachim and Anne. This was a commonplace by William's time: M. Clayton, *The Apocryphal Gospels of Mary in Anglo-Saxon England* (Cambridge, 1998²), pp. 21, 116, 167, 319, 323.

double deception out of the weakness of the flesh,[19] yet brought back the Holy Spirit to himself[20] by uttering a single word of confession. The Ninevites, who had deserved to be burned up by lightning for their heinous crimes, disarmed the wrath of God by a three-day fast.[21] The first of the apostles, guilty of the same offence as I, save that *he* sinned out of fear, *I* out of ambition, recovered his old position by shedding tears for a single hour.[22] It was these examples that emboldened me to take refuge with you, for it was you who by bearing a single child brought forth a remedy for the whole world.'

12. She said: 'Then confess to me, and patch up your belief in the true faith, which you vomited up for the Devil, so that I may report it to my son.' Theophilus had from childhood learned the formula of the creed, and he still remembered it. Now he recited it from memory, word-perfect. The Virgin went away, as if he had satisfied her; and he awoke.

Then indeed, feeling more hopeful of being forgiven, he started fasting as well as praying. He was continuing his vigil on the third night, when he fell asleep. Suddenly the Virgin appeared to him, speaking more pleasantly, looking more cheerful: God 'had breathed a happy sparkle on her eyes'.[23] 'I have won over my son,' she said, 'and come now to bring you, my man, full absolution for what you did. So stop sobbing, stop torturing yourself: through me the sentence of the highest Judge has been mitigated. As for you, make sure you remain loyal to Him who gave His favour, and beholden to her who mediated for you.' 13. Another might have been satisfied to have heard the words of the empress of heaven, and to have been found worthy of her promises. But he was not content with this generosity, and, happily daring, he ventured to ask more: he requested the document he had given to the Enemy, urging over and over again that nothing was accomplished unless the paper were given back; if it were not, he would die wretched and conscience-stricken. But the Lady, to gratify a guilty man reconciled through her, a captive freed through her, used her imperial authority to wring the document out of the Enemy; and three nights later she placed it on his breast as he slept, after giving him the kind of sweet admonition that the honeyed

[19] The double crime was David sleeping with Bathsheba, then arranging for the death of her husband Uriah the Hittite (2 Reg. 11–12). Dominic mentions only David's name, without specifying his crime. The crime, and the 'word of confession' (identified by its *titulus* in the Vulgate as Ps. 50), are specified in Ps.-Eutychianus 10 (485E).

[20] Cf. Ps. 50: 13: 'spiritum sanctum tuum ne auferas a me'.

[21] Ion. 3: 5–10. But neither lightning nor three days for their fast are specified in the biblical text, nor in e.g. the Commentary by Jerome (CCSL 76, pp. 405–10).

[22] Matt. 26: 75, of S. Peter. There is no specific mention in Scripture either of his losing his position or recovering it by repentence, but cf. Ps.-Eutychianus 10 (485E): 'Si non fuisset poenitentia, quomodo Petrus apostolorum princeps ... Christum Dominum non semel aut bis sed ter negans, postea duriter lugendo et indulgentiam tanti delicti meruit et maiorem honorem adeptus pastor constitutus est dominici rationalis ouilis?'

[23] Virgil, *Aen.* 1. 591 (transl. Austin).

eloquence of the Virgin can utter. He was getting ready to thank her and fall to his knees when sleep and the vision forsook him.

14. As it was Sunday, he hurried to church, and finding the bishop performing Mass he told him in the hearing of the people what had befallen him, holding nothing back. As he spoke his hearers wept tears called forth[24] both by his hideous deed and by the speed of his forgiveness. He consigned to the flames the grim and unlucky document, and went to communion. Then you might have seen God's grace smiling upon him: light brighter than the sun's played on his face as he took communion, and, two days later, he breathed his last, removed by a happy death from the wickedness of this world.

---

[24] For *inuitare* used thus cf. 10. 2.

2. Julian the Apostate[1]

1. I have now made a start on what I have to say. Henceforth I shall compose my unfolding narrative in such a way as to show that the blessed Virgin has poured out the bowels of her compassion on every rank, every condition of men, and on both sexes. And I shall adduce events differing in time, place and type,[2] like flowers woven into a garland[3] for the queen of heaven.

2. In fulfilment of this promise,[4] I shall start with bishops, the highest type[5] of men, and place Basil first. He, as is well known, was archbishop of Caesarea[6] in Cappadocia. A somewhat brusque rejoinder of his had enraged the apostate Julian, who, breathing poison and foaming filth, had vomited forth the threat that he would turn the city upside down when he returned from his projected campaign in Persia. Basil knew the tyrant for a stubborn and impious man, for they had formerly been at school together, and he devised twin counter-measures. First, the people were all to go to the church of the holy Mother of God, high up outside the town, fast for three days, and launch prayers at the sacrilegious emperor. Second, the public treasury was to be emptied smartly, to satisfy, if it came to it, the desires[7] of the insolent Caesar: gold will soften anything. 3. A large quantity of precious metal was accordingly brought by the citizenry and placed in the archbishop's chamber. Each portion was identified with the owner's own name and seal, so that if Julian did not come back the money could be returned to the owner in full; otherwise, Julian would be given it. Two days later

---

[1] Poncelet 318 (506). A similar account is given in Dominic 4 (ed. Canal, pp. 25–7), but William's version depends upon Dominic's own source, the Latin version of Ps.-Amphilochius, *Vita S. Basilii*, 35–7 (*BHL* 1024; *AASS Iun.* II, 944B-F): J. Wortley, 'The pseudo-Amphilochian *Vita Basilii*: an apocryphal Life of Saint Basil the Great', *Florilegium* 2 (1980), 217–39. This popular *Vita* is found e.g. in the late eleventh-century Worcester Passional, BL Cotton Nero E. I, ff. 61v–70; Jennings, 'Origins', p. 85; P. Jackson and M. Lapidge, 'The contents of the Cotton-Corpus Legendary', in *Holy Men and Holy Women in Old English Prose Saints' Lives and their Contexts*, ed. P. E. Szarmach (Albany, NY, 1996), pp. 131–46, at 135; P. Shaw, 'A dead killer? Saint Mercurius, killer of Julian the Apostate, in the works of William of Malmesbury', *Leeds Studies in English*, n.s. 35 (2004), 1–22. William abbreviates slightly. This miracle is summarised by Fulbert, *Serm.* 'Approbatae consuetudinis', ed. Canal, p. 60 ll. 130–2 (*PL* 141. 323A-B).
[2] William thinks of the *rank* of the persons concerned (see above, Introduction, p. xxxi).
[3] An 'anthology'. Cf. the use of *attexam* above, and *texuimus* in 40. 1.
[4] Mussafia, 'Studien' IV, p. 24, thought that William must have been referring to some passage in his own Prologue, but, as Carter saw (p. 24, n. 1), the reference can only be to the preceding paragraph. Though obscurely and indeed misleadingly phrased, it picks up the mention of different ranks, highest of which are (arch)bishops.
[5] Picking up 'type' in §1.
[6] Basil, abp. of Caesarea (d.379): *BHL* 1022–7; *Oxford Dictionary of Saints*, pp. 44–5. Julian the Apostate was emperor 361–3, Mercurius was martyred under Decius (c.250): *BHL* 5933–9. In fact Basil did not become abp. until seven years after Julian's death. The place is modern Kayseri (Turkey). The church was perhaps on the prominent citadel hill, rather than on the very high volcano 25 miles away. Ps.-Amphilochius (and following him Dominic) talk of a *mons Didymi*. As Ps.-Amphilochius was writing no earlier than the ninth century, it is difficult to know whether this has any authority.
[7] Cf. *GP* 43. 1: 'affluebantque sibi tanta quae quantumlibet ambitum possent et explere et uincere.'

Basil saw in a dream the most happy Lady, seated on a lofty throne near the cathedral, attended by large numbers of respectful servants from on high. She proceeded to utter a welcome order: 'Call me Mercurius, to go and kill Julian, who is breathless with rage against the Lord my Son.' Mercurius answered the call, took the message, and set off with his lance. He had been a spirited soldier,[8] who had suffered for Christ at Caesarea in pagan times, sacrificing the present life in hope of life to come.

4. When the archbishop awoke, he let the rest sleep on; taking a single man into his confidence, he set off from the mountain, where this had been taking place, for the city to get at the truth of the dream. Coming to the martyr's sepulchre, he found that the lance that was kept there in his memory had disappeared. The guardian, under questioning, swore by all that is sacred that it had been there the evening before. Not much later, after the rumour had spread and the people had been woken to give praises to Mary, the lance was found in its place, wet with newly shed blood. It is a fact, vouched for by historians,[9] that Julian died that night from an unseen wound. His evil ways had disturbed those above; now his fierce soul would trouble those below too.

---

[8] With 'festiuitatis egregiae miles' cf. GR 145. 2 'insignis festiuitatis miles' (where our translation 'charm' is probably wrong). But the phrase is mysterious.

[9] Dominic refers to Cassiodorus, *Historia Tripartita*, 6. 47 (*CSEL* 71, pp. 371–2), and tells at length the famous story (with the punchline 'You have conquered, Nazarene!').

3. Ildefonsus[1]

1. Toledo is a city in Spain, the seat of an archbishop in time past, but perhaps no longer:[2] some say that the primacy has been claimed by another city called Mérida, famous for housing the bones of the blessed martyr Eulalia.[3] As for Hispalis, it is in the hands of the Saracens, who call it 'Seville' in their foreign tongue.[4]

2. In Toledo Ildefonsus was at one time archbishop,[5] a pupil of St Isidore bishop of Hispalis,[6] who out of love for our Lady produced a sizeable volume on her perpetual virginity.[7] Written in the 'synonymous' style,[8] it is especially aimed at Jews and at Helvidius, who clamour against catholics, saying that Mary gave birth not to God but only a man, and after childbirth was not a virgin. Ildefonsus, ever vigilant and acute, routed their insane ideas by the brilliance of reason, and blotted them out with the lightning of gospel instances. How welcome this was to Mother and Virgin she herself showed when she appeared to the bishop as he watched in the church, and, holding out the book, thanked him with the characteristic sweetness that only those who have experienced it can judge.

3. Reinvigorated by this divine encouragement, the energetic man threw himself with especial intensity into greater displays of devotion. He urged at more than one Council that the Feast of the Mother of God should be held every year, on the eighth day before the Nativity of our Lord. It seemed only reasonable that one should pass from the service of the parent, as being already pregnant, to the service of the Son. Also, as the Annunciation of the Virgin was often deprived

---

[1] Poncelet 1117 (1720); J. M. Canal, 'San Ildefonso de Toledo. Historia y leyenda', *Ephemerides Mariologicae* 17 (1967), 437–62, at pp. 450–1, printing this miracle at pp. 459–61; Ihnat, *Mary and the Jews*, pp. 164–6. The main source is HM 1 (Dexter, pp. 15–17), itself based upon the *Vita Ildefonsi* falsely ascribed to Cixila, abp. of Toledo (*BHL* 3919; *PL* 96. 43–8), which William also knew. William supplemented these with Ildefonsus's own writing, and a text of the tenth Council of Toledo. The epilogue, in which William attempts to reconcile the death of Siagrius with the Virgin's characteristic mercy, is his own.
[2] It was still an archbishopric in William's day, the seat occupied by the famous Raymond (1124–52). His predecessor, Bernard de Sedirac/of Agen, had become Spain's first primate in 1088/9.
[3] Eulalia: *BHL* 2699–703; *Oxford Dictionary of Saints*, pp. 184–5. William may have known of this from Prudentius, *Peristeph.* 3. 186.
[4] Cf. *GR* 167. 2, without mention of Mérida, which was a metropolitan see from Visigothic times until 1120, when the dignity was transferred to Compostela.
[5] Abp. 657–67.
[6] That Ildefonsus was Isidore's pupil is stated by the *Vita* (*PL* 96. 43), not HM.
[7] Ildefonsus of Toledo, *De perpetua uirginitate beatae Mariae*: CPL 1247; ed. CCSL 114A.
[8] So the *Vita* itself ('libellum uirginitatis more synonymiae' *PL* 96. 47), but not HM. The reference is to the so-called *stylus Isidorianus*, whereby the same phrase is repeated several times using different words but with identical meaning: M. Winterbottom, 'Aldhelm's prose style and its origins', *Anglo-Saxon England* 6 (1977), 59–62; M. Díaz y Díaz, 'Literary aspects of the Visigothic liturgy', in *Visigothic Spain: New Approaches*, ed. E. James (Oxford, 1980), p. 69. William himself used it at times (e.g. in §3 'mercaretur dampnum, restauraret dispendium').

of rites of its own because of the Passion and Resurrection,[9] he was taking care to make good the loss and restore what was passed over. So a decree was made both during Ildefonsus' lifetime and also (as Toledo IX. c. 1) after his death.[10]

4. With the devotion of the bishop grew the generosity of the Virgin. On the eve of one such feast, when, as was his custom, he was spending the night alone in the church, with every one else shut out, he saw the Lady sitting on a throne next to the altar. She gave him a friendly nod to approach, and presented him with the white vestment that we call an alb, and the throne, decking out the gift with fulsome language. 'Here for you,' she said, 'are the throne and vestment that I have brought from paradise, where my son dwells. So, whenever you wish, you shall sit on the throne and put on the alb. But I warn you, do not let your successors dare to do the same, unless they want to find out to their cost what folly it is to attempt what is higher than one's due.'

5. After these kind words to Ildefonsus, the blessed Lady went away, leaving him the throne and the vestment. So long as he lived he made use of them, and behaved in a way that was worthy of them. But his successor Siagrius[11] made light of Mary's words; no doubt he thought them a mere old wives' tale. Anyway, he <one day> took his place on the throne to officiate at mass, and ordered the vestment from paradise to be produced. When his staff reminded him of the injunction from Heaven, he replied that he was as devout towards the holy Virgin as his predecessor, no less holy, and of the same rank. He had scarcely sat down on the throne and polluted the sacred vestment with his touch, when he fell of a sudden, and stained the paved floor with his subsequent death. The servitors who saw his temerity so swiftly punished were terrified, and hastened to put the throne and vestment back in the sacristy. No one to this day has been found ready to risk testing out the truth of the matter, and find out to their own peril whether the old story is true.[12]

6. But it is quite remarkable, indeed almost incredible, that (as in this story) the Mother of Mercy and Pity should have punished a man, however temerarious.

[9] Because their dates (Easter Sunday always falls between 22 Mar. and 25 Apr.) could interfere with the day of the Annunciation (25 Mar.). The new feast, held on 18 December, was later popular only on the Iberian peninsula. It is therefore significant that it was introduced at the abbey of Bury St Edmunds by Abbot Anselm (1121–48; see above, pp. xvi–xviii): *The Customary of the Benedictine Abbey of Bury St Edmunds in Suffolk* (The Suffolk Record Society, 1973), ed. A. Gransden, pp. 96–9, 122; id., 'The cult of St Mary at Beodricisworth and then in Bury St Edmunds Abbey to c.1150', *Journal of Ecclesiastical History* 55 (2004), 627–53, at pp. 648–9.

[10] In fact Toledo X, held on 1 Dec. 656, presided over by Eugenius III, Ildefonsus' predecessor: *PL* 84. 439–52, at 441. Ildefonsus was only created abp. in the following year. William will have found the conciliar *acta* in a copy of the *Pseudo-Isidorian Decretals* (*PL* 130. 527; P. Hinschius, *Decretales Pseudo-Isidorianae* … [Leipzig, 1863], no. 400), which he used in several of his writings: Thomson, *William of Malmesbury*, pp. 64–6, 131–2.

[11] So also HM, but no abp. of this name is known; Ildefonsus's successor was named Quiricus (667–80). The *Vita Ildefonsi* has Sisibut, who was actually abp. 690–3, exiled by the sixteenth Council of Toledo.

[12] William's own comment; HM says only that the alb 'hactenus seruatur' in the cathedral's treasury.

At any rate, every age has heard it repeatedly declared that she is the essence of mercy, the path of pity, the gateway to sweetness. Surely then the fount of clemency did not dry up, the way of pity did not get diverted, the door of sweetness did not close? Rather, it must be that she allowed in Siagrius' case, and sometimes allows in other cases, that men should pay the penalty for their sins, so that, when she feels pity (as she often does), she may not be thought to be straying from the path of justice. The wise man must make this distinction: the merciful Lady is never to be imagined to turn away from justice, although she is almost always perceived as inclined rather towards pity.

4. Toledo[1]

1. Reliable histories assert that Spain was at one time overburdened by the number of Jews there; and unambiguous rumour insists that it is no less polluted by them nowadays too.[2] For instance, it has more than once been reported that at Narbonne[3] they have a supreme pope, to whom Jews run from all over the world, piling gifts upon him, or deciding by his arbitration any dispute arising among them that requires someone to resolve it.[4]

2. Such a great number of them had swamped Toledo in the time of Reccared,[5] king of the Goths and ruler of Spain, that they attempted to claim equal rank with Christians in all respects, and used bribery to try to bring about the annulment of regulations passed against them by councils at Toledo. They tested the mettle of the pious king, but the unbelievers could find nothing in his breast that encouraged their arts:[6] their cash was beneath the notice of the self-controlled king. Hence the compliment to him in a letter he received from the blessed Gregory, that he did not sell justice for gold: rather he rated justice above gold. The letter is to be found in the ninth book of the *Registrum*.[7]

3. The reason for the discomfiture of the Jews is known to be this. On the day of the Assumption of the holy Lady, the people of Toledo took a holiday from all business, as the joyful occasion required, and went to church. The other rites had been completed amid the festal hubbub, and the priest was dripping the

---

[1] Poncelet 283 (914); Ihnat, *Mary and the Jews*, pp. 163–4. From §3, the main source is TS 1 (Dexter, pp. 39–40); William has prefaced this with a good deal of historical context. His knowledge of the anti-Semitism of King Reccared and the policies that flowed from it could have come from the canons of Toledo III (589), probably via Pseudo-Isidore (ed. Hinschius, no. 354), and perhaps a copy of the Visigothic Laws, although this is unlikely to have been available in the England of William's day: see the list of surviving MSS in *Leges Visigothorum*, ed. K. Zeumer, *MGH Leges* 1. 1. 35–456, at pp. xix–xxv. On the condition of the Jews in Visigothic Spain, see S. Katz, *The Jews in the Visigothic and Frankish kingdoms of Spain and Gaul* (Cambridge, MA, 1937), and W. Drews, *The Unknown Neighbour: The Jew in the Thought of Isidore of Seville* (Leiden, 2006), esp. pp. 7–32.
[2] We have not succeeded in identifying these histories. For persecution of the Jews in twelfth-century Spain, see Y. Baer, *A History of the Jews in Christian Spain* (English transl., 2 vols, Philadelphia, PA, 1965), chs. 1–2.
[3] Now more than 100km from the Spanish frontier.
[4] Apparently the earliest English reference to the dynasty of the Kalonymides, who traced their authority within Narbonne to Charlemagne and beyond: Katz, *The Jews in the Visigothic and Frankish Kingdoms of Spain and Gaul*, Appendix III; I. Levi, 'Le Roi Juif de Narbonne', *Revue des études juives* 48 (1904), 197–207; id., 'Encore un mot sur le Roi Juif de Narbonne', ibid. 49 (1905), 147–50; A. Graboïs, 'La dynastie des "Rois juifs" de Narbonne (IXe-XIIIe siècles)', in *Narbonne. Archéologie et histoire: Narbonne au Moyen-Âge* (Narbonne, 1973), pp. 49–56, esp. p. 50; J. Schatzmiller, 'Politics and the myth of origins; the case of the medieval Jews', in *Les Juifs au regard de l'histoire, Mélanges en l'honneur de Bernhard Blumenkranz*, ed. G. Dahan (Paris, 1985), pp. 49–61, esp. 54–8.
[5] 586–601. He is mentioned in GR 167. 1 ('Ricaredus').
[6] Cf. VW 1. 11. 2 (of King Edward the Confessor).
[7] Gregory, *Registrum* 9. 229 (*Epistola ad Recaredum regem*); CCSL 140A, pp. 805–10 (esp. p. 807 ll. 56–7: 'auro innocentiam praetulit').

secrets of the mass into the ears of God alone,[8] when behold a voice came down from above and was heard clearly by the congregation. It sounded like that of a woman carried away by grief. It kept saying: 'O the shame, O the pain, that the enemies of my son dwell amid His faithful! How shameful and disgusting it is that they are this day turning on His image with the same fury with which they once attacked Him in the flesh.' 4. Complaint on these lines was clearly enough heard, but when some people ran outside they could see no one anywhere, and everybody spoke in undertones, such was their amazement. Later, after mass and consultation with the archbishop, troops were told off to go to Jewish homes, and break the doors down if there was any resistance, to see if they had, as the voice had asserted, done anything that day to match their madness of old. Off the soldiers went, killing those who saw fit to stand up to them. They went into the synagogue, looted the holy of holies, and found a wax model caricaturing Lord Jesus, crowned with thorns, spat upon, and finally run through with a lance. As a result, the Jews they found then were put to the sword; the rest later fell foul of the laws. It was a fine exploit the Christians were engaged in: they could reckon up a laurel for themselves in heaven for each Jew they killed.

5. That is how the Jews of Toledo came to be wiped out. The rest of them all over Spain were either converted or expelled in the time of King Sisebut,[9] dedicatee of St Isidore's book on the Nature of Things.[10] But later, as happens in periods of decadence, they enormously increased again; the Christians made mock of them to be sure, but they were concerned with their own enrichment. They never thought of taking themselves off, as will be clear from the following instance.[11] For as I am speaking of Jews, I want to tell of something that happened in connection with the Jews of Toulouse: a pleasant story and one to make the reader smile.[12] And it will not be irrelevant: an injury to her Son was appropriately requited in a way that brought glory to the blessed Mary.

---

[8] I.e. uttering the *Secretum* (the 'oratio super oblata' spoken quietly by the priest following the *Offertorium*), as TS makes clear. Cf. the broader meaning ('mystery') at 30. 6 'in secreto missae'.

[9] Early in his reign (612–21) Sisebut ordered the forced baptism of the Spanish Jews, possibly offering them the alternative of exile: Drews, *The Unknown Neighbour*, pp. 16–17 and nn. One possible source for William's information is Isidore's *Historia Gothorum*, ed. C. Rodríguez Alonso (León, 1975), 60 'Qui [*sc.* Sisebutus] in initio regni Iudaeos ad fidem Christianam permouens ... potestate ... compulit'. However, this work was apparently rare in medieval England. Only one possibly identifiable copy is recorded, at Rochester Cathedral Priory in 1122/3 (*Corpus of British Medieval Library Catalogues* 4, ed. R. Sharpe *et al.* [London, 1996], B77. †58b 'Gothorum hystoria'); but this might have been the *Getica* of Jordanes. Another possibility is can. 57 of the fourth Council of Toledo, referring to those who 'ad Christianitatem uenire coacti sunt, sicut factum est temporibus religiosissimi principis Sisebuti'. The canons of this council were available to William in the version of the Pseudo-Isidorian Decretals that he knew (ed. Hinschius, no. 362). The alternative of expulsion could be William's embroidery.

[10] Isidore, *De natura rerum: CPL* 1188. A copy survives in Oxford, Bodl. Libr., MS Auct. F. 3. 14, ff. 1–19v, made at Malmesbury for William: Thomson, *William of Malmesbury*, pp. 83–5, 210.

[11] The 'instance' is meant to prove the continuing presence of Jews in the same general area.

[12] Cf. *GP* 153. 3 and n. (of bitter taste).

27

5. Jews of Toulouse[1]

1. Gascony, which, as expert geographers affirm,[2] borders on Spain, has as its metropolis Toulouse. The city is celebrated for housing the bodies of many saints, and particularly the excellent martyr Saturninus, who was sent flying all the way down the Capitol steps by an excited heathen mob;[3] they tied him to the flanks of an untamed bull and drove it down the steep slope, making of him a holy witness to Christ by his dire end.[4]

2. It was here that a large number of the accursed race lived in the time of the 'old' count William, father of the Raymond who was one of the prime movers of the crusade to Jerusalem.[5] The Jews were so out of control that in the wantonness of their wealth they took advantage of the prince's mildness, going so far as to mingle with the Christians and force their way into the church on feast days, greet what they heard there with guffaws, and take the tale back home. These occasions were marked by great insolence on their part and great indignation on ours.

3. It was against this background that on the Friday before Easter, when the story of the Passion is customarily read from St John, a witty Jew made open mock of one of our people, of good birth but excommunicate, for listening closely to the gospel. He went so far as to abuse Christ in foul language, saying that he was a wizard who had deserved execution; as for us, we were dustmen, fixated on the embers from funeral pyres, worshipping as we did men dead and gone, Jesus and those who witnessed to Him. The Christian was incensed (a noble wrath befits a noble man); he punched the Jew and left him dead at his feet. What prowess to be able to lay low a rascal with the blow of a bare hand! News of the event spread among the Jews. They lost no time in assembling, and started to bay round the ducal palace: you might have thought the Furies were howling. The count, taking cognisance of this contentious case, put it off to the

---

[1] Poncelet 1780; Carter, pp. 340–1; Ihnat, *Mary and the Jews*, pp. 168–9, 173–5. William's source has not been identified.

[2] Or 'those who know the area' (Carter), in either case a possible reference to Pliny, *Nat. hist.* 4. 110.

[3] 'gentile tumens' echoes Statius, *Theb.* 8. 429, where the meaning is 'in pride of race' (transl. Shackleton Bailey). William has deftly introduced a Christian note: 'excited like heathens.'

[4] So Gregory of Tours, *In gloria martyrum*, 47 (*MGH Script. Meroving.* 1/2, p. 70): 'Qui impulsu paganorum bouis petulci religatus uestigiis per grados capitulii precipitatus praesentem finiuit uitam, capitis conpage dispersa.' Even closer to William's wording is the twelfth-century *Le guide du pèlerin de Saint-Jacques de Compostelle*, ed. J. Vielliard (Mâçon, 1950[2]), p. 48: '... tauris acerrimis ac indomitis alligatus, atque a summa Capitolii arce ... per omnes gradus lapideos precipitatus ... dignam Christo animam reddidit'. Carter suspected that William and the Pilgrim's Guide relied upon a common source derived from Gregory.

[5] So also *GR* 388. 1, wrongly: Raymond's father was Pons (d. c.1060), whom William has probably confused with *his* father William III Taillefer (950–1037). See C. de Vic and J. J. Vaissète, *Histoire générale de Languedoc, continuée jusqu'en 1790 par E. Rosbach*, ed. E. Dulaurier, E. Mabelle, and E. Barry (16 vols, Toulouse, 1872–1904), III, esp. pp. 415–566 (on Raymond IV).

next day. When the Jews objected that this was the Sabbath day, on which they were not allowed to transact any business, let alone go to law, the case was set for the following Monday.

4. Meanwhile the Jews, directly or through patrons, badgered the count, promising gold and suppressing nothing that might bring us into disrepute. What does the accursed hunger for money fail to obtain?[6] The count, already more or less won over to love the wicked Jews, threatened punishment for the great man who had disturbed the peace of his court. This could not be kept from the nobles, who formed a cabal: it would set (they said) a very bad example for the future if the lord count should punish a Christian, even verbally, for killing a Jew, especially one so well born, who, like Mattathias, had had zeal for the law of God.[7] An act that anyone else might take as a cause for praise, the count was willing to cheapen in return for gold. He should face up to the situation and ward off the injury. 5. Not only would they themselves not tolerate that a punishment inflicted on a Christian should damage our faith: they would exact the same penalty from the Jews annually. One of them should in future be put on display on that day to bare his neck to a Christian and take a cuff or a blow, to teach the Jews how foolish it was to abuse Christ. If the count did not countenance this, he should be abandoned by them all, as someone who overlooked injuries to Christ, a half-Jew in fact. This was to be proclaimed with a single voice: everyone is involved if the next-door house is in flames.[8] Well, the day came, the parties took their places, the complaints were advanced and examined. The chief men, as usual, proceeded to judgement. When the decision was announced, the count was astonished; he had imagined that his treasury would reap the benefit from their favourable view.[9] But he was defeated by this united stand and gave in, preferring confrontation with the Jews to the risk of so many noblemen seceding.

6. So that is the custom there to this day. A Jew chosen by lot proffers his neck to a Christian, his head previously shaved by his friends, so that he cannot be grabbed by the hair, and smeared with honey, so that the slippery substance frustrates the blow: though the Christians for their part always find a way of getting round the Jews' devices. Noble youths pay a lot to be the one to strike, or if possible shatter, a head thus put on public show. In planting that punch, they show their own prowess – and avenge the injury done to Christ.[10]

---

[6] Cf. Virgil, *Aen.* 3. 56–7 (*GR* 108. 3 and n.).
[7] I Macc. 2: 27.
[8] Horace, *Epist.* 1. 18. 84.
[9] I.e. that the man would be punished with a fine.
[10] Similarly Adhemar of Chabannes, *Chronicon* 3. 52 (*MGH SS* 4, p. 139), c.1020. It was apparently still practised in William's day: *Cartulaire de l'abbaye de Saint-Sernin de Toulouse*, ed. C. Douais (Paris, 1887), pp. 200–1, in a document dated certainly 1106–39, by the editor c.1106 or c.1110.

6. St Bonitus and his vestment[1]

1. There is a city in the Auvergne (once the border between Gauls and Goths) then called *Arvernus*, but nowadays Clermont. Here of old, as we learn from Gregory of Tours,[2] all the Roman nobility assembled. In our time a very famous council was held there, at which the Christians' crusade to Jerusalem was promulgated.[3]

2. Of this city Sidonius, distinguished for his ancestry and his writings, was first prefect and then bishop. Another bishop (I do not commit myself as to whether he came after or before Sidonius, for fear a mistake might damage belief in my reliability) was the holy Bonitus,[4] a devotee of the blessed Mary and one who loved her with a singular passion. He never interrupted his virtuous practices, and had made it his unvarying custom to spend all night in the church of St Michael, there being an altar to our Lady in that place of prayer. Here he made of himself a living sacrifice to God,[5] requesting forgiveness for past misdeeds and guard against ones in the future. Recollection of his guilt brought forth tears, that flowed the more freely because of his affectionate love for the Mother of God. All this took place not in front of the altar, for he thought himself unworthy of that, but in a secluded corner of the church, where he could escape the notice of the populace, even when there was a milling crowd. So this was where he poured out his prayer, which God received the more gladly because in the eyes of man it was uttered with such abasement and submissiveness.

3. So one night, when he was carrying out his usual observances, he saw a long procession wending its way. In front went standard-bearers, and behind them a whole ritual procession in due order, like the one the sedulousness of the devout has devised for use in church. There were men in albs, from whose forms the inmost light poured forth, casting its radiance near and far alike.[6] The confined space seethed, so numerous were the blessed ones – not bodies, though, but spirits. Sweet was the harmony of voices that charmed the bishop's ears; the repeated[7] song filled the air with music.

---

[1] Poncelet 175. The main source is one of Carter's MB collection: the rhythmic *Vita* 'Praesul erat Deo gratus' (*BHL* 1420, pr. G. Lozinski, *De Saint Bon … par Gautier de Coincy* [Helsinki, 1938], App. II, Version A, p. 104, and Crane, no. 38), to which William has added historical and geographical context and numerous narrative details. For instance, the MB version makes no reference to Bonitus' see or the historical period in which he lived.

[2] *In gloria confessorum*, 5 (*MGH Script. Meroving.* 1/2, p. 301).

[3] The Council of Clermont, 1095, of which William gives a detailed account in *GR* 344–7.

[4] Sidonius was bp. 471–86, Bon or Bonitus 690–c.706. Bonitus's feast (15 Jan.) was observed at Malmesbury: F. Wormald, *English Monastic Kalendars after AD 1100* (Henry Bradshaw Soc. 77, 81: 1939, 1946), p. 97. It does not appear in any other surviving English medieval kalendars, but it was also observed at Norwich Cathedral Priory (inform. from N. J. Morgan).

[5] Cf. Rom. 12: 1.

[6] For *lux intima* cf. *Comm. Lam.* III, 209.

[7] Perhaps 'echoing'.

He had never in his life known anything so sweet. He fled out of fear rather than gazing out of love. The stone still preserves the traces of his flight, hollowed out as it is where he pressed back against the wall. I believe, and my faith is not misplaced,[8] that the flint-hard rock yielded before the fear of the man of God.

4. After them came the lofty Lady of the angels, led along by patriarchs and prophets. The rest of the saints took their places at a distance, like subordinates, awaiting the nod of the Lady. She ordered a celebration of mass. When they asked who she desired to officiate, she said: 'Let Bonitus sing mass. It is he whom I judge worthy.'

It was in vain that Bonitus now tried to go on hiding or to offer excuses. He was pulled out of his corner and placed before the altar. The holy vestments were brought out of the Lady's casket,[9] and the bishop was told to hurry himself. All the saints were competing in pious rivalry as to who was to help him put on his alb, who to hand him his girdle, who to smooth out the creases in his vestment. Nor is it surprising that they competed to serve one whom out of them all the Lady had chosen to pronounce worthy. 5. At first he officiated in fear and trembling, but gradually he put aside his fright and grew confident and fearless. So he made a good job of the office, and was told to draw near. The Lady feels beholden to her servants even for the slightest service, and knows how to give no slight recompense; she ordered Bonitus to go away with the vestment as a gift, and to preach to others how generous is Heaven. He made public what had taken place without overcolouring it, but he never became puffed up by empty flattery.

6. If some reader of slender faith asks for witnesses of this story, I shall bring forward for him the whole clergy and people of Clermont, and to cap them Herbert, bishop of Norwich, of revered memory,[10] who was found worthy to see the vestment itself;[11] but though he made every enquiry he was unable to find out what kind of fabric or weave it is made of. The difficulty of learning these details shows how misguided doubters are. So too does what befell Bonitus' successor.

7. This man, in the course of a good life, had knocked at the door of religion without yet perfectly attaining the deepest secrets. When he conceived the hope

[8] Cf. Virgil, *Aen*. 4. 12.
[9] *Scrinium* can mean a shrine or any kind of chest or casket. Here, one imagines that the reference is to a box large enough to contain a set of vestments, perhaps carried by Mary herself.
[10] 1094/5–1119. Presumably William had the story directly from this man, of whom he has more to say in *GP* 74. 14–19. But see Crane, no. 38; the end of the poem talks of the impossibility of identifying the textile, though William attributes this information to Herbert.
[11] First recorded in the late tenth century as the gift, made in 988, of Adelaide, wife of Hugh Capet, to Gerbert, abp. of Reims: L. Bréhier, 'Deux inventaires du trésor de la Cathédrale de Clermont au Xe siècle', *Etudes archéologiques suppl. à la Revue d'Auvergne* (Clermont-Ferrand, 1910), pp. 34–48. Regarded as having miraculous powers by the eleventh century at earliest, by the twelfth it was being displayed annually to the populace on the saint's feast. Vincent of Beauvais (*Speculum historiale*, 7. 97) says that this was still being done in his own day.

of being rewarded in the same way,[12] he went into the church by night, taking no one with him. But sleep soon overcame the eyes of the presumptuous man; he fell to the floor then, and in the morning found himself back in his own room; no one knew whose hands had carried him from the church. A second removal followed a second presumption, and the third time he gave up. From then on he devoted himself to holy works rather than hope of miracles, thanking St Mary for not driving him out with contumely but instead taking him away gently in his well-meant sin.

8. Indeed, our good Lady and merciful Empress takes the trouble to seek out opportunities to spare her servants when they do wrong. And I make so bold as to say that if she could have found a reason to conceal, mitigate, and excuse in the eyes of her son the temerity of Siagrius, whose fate I related above,[13] she would not have allowed him to be punished. But in Bonitus' case, however great his fault,[14] it had been blotted out and obscured by many good actions, and Lady Mary was glad to come to his aid, ensuring that someone who had done wrong in all innocence was dealt with gently.

---

[12] I.e. as Bonitus.

[13] See 3. 5.

[14] The phrase is ill-expressed: *quantulamcumque* is ambiguous, and *superfluitatem* imprecise.

7. St Dunstan and the Virgin's choir[1]

1. Greater Britain, which is now called England and by some, because it is surrounded by the ocean, another world,[2] has in its eastern part the city of Canterbury, the seat of archbishops. The city is famous for the many saints whose ashes lie there, and behind its unbroken circuit of walls, though it has more than once experienced war, it is vibrant and powerful.[3]

The first holder of the see was Augustine, follower of Gregory the Great;[4] he presided over the church of the Lord Saviour, which he found there, of antique Roman construction.[5] Outside the city he established the monastery of the apostles Peter and Paul. Hadrian, its abbot some years later, built adjacent to the greater church an oratory dedicated to Mary, holy Mother of God.[6] I have included this fact because it is highly relevant to my purpose.

2. The twenty-second archbishop of the city was Dunstan,[7] a man who held to the right if any man ever did; you would find it easier to marvel at him than to give him the praise he deserves.[8] Among the saints he was especially attached to the blessed Mary and the apostle Andrew;[9] he gave them every possible attention, building churches in their honour and equipping the churchmen. The saints to whom he was dear were not slothful in repaying their client in every manner he wished. The apostle was so visible to him that he often confronted him face to face and taught him how to avoid adversities and be moderate in prosperity.[10]

3. He often spent long nights watching in the oratory of the holy Mother of the Lord which I mentioned, and miraculously saw her in person while awake.[11]

---

[1] Poncelet 45 (150). The main sources are *GP* 19. 9–11 and *VD* 2. 27–8, conflated. William also refers to, but apparently does not use, the early *Vita Dunstani* by B., and makes marginal use of the later one by Osbern of Canterbury. He does not seem to have used the Life by Eadmer. There is detailed discussion in Carter, pp. 349–56.

[2] *GR* 54. 1 and n.

[3] A summary of *GP* pr. 1.

[4] *GP* 1. 1.

[5] For 'he presided over ... Roman construction' the source is Bede, *HE* 1. 33. The monastery was by William's time dedicated to St Augustine.

[6] Similarly *VD* 2. 28. 1. According to Bede (*HE* 5. 20. 1), Abbot Hadrian was buried 'in monasterio suo in ecclesia beatae Dei genetricis'. This was a funerary chapel, actually commissioned before Hadrian's time by King Eadbald and consecrated by Archbp. Mellitus (619–24; Bede, *HE* 2. 6. 2), sited to the east of the main church and on the same axis. It was demolished by Abbot Scollandus (1070–87) and replaced by his new abbey church: *St Augustine's Abbey Canterbury*, ed. R. Gem (London, 1997), pp. 37, 111. William's statement that Hadrian built an 'oratory' adjacent to the greater church was therefore probably no more than intelligent guesswork.

[7] Twenty-third, according to his own listing in *GP* 1–14.

[8] Cf. *GR* 54. 1, of Bede.

[9] For St Andrew's advocacy of Dunstan, cf. *VD* 1. 24. 3, 29. 2; 2. 24. 5–6.

[10] Similarly *GP* 19. 10.

[11] Cf. *GP* 19. 10. But in *VD* 2. 28. 1–2 he was on his way to the oratory, and applied his eyes to cracks in the walls to see the vision.

Around the Lady sat a company of virgins, whose faces and dress betrayed their divine nature. All of these were being encouraged to praise Christ by the Lady Empress, who was singing in a charming voice the following verses:

Companions, let us sing, let us sing in honour of the Lord!

Let the sweet love of Christ resound from our pious lips.

4. The blessed virgins responded to the lead given by their mistress by singing the verses that follow:

The first man in his pride plunged from a great light to the depths,

Thus when the first man swelled up, he plunged to the depths.

For the guilt of one all his descendants perished;

All are saved thanks to the merit of one.

It was a woman alone who opened the door to death,

And a woman alone by whom life returned.[12]

5. While the blessed instructress who was leading the song frequently repeated the earlier[13] verses, the holy virgins tactfully chided the bishop for his silence and urged him to sing by sweetly admonishing him. He pleaded ignorance: no mortal knew how to bring out such a concordant song.[14] But they kept on at him to <take part>[15] if only to honour his own mother, whom he could see there dressed as beautifully as the others. <And eventually> he burst out into this song of praise: 'O King of glory, born of the Virgin Mary, save the race of Christians who are pilgrims on this earth', and the rest, which you can find, if you will, in the Life of Dunstan.[16]

6. Great proofs are these to show to men the sweetness of the blessed Mary, displayed by her to a servant who won her favour by long service. And great the praise redounding to the man, that, though not yet free of the muddy frame of the body, he saw with his eyes and heard with his ears what other holy men, in their great longing over many years, can only hope will be granted them in a future life. Let others think what they will; I should prefer to the whole world

---

[12] Sedulius, *Hymn*. 1. 1–8 (*CSEL* 10, p. 155), as in Osbern, *Vita Dunstani*, 40 (Stubbs, *Memorials*, p. 118), not *VD*, which omits lines 3–6. The version of lines 7 and 8, however, is different from Osbern's and the same as *VD*. It is possible that William was referring to his own copy of the complete text.

[13] I.e. the couplet 'cantemus ... pio'. The girls want Dunstan to join them in their sung response.

[14] Presumably a reference to the music, since the text was already ancient.

[15] The text is slightly lacunose. William drastically summarises his own version as given in *VD* 2. 27. 1: 'iuuenis ... arguit tacentem, cum uel propter matris gloriam debuisset in Christi erumpere laudem'; the youth teaches Dunstan, who then sings the hymn. B's addition of 'suauibus concentibus associaretur' is not foolish, but it will not necessarily be what William wrote.

[16] Presumably William refers to the *Vita S. Dunstani* by B., 29. 5 (*Early Lives*, p. 86), but its text, and that in Eadmer, *Vita S. Dunstani*, 29 (Stubbs, *Memorials*, p. 206), and *VD* 2. 27. 2, are different: 'O rex gentium dominator omnium, propter sedem maiestatis tuae da nobis indulgentiam, rex Christe, peccatorum.' William is closer to the version in Osbern, 40 (Stubbs, *Memorials*, p. 118): 'O rex dominator gentium salua genus Christianorum in terra adhuc peregrinantium'. It seems to have been of English origin.

a single glimpse of her, and weighed in that balance I count as nothing all the miracles anyone has done or will do.[17] If anyone says I err, I err willingly and with pleasure; and I have no wish ever to be freed from this error.

[17] The paragraph to this point is taken over almost verbatim from *VD* 2. 28. 3 (where see nn.).

8. Chartres saved by the Virgin's shift[1]

1. My pen must next leave England and stray away to Chartres, to relate what took place there, thanks to the help of the blessed Virgin, to counter Rollo and the Normans. For though he had ravaged almost all Gaul, particularly along the sea coast, with nothing able to resist his mad assault – the sword of Gaul was no match for the Norman axe – he was brought to a halt at Chartres.

2. The citizenry did not trust weapons or walls; instead they implored the blessed Mary for aid, and displayed to blow in the winds above the battlements, like a standard, the chemise of the glorious Virgin.[2] One of the Charleses had had it brought for him from Constantinople,[3] and housed it in Chartres. When the enemy saw it they burst out laughing, and directed their arrows at it through the empty air. But before long, blinded by an avenging God, they found themselves unable to move forward or back. The townsmen were delighted to see it, and leapt down from the walls, killing Normans to their hearts' content so long as fortune favoured them. But Rollo got away; God was keeping him back to believe in Him later.

---

[1] Poncelet 76 (695). The siege took place in the summer of 911. William follows closely his own account as given in GR 127. 2–3. The main source for that seems to have been Dominic 5 (ed. Canal, pp. 27–8), with perhaps some reference to William of Jumièges, *Gesta Normannorum Ducum*, 2. 8–9, 12 (14–15, 18), ed. E. van Houts (2 vols, Oxford, 1992, 1995), I, pp. 61–3, 66–7. The various versions of the siege and associated legend, and the later influence of William's account, are discussed by Carter, pp. 358–68; see also Fassler, *The Virgin of Chartres*, pp. 16–23.

[2] According to the earlier sources, the tunic was borne at the head of a force, led by the bishop, which issued forth from the city against the attackers. Dominic alone says that Rollo's army was blinded by the sight of it.

[3] Charles the Bald, according to GR 127. 2, where William seems to imply that the emperor found the item in Constantinople in person, though he (or another) corrected this in the B version. There is no mention of this in the earlier sources, nor in D. Iogna-Prat, 'Le culte de la Vierge sous le règne de Charles le Chauve', in *Marie: Le culte de la Vierge dans la société médiévale*, ed. D. Iogna-Prat, É. Palazzo and D. Russo (Paris, 1996), pp. 65–98. Dominic refers only to 'tunicam ... quae tunc temporis in thesaurario basilicae dignissime seruabatur'. It is known to have been venerated at Chartres by the late tenth century (Fassler, *The Virgin of Chartres*, pp. 21, 38, figs. 2. 1–2).

9. Milk: Fulbert of Chartres[1]

1. Later on, Fulbert was bishop in the same city. His assiduity and learning showed itself especially in his love of St Mary. For example, not content with the traditional rites in honour of the ever-virgin, he took particular pains by personal example to see that her Nativity should be celebrated throughout the Latin world.[2] To cap her praises, he composed a sermon[3] and responsories[4] which are so well known that they do not need to be recorded[5] by me.

2. The excellent Lady, knowing how much she owed to him, and never slow to act, made due return.[6] Once, when he was lying sick and almost at death's door, she visited him in person, and made milk from her breasts fall on his face in his despair, after a friendly exchange in which she asked him kindly why he was so fearful at the apparent nearness of death. Recognising her face, he replied that he had hopes of *her* mercy, but was afraid of the judgement of her Son: though merciful and well-disposed, He is also truthful and just.[7] She said: 'Do not be afraid, my Fulbert, do not be afraid. I, to whom you have so long given your service, will mediate between you and my Son. And to reassure you about the future, I will now ensure that you make a good recovery from this illness.' No sooner had she spoken when she exposed her breast and let fall upon him three drops of the precious and fragrant liquid, before departing. Fulbert was forthwith restored to complete health, and ordered the heavenly substance to be taken up in a silver vessel and preserved as a memento of the event.

---

[1] Poncelet 667 (1221), the source unknown; cf. William's earlier brief remarks on Fulbert and his devotion to the Virgin in *GR* 186 and 285.

[2] The Feast of the Nativity had been celebrated in the West long before Fulbert, who however showed his support for it by dedicating to it the cathedral which he began to rebuild after a fire in 1020: Fassler, *The Virgin of Chartres*, pp. 79–81. William's words overlap with those of Fulbert, *Serm.* 'Approbatae consuetudinis' (ed. Canal, p. 56 lines 8–15; *PL* 141. 320B-C): 'Unde post alia quaedam ipsius antiquiora solemnia non fuit contenta deuotio fidelium, quin natiuitas solemne superadderet hodiernum. Hac itaque die peculiariter in Ecclesia recitandus esse uidetur ille liber, qui de ortu eius et uita scriptus inueniebatur, si non iudicassent eum patres inter apocrypha numerandum. At quoniam magnis ac sapientibus uiris ita uisum est, nos alia quaedam sed non aliena legentes, ecclesiasticum morem debitis officiis exsequamur.'

[3] See above, p. 1 n. 3. It seems that William knew only Fulbert's sermon 'Approbatae consuetudinis', though at least three other Marian sermons attributed to him survive in English copies: Canal, 'Los sermones marianos de san Fulberto de Chartres', *RTAM* 29 (1962), 39 (a single copy), 41–2; Fassler, *The Virgin of Chartres*, pp. 112–15.

[4] Presumably meaning the *responsoria* in honour of the (Nativity of the) Virgin, 'Solem iustitiae regem', 'Stirps Iesse' and 'Ad nutum Domini', printed together as 'Hymnus XI' in *PL* 141. 345A; Y. Delaporte, 'Fulbert de Chartres et l'école chartraine de chant liturgique au xie siècle', *Études grégoriennes* 2 (1957), 51–81, at pp. 55–6; Fassler, *The Virgin of Chartres*, pp. 122–8.

[5] There is a play on *nota* and *notas*.

[6] Alluded to in *GR* 285. 1.

[7] Cf. *Comm. Lam.* II, 1097–8: 'Deus est misericors et miserator, et patiens et multae misericordiae, sed est et uerax.'

3. Who would believe this story, were it not so widely told that it seems shameless to disbelieve all those who agree on it? Lord, it is apparently not enough if she looks after those who love her with help that never fails: she must needs also give them milk to satisfy their bodies![8]

In any case, the air of the city of Chartres still breathes the devotion of Fulbert, second to none as it is in all Gaul for learning and the number of its clergy. What is more, it is so fervent in venerating St Mary that if any one, even a common man, calls her simply 'St Mary' without adding 'Our Lady', it is an offence that brings condemnation and almost merits capital punishment; everyone brands it with a gesture of contemptuous reproach.

[8] An awkward phrase: the Virgin gives her milk as a general gives pay to his men.

10. Milk: monk with quinsy[1]

1. A monk experienced a similar beneficent gift of milk, and has long since won everlasting fame for the mercy shown him by the Mother. Because this is so like the previous miracle, I shall tell of it here by anticipation, even though I may seem to be transgressing against the grouping by persons.[2]

There was a monk in times past who was devoted to sweet St Mary. She was not yet receiving such elaborate service from the clergy in public gatherings,[3] and anyone who sang her Hours in private was revered as a prodigy. 2. Our monk used to collect them up wherever he found them, and sing them in church after the canonical Hours when every one was on the way out. He observed this practice without wearying, by day and by night, often standing, more often praying on bended knee; he never sat or lay down, for fear lest indulging the body should sap the virtue of the prayer.[4] He thought it sweet to speak of her, sweet to reflect on her. He sought out opportunities to tell of her miracles, and rejoiced to be questioned about them. He had tears ready to summon up at every mention of her.[5] His marrow was quite melted for love of her, and he was moved to the depths of his being at the thought of her sweetness.

3. Such constant and heartfelt attentions made the Empress his friend. To set the scene for showing this, she allowed him for some time to suffer an uncomfortable swelling on his neck. It grew by the day, and crept up to his throat, cutting off the passage of food down it.[6] Not being able to eat, he took to his bed. The doctors' name for this very serious illness is quinsy.[7] If the neck swells on the outside and grows red, they think it curable. If not, and the swelling remains inside the throat, they pronounce that death is certain to follow. This was the ailment that weighed heavy upon him; he could hardly breathe, and lay unable to move. They were not far from giving him up for dead. Some even swore he had already expired. Others were loud in putting the other view, pointing to the strong pulse as proof of the folly of the pessimists.

---

[1] Poncelet 461 (1660). According to Carter this is expanded from the version in TS 11, which he identifies with the text pr. Dexter, pp. 54–7. However, he also identifies this text (which is in verse) as in MB and this is certainly correct. It may be that these versions were one and the same, i.e. that one adopted the version of the other. As the MB version is in verse, like the rest of MB, it would seem that TS lifted from MB rather than the reverse.

[2] See above, 2. 1–2, and the Introduction, pp. xxxiii–xxxiv.

[3] I.e. as she does nowadays.

[4] A striking adaptation of *GR* 213. 2 = *GP* 74. 21.

[5] Or: 'every time he remembered her.'

[6] The text is probably unsound. Instead of the otiose *fautium*, one expects a mention of the monk's voice, given what Mary says of its loss at §4 below.

[7] Cf. Pliny, *Nat. hist.* 26. 6, with similar wording, though if William refers to this, then he has confused quinsy with carbuncles. Cf. a similar confusion in *GP* 68. 8 (with note).

4. All this time he was being watched over by Heaven: the most holy Lady was holding him up in her arms. She had come swiftly in her mercy, for her aid is the more remarkable the more signal the danger. She let the nectar from her breasts drip into the mouth of the sick man, while uttering these words of consolation: 'Do not be afraid, my dear one; you are not going to die. I did come tardily, for I had other servants of mine to attend to. I should not have allowed the neck, through which my praises have so often sounded forth, to swell up in this ugly manner, or the voice with which you used to greet me to fall silent. But I come, I do come, friend, and will make up for my slow arrival by the speed of the cure. This gift of health here on earth will be surety for the eventual prize, a guarantee of the eternal joy, that you will have for ever after your death, in the company of me and my Son.'

5. As she spoke, she drew her hand across his neck and throat, touching the affected spot with her bejewelled fingers. Health swiftly accompanied the healing hand. The tumour went down and softened, the deadly pus was expelled. The monk's first feeble impulse was to try to grovel at the knees of his healer. But she gradually slipped away. He sprang to his feet, but when he tried to worship and embrace his saviour he grasped only the empty air.

When the rest expressed their astonishment, he flew at them: 'You unlucky ones, who did not honour the queen of glory or even offer her a seat! Did you not see her lying here unworthily in the straw and rolling in the dust?[8] You did not even keep quiet in reverence for her: she was put off by the row you made, and went away.' These words, when his restored health and the tears that followed made them credible, not surprisingly fired many to love of our Lady.

6. What of the milk? I have no idea if it is misguided to think she still has milk in her breasts to revive her servant. So let us take the safer line and believe that to be the milk of kindness and mercy, in which she knows how to abound more than all saints, and that such things can be seen only by means of bodily images, and expressed only in bodily words.[9]

---

[8] Yet Mary had been suckling the monk.
[9] For similar comment on the necessity of conveying divine attributes by means of corporeal images, see *Comm. Lam.* I, 2997–3002 and p. 332 (comparing 17. 5 below).

11. Jerome of Pavia[1]

1. You too, Jerome, shall enter these pages,[2] and swell the number of bishops. You were once a priest outside Pavia.[3] Yet though you lived far from the city you were not all that rustic in character. You served the holy Virgin Mary devotedly, passing nights as well as days in this zealous activity. You followed in the steps of the ancient Jerome particularly in that what he had made a start on by his sermons you completed by your behaviour: you did not fall short of him in dutifulness or bring discredit to his name. This did not escape the kind heart of the kind Rewarder, but she recompensed you an hundredfold.[4]

2. When the bishop of the city went the way of mortals and came to the end of his life, lay and clergy were of one mind: Heaven must be asked for help, and for an answer to the question, whom did God wish to be bishop. Their prayers were not answered for a little while, so they followed up their petitions with fasting.

Then the Lady gave a certain pious man the privilege of a clear vision of her, in which she seemed to press upon him these words: 'Have no doubt about the bishop: make my chancellor[5] bishop.' When the elder asked the name of the chancellor, she gave him yours. Happy man indeed, who as chancellor [*cancellarius*] of so excellent a Lady never went beyond the bounds [*cancellos*] of justice! That can be the only possible judgement on you, considering that she, who as sanctuary of God Himself has knowledge of all secrets, praised you so highly! Raised to a lofty position, you subsequently did everything possible to promote virtue and show your love of the Benefactress.

---

[1] Poncelet 99. From HM 13 (Dexter, p. 28), which however does not specify that Jerome was a priest from the country district near the city. William may have had another source for this, but what it could have been is unknown. The brief *Vita* in *AASS Jul.* 5. 322 says that Jerome had served as sacristan in the Pavian church of S. Maria de Pertica (built in 677, now destroyed). The *Cronica breuis de sanctis episcopis Ticinensibus*, ed. R. Maiocchi and F. Quintavalle, in Muratori, *Rer. Ital. Script.*, 2nd edn, 11/1 (1903), p. 62, says that he had served as priest and sacrist in S. Maria ad Perticas, where he was devoted to the Virgin and performed miracles; that he was elected bishop through the merits of the Virgin, who prompted an angelic revelation to King Desiderius, rebuking him for the prior election of a certain Augustine. On being conducted to the king, Jerome hung his cope on a sunbeam. In the early fourteenth-century *De laudibus ciuitatis Ticinensis*, ed. Maiocchi and Quintavalle (Muratori, *Rer. Ital. Script.* 11/1 [1903]), which used the *Cronica breuis* as a source, the same miracle is referred to, 'sicut habetis in libro de miraculis sancte Marie uirginis' (p. 12).

[2] Cf. *GR* 4. pr. 5. (Saint) Jerome was bp. of Pavia 778–87; *BHL Suppl.*, p. 424.

[3] MW suggests that *suburbanae* is an error, by William or a scribe, for *insubrianae* or a similar adjective from *Insuber* ('Insubrian'). Jerome's *Vita* (*AASS Jul.* 5. 321B) has 'Papiae in Insubria'.

[4] Cf. Jerome, *Epist.* 66. 7. 4 (*CSEL* 54, p. 656, line 1): 'parua dimisimus et grandia possidemus, centuplicato faenore Christi promissa redduntur'.

[5] Whatever William thought it meant, he took the term 'chancellor' here from HM 13. It is used again in 25. 5 (from HM 3), of a clerk of Fulbert's, and of an ignorant priest in 29. 6 (from HM 9); in both these cases Mary protests at the treatment of her favourite.

3. That city, which had once nurtured the blessed Martin,[6] was previously known as Ticinum, because a river of that name[7] washes its walls. But under King Theodoric (the legitimate ruler of Italy in the time of the emperor Zeno, though later its tyrannical oppressor) its walls were extended and its buildings made grander, and it came by a stroke of chance to change its name. The king's daughter, provoked by the report of these developments, was on her way to the city with a large company of attendants. When she saw from some way off the size of the buildings and the sky-menacing battlements of the towers,[8] she said: 'Goodness [*papae*], what a wonderful place!' The girl's remark was seized upon. Everyone dropped the proper ancient name, and both newcomers and inhabitants always speak of *Papia*.[9]

11a. Syrus[10]

1. It was in Pavia that Syrus, one of the seventy[11] disciples, first sowed the seeds of the Gospel. He was poor in the number of his followers, but rich in knowledge of Christ, whom he carried in his breast. He set off by himself to the city, accompanied only by Eventius;[12] but he was brought to a halt on the near side of the river, whose rapid current made crossing impossible. By chance a poor man was rowing a fishing boat with all his skill, now avoiding the waves, now frustrating them by passing between them. Syrus hailed him to bring his craft inshore, but the silly rustic took no notice. 2. Then he removed his cloak and laid it on the water, and with a swift leap took his stand on it as though it were dry land. The winds proved kind, and soon carried the cloak into deep water, before bringing Syrus safe and sound to the further bank. He had been relying on his staff to propel him, his footing secure as he warded off the rolling waves.

---

[6] Sulpicius Severus, *Vita S. Martini*, 2. 1 (ed. Halm, p. 111). What follows is not in the HM version.
[7] The Ticinus (now Ticino). So *De laudibus*, p. 2.
[8] Cf. VW 1. 8. 6 and n. 4.
[9] Zeno reigned 474–5, 476–91, Theodoric ruled Italy 493–526. The two men had dealings from 483, when Theodoric became *magister militum*. He entered Italy, with Zeno's encouragement, in 488. Pavia changed its name in the eighth century. William's account of this, otherwise unknown, bears some resemblance to that given in the *De laudibus*, p. 2, which describes how St Syrus prophesied its future greatness: 'tale sortita est nomen ut quod a "pape", quod est "mirum", Papia mirabilis diceretur.'
[10] The source of the story of St Syrus (bp. of Pavia 283–339), which has nothing to do with Mary, is unknown. It does not appear in the saint's main *Vita* (BHL 7976; ed. B. Mombritius, *Sanctuarium* [rev. edn in 2 vols, Paris, 1901/repr. Hildesheim, 1978], II, pp. 542–7), or in the *Cronica breuis*, p. 60. But note *De laudibus*, p. 2: 'uolante ad populum fama miraculorum, que in itinere beatissimus pater patrauerat Syrus, comite sibi decoro leuita Yuentio'.
[11] Luc. 10: 1–24. The number was 72, according to MS S. Syrus does not appear in any of the received lists of the 70 or 72 disciples (PG 92. 519–24, 543–6, 1061–6, all giving 70). Perhaps William or his source confused him with Silas, bp. of Corinth, who does appear in the earliest lists.
[12] Properly Inuentius (Invenzio), Syrus's successor but one as bp. of Pavia (353–92).

42

The citizens who witnessed the incident greeted Syrus with enthusiasm, and he had no difficulty in getting all or almost all to believe his preaching. The miracle had been compounded by the state of his clothing; a few little drops had dampened it, and it only needed a shake from those holy hands to become quite dry.

11b. Augustine[13]

1. There[14] rests Augustine, that untiring torrent of eloquence, clear-voiced trumpet of the word of God. When, as is well known, the Vandals besieged the city of Hippo, where Augustine was bishop, he died to the world and was taken into heaven.[15] But after his death the same Vandals took over the whole of Africa and stained it with the Arian heresy,[16] banishing all the catholic bishops to exile in Sardinia, as we read in the Life of St Fulgentius.[17] The bishops who faced exile, unwilling for the bones of so great a father to be polluted by contact with heretics, removed them from their tomb and buried them in Sardinia. But here is a wonder for you to listen to, handed down by the Fathers of the Church. While the holy body was being dug up, a snake was seen to come out of the tomb, a dreadful sight. Harming no one, and harmed by none, it dragged itself along in scaly coils, and slipped away who knows where;[18] perhaps this was just chance, or perhaps it was a natural phenomenon, for students of nature claim that from the spine of a wise man after his death is born that wisest of animals.[19]

2. Many years passed, and Liutprand, king of the Lombards, purchased <the bones> from Sardinia, weight for weight in gold, and placed them in the crypt at Pavia.[20] I have heard from a most truthful man, one who would blush to tell a lie,[21] that at his head a fountain of clear water flows forth. It never fails to please the eye by the clarity of its water and the taste of those who try it with its honeyed sweetness. And on the saint's feast day, the water overcomes all obstacles and triumphantly covers the whole floor of the crypt. Then, the festival over, it goes back to its channel. I believe that God is in this manner giving an indication of the richness of the teaching by which the great man waters the entire world.

[13] Put together from several sources, described below.
[14] I.e. in Pavia.
[15] Cf. Possidius, *Vita Augustini*, 28–31 (*PL* 32. 57–66).
[16] Cf. *Comm. Lam.* I, 271–2: 'heresis Arriana totum fedarat orientem'.
[17] Ferrandus, *Vita Fulgentii*, 20 (*PL* 65. 157B).
[18] Cf. Virgil, *Aen.* 5. 84–93.
[19] Cf. Isidore, *Etym.* 12. 4. 48, and the Bestiary account that derives from it: W. B. Clark, *A Medieval Book of Beasts: The Second-Family Bestiary: Commentary, Art, Text and Translation* (Woodbridge, 2006), 109 (p. 203). But neither account makes reference to wisdom.
[20] Paul the Deacon, *De gestis Langobard.* 6. 48 (*MGH Script. Rer. Langobard. et Ital. saec. vi–xi*, p. 181): 'dato magno pretio'. Liutprand reigned 712–44. See also *GR* 184. 1 n. The church is San Pietro in Ciel d'Oro, in whose crypt the shrine allegedly containing Augustine's bones (made c.1362) is still to be seen.
[21] Cf. *Comm. Lam.* I, 2625–6, *GP* 83. 12.

11c. Boethius[22]

1. There too lies Boethius. He was indicted before King Theodoric (mentioned above)[23] for working against his interests in writings sent to the emperor of Constantinople, and exiled to Pavia. In prison he composed and published books on the Consolation of Philosophy.[24] When he was about to clear his name by the mediation of his friends, he was foully killed in a public assembly. His bodily remains were buried in the same church [as Augustine].[25] His spirit had long since deserved a trophy in the eyes of God, for (we are told) he lived a holy life, and we can judge from his writings on the Trinity[26] that he was sound and catholic of faith. In fact the locals have no hesitation in pronouncing him a saint, and call him Severinus, his *agnomen*.[27]

2. The purpose of all this[28] is to make clear the sweetness that the merciful Mother of God showed to her chancellor[29] by making him bishop of so celebrated a city, and thus adding a brilliant topaz to the great choir of saints who form, as it were, a well-worked diadem for the eternal King. Let the memory of our Lady, then, be sweet in men's hearts; let all their inmost parts melt out of love for her, for she well knows how to grant good to her servants in this life, so that they may the more confidently hope for eternal good.

---

[22] Some information from one of the *Vitae Boethii* often prefixed to his works: ed. R. Peiper (Leipzig, 1871), pp. xxix–xxxv, at xxxv. But William seems also to have had access to a Pavian guidebook or else to a traveller who had been there (for such a traveller see 11b. 2).

[23] 11. 3.

[24] CPL 878.

[25] So the Pavian authorities, e.g. *De laudibus*, pp. 12–13. See above, 11b. 2.

[26] This title usually designates the five *opuscula sacra*: CPL 890–4; ed. C. Moreschini (Munich, 2000).

[27] The feast of Severinus Boethius was, and is, kept on 23 October.

[28] I.e. all of 11–11c.

[29] I.e. Jerome.

12. Guy of Lescar[1]

1. What I now relate took place in Spain, the blessed Virgin Mary as ever working her will. She is manifested to be the Lady of all nations in every part of the world; she holds sway as empress of the world, on earth above through the love, and in hell through the terror, she inspires. She is well used to bringing the chained out of the pit of misery;[2] and those whom a dark prison encloses 'in both men',[3] the queen of heaven is in her mercy accustomed to free.

2. A king they used to nickname 'the Small' was pre-eminent in Spain;[4] his wealth and arms always redounded to the dignity and excellence of the name of Christian. Taking an army within the bounds of Further Spain,[5] he laid low a great multitude of Saracens. After bringing over to his side thousands from many peoples at the town called Fraga,[6] he used his active valour to subjugate vast swathes of wild Iberia. And the people of God rejoiced to see such a great heritage won for Christ.

In this stronghold the king had left to guard and protect the saints the virtuous Don Guy, bishop of Lescar, so that through him holy religion might increase in that nation, while his life served as an example to the neighbourhood.[7] The

---

[1] Poncelet 800; detailed commentary by Carter, pp. 391–6. This is not taken from one of the earlier miracle collections; the events were very recent, and seem to have come to William by word of mouth. William's account of what happened is brief, vague and misleading. A more accurate account of the events is given in the contemporary *Chronica Adefonsi Imperatoris*, ed. L. Sánchez Belda (Madrid, 1950), 51–9, and Ibn el-Athir, *Annales du Maghreb et de l'Espagne*, trans. E. Fagnan (Algiers, 1898), pp. 553–5. Another version, not mentioning Bp. Guy, is given by Orderic Vitalis, *Historia Ecclesiastica*, 13. 8–10 (ed. M. Chibnall [6 vols, Oxford, 1969–80], VI, pp. 410–19. A reliable modern one is in M. Defourneaux, *Les Français en Espagne aux xie et xiie siècles* (Paris, 1949), pp. 164–5. Fraga was actually in Muslim hands; Alfonso laid siege to it over a long period. Its attempted relief by a large army of Muslim from other parts of Spain and the Maghreb led to the main battle on 19 July 1134. Alfonso was resoundingly defeated and forced to withdraw, dying later in the same year. William gives the impression that Guy had been left to guard Fraga, which was certainly not the case. According to the *Chronica Adefonsi* (56; ed. Sánchez Belda, p. 46) he was captured during the battle. It describes his captivity thus (59; ed. Sánchez Belda, p. 48): 'Episcopus uero de Lascar captiuus ductus est in Valentia; et afflixerunt eum multis tormentis ut denegaret Illum qui pro nobis suspensus est in ligno et baptismum, et circumciderunt eum secundum legem suam. Post haec, dedit obsides pro se, et reddidit tria milia Morabetinos aureos, et reuersus est in Lascar in sedem suam.'

[2] Ps. 39: 3.

[3] I.e. body and soul.

[4] William presumably had in mind Alfonso VII of Galicia (called 'little' by Orderic, 13. 7; ed. Chibnall VI, pp. 408–9), whereas the king involved at Fraga was Alfonso I ('the Battler') of Aragon and Navarre (1104–34). The erroneous variant 'Petrus Sanctio' in Pv presumably refers to his predecessor and older half-brother, Peter I (1094–1104).

[5] Prima facie, one would expect William to be following ancient Roman usage; but for the Romans 'further Spain' was Baetica (earlier Baetica + Lusitania), i.e. in the south, whereas Fraga is in the north.

[6] The town is about halfway between Barcelona and Saragossa.

[7] Guy de Loth, bp. of Lescar, 1115–41. Lescar is on the French side of the Pyrenees, c.100km east of Bayonne, c.200km west of Toulouse, now virtually a suburb of the town of Pau. The present church is Guy's work (Lescar ceased to be a bishopric in 1801). Apart from the *Chronica Adefonsi* (see above, n. 1), his presence at Fraga is mentioned in a legal document pr. R. del Arco, *Referencias a acaecimientos*

distinguished bishop governed his subjects with spirit; he knew them to excel in bodily strength and to be equipped like proper men with the weapons of secular warfare.

3. Suddenly a swarm of treacherous infidels, who had always warred against the dignity of the name of Christian,[8] swooped down on those manning the fortifications. The enemy strove openly with all the accoutrements of military glory, while treacherously laying traps for the walls and way of life[9] of the holy men; and lo and behold! the absence and departure of the pious king became known at the very same moment when the hostile infidels, bent on levelling the battlements to the ground, were everywhere coming on thicker and faster. Guy, that man of the Lord, was taken out of the place secretly at night, hoping to get back to the city of Lescar with no baggage and clad in a pilgrim's clothes; but he missed the way and fell into the hands of the heathen.

4. The Lord's priest was shut up in a stinking dungeon deep underground. The hands that had been accustomed to administer the Lord's sacraments were shamefully put to women's work. The chaste hand of the bishop, that had so often consecrated the holy chalice of the New Testament[10] and divided the body and blood of our Redeemer among a purchased[11] people, had every day to hold a woman's spindle in his dark prison, while a pagan hag systematically took in the thread from the common-or-garden silk.[12] He had so worn away both hands between thumb and index finger that there was no flesh left, right through to the bone, that had not been ruined by labouring at this task. The famous bishop was treated(?) like this for a whole year. They tried to get him to deny the Lord and by making a sacrilegious profession to become a profane worshipper of idols.[13] But he maintained his catholic faith without blemish; in the words of the apostle, he believed with the heart unto justice and confessed to God with the mouth unto eternal salvation.[14]

5. But in his prayers he always remembered the Virgin Mother, who bore God and man in so unusual a birth.[15] While he was pondering on her one night as

---

históricos en las datas de documentos aragoneses de los siglos xi y xii (Estudios de Edad Media de la Corona de Aragón 3: 1947–48), p. 332.

[8] Cf. GR 359. 2.

[9] There is a laboured play on moribus and muris.

[10] Cf. Luc. 22: 20: 'hic est calix nouum testamentum in sanguine meo quod pro uobis funditur'.

[11] I Pet. 2: 9, i.e. 'redeemed'.

[12] William's account of the bishop apparently weaving using a spindle may result from real knowledge or confusion. A spindle was not usually, but was occasionally, used for weaving silk. The role of the old woman is obscure; presumably she took the silk from the full spindle for storage elsewhere.

[13] Elsewhere William took care to explain that Muslims were not idolaters: Thomson, William of Malmesbury, p. 169.

[14] Rom. 10: 10.

[15] Guy's cathedral had been rededicated to the Virgin Mary not long before these events: L'Abbé Laplace, Monographie de Notre-Dame de Lescar (Paris, 1863); P. Raymond, 'Notice sur un mosaique

usual, only half awake, a woman unique in her ineffable beauty, wonderful for her unique appearance, appeared to him. He knew for sure in his vision that this was the Lady of heaven and queen of the angels. From a great halo of dazzling light, she said to him: 'Do you know, amid your present tribulation, who I am who have come to you?' 'I do know,' he said, 'my Lady. You are the Mother of God and the uncorrupted Virgin.' 6. She replied: 'Quite right. Why then do you not ask me earnestly as a suppliant to snatch you from this pit of misery?' 'I am doing that,' he said, 'so far as I can manage.' The empress of the world approached the bishop a second time, with these words: 'You do not redouble your prayer as you should, or ask help as would be expedient. If you begged me for love of St Anne, my beloved mother, and by your deep-felt prayers won her as mediator for you with my only-begotten Son, you would walk free of your prison chains and swiftly win the grace of bodily freedom. You would escape the hideous solitude of this ugly prison, the yoke of injurious servitude would be lifted from you, and you would be taken away from this misery of death.'

7. Ah, mistress of heaven, saving refuge for the faithful, with what unspeakable complaisance you deign to fulfil what the Holy Spirit predicted in the Law: 'Honour thy father and thy mother, that thou mayest be longlived upon the land'![16] O chamber full of the sweetness of supernal grace, how honeyed the liquid of heavenly balsam that oozes from the words of your mouth, a saving drop of which slipped pleasantly into the ears of the bishop, and gave him a novel cure in his half-dead state! What welcome delight you instil in this man, whom, Virgin Mother, you refresh with food so sweet that from its fragments you make an antidote for minds that have suffered spiritual wounds! Blessed be your mother Anne, who bore you though a virgin, and blessed be the womb from which your virginal flesh proceeded!

8. O dwelling-place of life, from which came forth the redemption of the earth, how efficaciously you pass on(?) to us in particular(?) the teaching of your son, which has by now been spread to the four regions.[17] Of you, holy Virgin, and of the blessed Joseph your husband we read that your son came to Nazareth and was subject to you,[18] humbly gentle and obedient. For[19] it is appropriate for those who flower in the profession of chastity to yield as fruit the simplicity of

---

dans la Grande Abside de la Cathédrale de Lescar', *Revue archéologique du Moyen Âge*, nouv. ser. 13 (1866), 305–13 and pl. IX; P. de Marca, *Histoire de Bearn* (Paris, 1640), pp. 446–60. Carter (p. 396) notes that there seems to have been particular devotion to the Virgin there even before Guy's episcopate. His predecessor Sancius used to give forty modii of wheat to the canons on the Feast of Mary's Nativity: *Gallia Christiana* 1 (1870), col. 1290.

[16] Exod. 20: 12.
[17] East, west, north and south (as e.g. Isidore, *Etym.* 13. 1. 3).
[18] Luc. 2: 51.
[19] The logic is not obvious.

an innocent life. Just as the Lord Jesus Christ paid honour to you, blessed Virgin Mother, so do you pay honour to your own famous mother. You encourage us by your example to take refuge in her protecting arms, and wish your son to be entreated in her name, so that you may be seen to have honoured your mother. You give us this example concerning her so that by her mediation we may attain to the prize of life in heaven, and so that any and every Christian may call upon her help in honour of you, just as each day the whole world invokes you as its mediator, to the praise and glory of your Son.

9. The bishop privately weighed up the glorious admonition of the blessed Virgin, going over all her sweet and well-chosen words. Accordingly, he supplicated the blessed Anne with tears,[20] and also asked her glorious daughter Mary, Mother of God, for her aid. He begged them both with sighs and groans, praying to the mother for love of her daughter and begging the daughter's favour for love of her mother. He appealed to Jesus son of the Virgin Mary, and invoked Christ, grandson and lord of Anne, to snatch him from captivity in prison and restore him safe and sound to the sons of the church of Lescar.

The famous bishop went on praying like this, and behold! at first light the next morning hostages came from the Christians, paying out to the Saracens gold coin for his ransom. The great man was taken out of the horrid place of his solitary confinement, restored to his fellow-citizens in triumph, and reinstalled with due ceremony on the episcopal throne.[21]

10. So in the end it was made clear how effective was the image of truth that forewarned him in the vision; divine inspiration made him ready to learn in his holy prayers, and the blessed Mother of God brought him back to his old liberty and freedom of action. And we should be careful to note and commit to memory that the queen of heaven impressed upon us the example to love her mother St Anne wholeheartedly, and to bend the necks of our minds and bodies to do her service with all devotion.

---

[20] An early instance of her cult; her feast was not widely established until the end of the twelfth century: B. de Gaiffier, 'A propos de Guy, évêque de Lescar et du culte de Sainte Anne,' *AB* 88 (1970), 74; H. E. Bannister, 'The introduction of the cult of St Anne into the West', *EHR* 18 (1903), 107–12; A. Wilmart, 'Chants en l'honneur de Sainte Anne', in his *Auteurs spirituels et textes dévôts du moyen âge latin* (Paris, 1932), pp. 46–55; *Oxford Dictionary of Saints*, pp. 24–5.
[21] His captivity cannot have lasted nearly as long as William says, since he was in Saragossa on 6 Dec. 1134, when he witnessed a charter of Alfonso VII: J. M. Lacarra, *Documentos para el estudio de la reconquista y repoblación del Valle de Ebro, Prima serie* (Estudios de Edad Media de la Corona de Aragón 2: 1946), no. 86 (pp. 538–9). Carter (p. 396) suggests that William or his source garbled the fact that Guy's captivity finished near to the year's end.

This story I have been telling you was told about himself by the Lord Bishop Guy of Lescar to an archdeacon called Elias, who had been with him among the cardinals in the curia of the Lord Pope, and was his colleague and companion on the way back from Rome.[22]

---

[22] Guy, employed from time to time as papal Legate, is known to have been in Rome in 1138, from whence he was sent back to Spain by the pope to issue summonses to the Second Lateran Council of April 1139 (*Historia Compostellana* s.a. 1138, in *España Sagrada* 20 [Madrid, 1765], pp. 597–8; Carter, p. 49). It is reasonable to suppose that he was in attendance at that Council, and Carter thought that that was the most likely occasion for him to have met Elias. This, however, seems too late for the writing of *MBVM* (see above, pp. xv–xvi). Presumably this Elias was English and told the story to William. Of two known archdeacons named Elias at the right time, the more likely candidate for identification as William's informant is the man who was archdeacon of Brecon in the diocese of St David's. He is only known from one reference, dated 1115–c.1125 (P. le Neve, *Fasti Ecclesiae Anglicanae* 9, ed. J. Barrow [London, 2002], p. 54, no. 17). However, his successor occurs in documents probably of the 1140s, so there is no difficulty in believing that Elias was still active in the 1130s. His bishop, Bernard, was campaigning in the 1120s and again in the late 1130s for his see to be made an archbishopric. Urban bishop of Llandaff was making bold claims in Rome in the early 1130s, and doubtless St Davids needed to keep a watching brief to prevent Llandaff encroaching on it. According to the Life of St Caradoc perhaps by Gerald of Wales, William of Malmesbury ('monachus et historiographus insignis') was present for the saint's translation, which occurred 'multos annos' after his original burial at St David's in 1124 (*GP* II, p. xix n. 1). Perhaps it was on this occasion that he spoke with Archdeacon Elias.

13. Abbot Ælfsige[1]

1. William, who became king of England after being duke of Normandy, showed high spirit when facing up to all others; he was afraid only of Cnut, king of the Danes, who made him bridle his ambition and moderate his hauteur.[2] On other occasions he displayed undue arrogance, but when he was courting the favour of the Danes by embassies or presents, 'his cares melted into peace of mind'.[3] It was Englishmen, clerks or laymen, who often had to undertake the burden of such embassies, for William was happier to expose foreigners to danger than his own people; and besides it was easier for the English to do business with the Danes because their languages were mutually intelligible.[4] Indeed, during the long Danish sojourn in England in the old days, the two had almost been welded into a common culture.[5]

2. So it was that, when William was particularly alarmed by a well-founded rumour that Cnut was about to arrive on the scene, he sent off to Denmark an abbot, Ælfsige, a man of known eloquence and no small piety.[6] He was to put Cnut off somehow if the story was true; if not, he was to report back. The ambassador took his instructions to heart, and, protected by the aid of the Mother of God, to whom he was especially devoted, had fair winds to take him over the sea.

In Denmark it was demonstrated how effective eloquence was. Alone and alien, he managed by the power of persuasive words to 'loose the girdle'[7] of the foreign king, who was ready to go, and indeed on the very point of departure. But I cannot believe that Mary did not give her help; with her shield ever protecting him, he was able to carry out his plan and come back home unharmed, though

---

[1] Poncelet 260 (1781), an immensely popular story; see Carter, pp. 399–406, and M. Clayton, *The Cult of the Virgin Mary in Anglo-Saxon England* (Cambridge, 1990), pp. 47–50. William's main source was TS 15 (Eadmer, *De conceptione beatae Mariae,* ed. H. Thurston and T. Slater [Freiburg im Breisgau, 1904], Appendix F, pp. 93–5; Dexter, pp. 37–8), which he tried to improve on, enlarging upon the details of Ælfsige's mission, and attempting to bring greater chronological precision by specifying the threatened Danish invasion (there were three possibilities). But in identifying it as the invasion scare of 1085 he was mistaken, since Ælfsige's mission must be dated in or near the year 1070. Ælfsige (Æthelsige, Elsinus) was abbot of St Augustine's, Canterbury, 1061–?1067, of Ramsey 1080–87: *Heads*, pp. 36, 62. Cf. H. Thurston, 'The legend of Abbot Elsi', *The Month* 104 (1904), 1–15; Southern, 'The English origins', pp. 194–8; M. Lamy, *L'Immaculée Conception: Étapes et enjeux d'une controverse au Moyen-Âge (XIIe-XVe siècles)* (Paris, 2000), pp. 90–3; Ihnat, *Mary and the Jews*, pp. 142–5. For the liturgical use of the story, see S. Corbin, 'Miracula Beatae Mariae semper Virginis', in *Cahiers de civilisation médiévale* 39–40 (1967), 409–33.

[2] Similarly at *GR* 258. 3.

[3] Cf. Claudian, *Carm. min.* 29. 23: 'Venus, humanas quae laxat in otia curas', and Prudentius, *Psych.* 729: 'in otia soluere curas'. A similar echo is at *GR* 154. 3 (see n. ad loc.), more apt there.

[4] Cf. *VW* 1. 10. 3, 2. 12. 2; *Comm. Lam.* I, 337–40.

[5] Cf. *GR* 9. 2, 125. 1.

[6] TS specifies his abbacy of St Augustine's Canterbury. It is hard to understand why William did not reproduce this, unless he thought that Ælfsige was already at Ramsey.

[7] Is. 5: 27.

the Devil did grudge the Virgin's servant a return as fortunate as his journey out, and tried in mid-ocean to spread a pall over the man's happiness.

3. They set out to sea in fair weather, and were cheerfully building on their success[8] when suddenly the winds turned treacherous and everything changed.[9] The day grew dim, night came on fast, all the elements conspired to pour out their fury.[10] The sailors threw everything they had into it; but all the fruits of their experience went for nothing. Despairing of what man could do, they turned to prayer. Everything thought and known to be sacred was invoked. The abbot in particular called aloud on St Mary, 'my helper, my protector, my patron'. Those bowels of mercy could not be inactive for long; she who comes speedily to all who call on her did not delay. Torn between hope and fear,[11] he saw walking on the water a man who looked from his dress and visage to be a bishop. 4. As Ælfsige gazed anxiously, he came nearer, and said: 'If you wish to be freed from danger, vow to St Mary that you will celebrate her conception every year.' Asked for the day and the rite, he answered: '8 December. The ceremony should be same as at the Nativity, but with the word 'Nativity' changed to 'Conception'. The abbot leapt for joy and gladly assented; the other thereupon vanished.

Fair weather returned; the adverse winds became obedient once more, and after some days brought the ship gently over subservient waves to the coast of England. Everywhere he could, and specifically in the monastery of Ramsey, where he then dwelt, Ælfsige taught the observance of that festival.[12]

---

[8] Cf. Claud. *Cons. Stilich.* 1. 2.

[9] Similar storm descriptions are in *VW* 2. 19. 2 and *GP* 224. 4–5.

[10] Cf. Claudian, *Tert. Cons. Honorii* 98.

[11] Cf. Virgil, *Aen.* 1. 218, also in the context of a storm.

[12] A feast of Byzantine origin, it had already been observed in England, almost uniquely in the West, since the early eleventh century: Clayton, *The Cult of the Virgin Mary in Anglo-Saxon England*, pp. 42–7; but it seems to have been dropped c.1100, for reasons that have been disputed by modern scholarship: E. Bishop, 'On the Origins of the Feast of the Conception of the Blessed Virgin Mary', in his *Liturgica Historica* (Oxford, 1918), p. 249; T. A. Heslop, 'The Canterbury Calendars and the Norman Conquest', in *Canterbury and the Norman Conquest: Churches, Saints and Scholars 1066–1109*, ed. R. Eales and R. Sharpe (London, 1995), pp. 53–62; R. W. Pfaff, 'Lanfranc's supposed purge of the Anglo-Saxon Calendar', in *Warriors and Churchmen in the High Middle Ages: Essays presented to Karl Leyser*, ed. T. Reuter (London, 1992), pp. 95–108, at 104; J. Fournée, 'Du *De Conceptu Virginali* de Saint Anselm au *De Conceptione Sanctae Mariae* de son disciple Eadmer ou de la Virgo purissima à la Virgo immaculata', in *Les mutations socio-culturelles au tournant des XIe–XIIe siècles*, ed. R. Foreville (Paris, 1984), p. 713, and J. Rubenstein, 'Liturgy against history: the competing visions of Lanfranc and Eadmer', *Speculum* 74 (1999), 279–309, at p. 305; Lamy, *L'immaculée conception*, pp. 33–7.

14. Guimund and Drogo[1]

1. I am prompted by its similarity to put another miracle next, even though it took place at a different time and involved a different person.[2] Guimund and Drogo, two of the king of England's chaplains, were sailing to Jerusalem with a view to taking up the religious life. The winds had been sluggish for many a day, and the sailors, using what light breezes there were or just pulling on their oars, had made little progress.[3] One begged help from St Nicholas, others from various other saints. Then Guimund, being a humorous fellow who seasoned almost all adversities with a pleasantry and turned them into a joke, said: 'Why call on these Greek saints, who are two a penny in this part of the world? They would help their own Greeklings; they take no notice of us Latins. Come on, let us all invoke St Mary instead, who for love of her Son is no accepter of persons. She aids all Christians, but she will show her heavenly favour especially to pilgrims on their way to avenge wrongs done to her Son.'[4]

2. They all agreed with the great man's suggestion, and at once made a collection of money to be given to the poor for love of the Lady. Guimund had scarcely received the container with the money in it when a much stronger wind filled the sails. It went on blowing, and carried the ship gently forward over calm seas, till it brought it safe to land at Jaffa, with no losses to the crew.

---

[1] Poncelet 1783. The story is original to William, who may have had it directly from Guimund. This man was chaplain to Henry I and first prior of the Augustinian house of St Frideswide, Oxford (1122–c.1139): *Heads*, p. 180. William, who had visited St Frideswide's not long before 1125 (*GR* 179. 4), refers to him warmly in *GP* 178. 4. Drogo was chaplain and Keeper of the Great Seal in the early years of Henry I's reign (*Regesta Regum Anglo-Normannorum II 1100–1135*, ed. C. Johnson and H. A. Cronne [Oxford, 1956], nos 684 and 687, dated 1105). The pilgrimage took place between 1100 and 1122.

[2] I.e. one of a different rank.

[3] William is writing a fancy piece of marine description. *per inania* seems to mean nothing in particular (there is perhaps a casual reminiscence of Ausonius, *Carm.* 16. 58), and oarsmen 'only scraping the very backs of the salt sea' not much more.

[4] Another example of Guimund's wit is the story in the cartulary of St Frideswide's Priory, pr. S. R. Wigram (2 vols, Oxford Historical Soc. 28 [1894], 31 [1896]), I, p. 9, and by Carter, p. 411.

15. Devil in three beast-shapes[1]

1. Of no little importance in the eyes of monks is the man to whom the care of the church treasures is assigned; he takes his name from what he does, being called 'secretary' because he is responsible for the secret treasure.[2] There was once an office-holder of this type in a monastery in France,[3] though I cannot recall the name of place or person. He loved what is good and avoided what is evil, being discreet and honest on both counts. In him flourished and every day grew a unique uprightness and upright uniqueness.[4] In particular he was sedulous and painstaking in the service of the blessed Mary, who loved *him* dearly, as the following story will make quite clear.

2. As is the way of mortal men (for there is not and never has been anyone so tirelessly active in religious works that he does not sometimes seek out and let in some means of relaxing from his cares), he one day overindulged in wine in a secluded corner of his store. Well over the eight,[5] he proceeded at dead of night to go into the church through the cloister. Drink had overwhelmed his senses, and neither foot nor tongue could do its job unaffected. The Devil had been looking for an opening like this for a long time; now he confronted the man in the shape of a bull trying (as it were) to gore him with a toss of his horns.

3. And now behold! a beautiful girl appeared, her long hair thrown back loose on her shoulders, holding a little napkin. She drove the monster away partly by her wonderful face,[6] whose brilliance outshone the sun, and partly by a forceful gesture. The monk went on. But as he neared the church door the Devil, attacking in the shape of a slavering hound, arrayed his sharp and devilish teeth against him. But the maiden ran up and imperiously drove the maddened beast off. He tried a third assault, presenting the form of a lion; the secretary was just rejoicing to have got into the church safely when the Devil was upon him, threatening to catch him in his unspeakable gaping jaws. The maiden could stand it no longer, but shook her stick at the Devil and struck him three or four times,[7] redoubling her blows and making them sharper with words:[8] 'Take that, and go away. I warn you and order you not to harass my monk any more. If you dare to do so, you will suffer worse.'

[1] Poncelet 66 (1162). Based upon TS 9 (Dexter, pp. 46–8). For the Devil appearing successively in the shape of three beasts, cf. *VD* 1. 18.

[2] Also known as sacristan.

[3] TS does not even specify the country.

[4] *singularitas*, a term used by William with a wide range of meaning, here with reference to the individual monk's cultivation of monastic virtue: cf. *GP* 45. 6; *Comm. Lam.* II, 224, III, 1220, elucidated by M. Winterbottom, *William of Malmesbury on Lamentations* (Turnhout, 2013), p. 181 n. b.

[5] Cf. *GR* 419. 4: 'immodice mero ingurgitati'.

[6] Cf. *VW* 3. 28. 2 and n., to which should be added *VW* 1. 1. 9; see also 51. 4 below.

[7] *terque quaterque* is Virgilian; see *GR* 235. 2 n.

[8] An unidentified hexameter.

4. Having got rid of him, she took the monk's hand and led him up and down uneven stairways, keeping him steady in his tottering course, though it is fair to say that fear of what he had seen had by now rid him[9] of some of his drunken stupor. Hand in hand they gradually approached the monk's bed. The girl took off the coverlet, put him to bed, and tucked him up carefully, laying his head gently on the pillow. Then she pressed the sign of the cross to his forehead as he lay there, and said: 'Tomorrow you will go for confession to my monk so and so' (and she gave the name) 'who is known to me[10] and has done me most welcome service. You will tell him what you did and how you were freed, and you will do what he orders with no delay.' His head had cleared by now, the fumes of liquor had altogether vanished; and he said: 'Dearest girl, I am ready to obey you and do your bidding gladly. But I do ask you to find me worthy of learning your name.' 'I am Mary,' she said, 'mother and daughter of the King of kings, who bore Him who made me and all things.' She spoke, and deprived the monk of the sweet sight of her, just as he was about to thank her.

5. I draw a veil over what ensued. The listener can easily understand what exultation both monks felt, one to see himself freed, the other to hear himself praised. How glad I am to spread myself here in meditation on the clemency of the Lady! It was not enough for her to have driven the Enemy away from her servant: she must needs lead him by the hand after he had been rescued! It was too little to lead him by the hand: she must needs put him to bed – and into the bargain warn him to confess!

To this pity then let the praises of all the saints yield place.[11] Since the Passion of the Lord no writing has ever told of such an act of honeyed mercy. She alone, after her son, feels pity, she alone is gracious; for she can both sustain the bodies of her devotees and cleanse their souls.

---

[9] Cf. below 18. 2 (*digessisset*).
[10] 'To you' in TS 9.
[11] Cf. *GR* 372. 2: 'cedant ergo poetarum preconia'.

16. The drowned sacristan[1]

1. There was another sacristan, devoted to the queen of the world, who would all the same have met a disgraceful end if she had not come to his aid in person. He was given to obscene practices, and burned for a neighbouring woman whom his roving eye and a recklessness that had no share in good counsel had marked out as his prey. Past the church flowed a river, beyond which the woman lived. He used to make clandestine forays there, but as the crossing inevitably took him past the altar, he never went by his Lady without a greeting: 'Hail Mary, full of grace', and the rest.

2. This went on for a long time. But then God in the rigour of His mercy decided to put a stop to such wicked behaviour. The monk, after greeting the Mistress, came to the river. He thought he had found the familiar ford; but he missed his way and fell into deep water, where he was sucked down and drowned.

Meanwhile, the bell that by custom interrupted the slumbers of the monks was late in sounding, and some in the dormitory expressed surprise. The repeated sound of cock crow throughout the village reproached the sacristan as a sleepy head. So some monks got up and burst into the church; but they could not find its guardian. Young people are curious by nature, and they looked for the missing man all round the monastery, finally coming to the river. Following his tracks, they found the body trapped in the water and brought it to dry land. 3. Grievous the cry that went up; the air was filled with wails and lamentation. While this was going on, the body shook itself, and at the first attempt got up on to its feet.[2] Unheard of joy called forth fresh tears, and amid embraces and kisses they asked him how he came to die and return to life. He revealed the course of events, and then said: 'When I had drowned and vomited up[3] my life in gasps, angels and demons surrounded me, contending with each other for my soul. In the end victory went to the dark spirits. The angels, discomfited because they were unable to say much good of me, were on the point of departing when (lo and behold!) my Lady, Mother of the Lord, appeared on the scene, her countenance flashing. She enquired of the demons why they were so angry with me, and calmed the angels down. 4. They presumed to reply that I deserved to be punished, because I did not repent my sins, but while still in their grip had died the death of a shameless casuist, a greedy extortioner, and a wicked plunderer.[4] She replied indignantly:

[1] Poncelet 201 (398). Based upon HM 2 (Dexter, pp. 17–18). The only differences are that HM has the sacristan pass before the altar saying the 'Aue Maria' independent of his visits to his lover, and has him drown on his way to her, not returning.
[2] Cf. Sen. *Epist*. 121. 8 (of an overturned tortoise): 'nec ante desinit niti, quatere se, quam in pedes constitit'.
[3] Cf. VW 2. 15. 5, GR 261. 3 (*spiritum*), both also of drowning.
[4] The accusations are surprising, though one must remember that the devils are just making them up; the only sin mentioned earlier was his sexual relationship with the nearby woman. It is also difficult to imagine how a mere sacristan could be a 'causidicus'. There is nothing of this in HM.

"You lie, wicked demons; I know he never left the monastery without greeting me. One who died almost at the moment of saluting me met no bad death. If you have a just cause of complaint, let us go to law with my Son as judge." When in this dispute no judgement had been reached, no sentence handed down from on high, I suddenly found myself here with you, goodness knows how.'

5. Thus restored to perfect health, he lived a holy and discreet life before dying a beautiful and fortunate death, in the fullness of his days.[5]

---

[5] It is not clear how to take either pair of comparative adverbs ('sanctius et circumspectius ... felitius et pulchrius').

17. Monk of Cologne[1]

1. Two miracles that I am now bursting to tell of took place in the time of Louis the most pious and august emperor, son of Charlemagne: the first in Cologne, the second in Germany. They are vouched for in writing, though they have not been particularly noised abroad.

Cologne was once known as Agrippina; later it was called Cologne (*Colonia*) by the emperor Trajan, who was made emperor there and established colonies of Roman citizens.[2] Here is to be found a monastery dedicated to the prince of the apostles,[3] famous for its many good monks. One monk, however, was notorious for his loose life. He had in fact something to show for his misbehaviour: a son, whom he had had tonsured in the same house.[4]

2. As he lay dying, he was spied by demons, always ready and willing to torment men. They grabbed his soul, whisked it away, and belaboured it with whips. But St Peter saw what was happening from on high, and in his sorrow supplicated Lord Jesus to forgive his monk. The Judge of inflexible justice answered: 'How can I annul the sentence of a prophet, especially one that I inspired?[5] To the question "Lord, who shall dwell in thy tabernacle? or who shall rest in thy holy hill?", the reply was: "He that walketh without blemish" and the rest.[6] Now since this monk was not without blemish and had not justice, how shall he enter into my tabernacle?'

3. This was true enough, and Peter, rebuffed, deployed the glorious Mother of God to mediate, because he knew that to her the Son would refuse nothing at all, however great, however difficult. She tried to prostrate herself before the throne, but the glory of God prevented her and raised her to her feet. Asked what she wished, she requested the release of the monk. The Lord said: 'It is impossible either for the prophet to tell a lie or for you, my sweetest mother, to be cheated of your wish. So I shall compromise. Let this soul return to its body, and from then on let him show more restraint, so that, as you wish, Mother, he may enter my tabernacle cleansed of blemish.'

4. Hearing this, the apostle Peter threatened the Devil by brandishing in his face the great key he had in his hand, and made him turn tail. The soul he entrusted to two beautiful boys. They in their turn handed it over to a monk of

---

[1] Poncelet 103 (387). Taken from HM 7 (Dexter, pp. 21–2). William's statement that the miracles took place during the reign of Louis the Pious is unique and, in the case of the first, can hardly be right (see n. 3 below).

[2] So also *GR* 175. 1 and n.

[3] St Peter's Abbey, in fact founded in 840: Cottineau I, p. 840.

[4] The son, but not his tonsure, is mentioned in HM.

[5] I.e. David as psalmist.

[6] Ps. 14: 1–2 (continuing with 'et operatur iustitiam', 'and worketh justice').

that house, long since dead,[7] to be brought back into the body. On the way, the old soul asked the new one to sing in return a Miserere every day for his soul, and sweep clean his tomb at the very entrance to the church. Then the soul felt itself to be there, poised over the roof of the house in which the lifeless body lay. Inside, it was being lamented by a group of brothers, in particular his son. The soul entered the body and raised it from the ground, so that the great sorrow became material for praise.[8] Restored to health, the monk narrated at large the tale I have told.

5. Here, maybe, some carper will charge me with peddling childish nonsense, for saying that spirits without body spoke to each other, and that St Peter had a key. I agree about the conversation, for there can be nothing spoken in the absence of the plectrum of the tongue or the organ of the voice.[9] But though we are well aware that blessed spirits learn and search out secrets merely by their innate perspicacity, and that there is no need for a tongue where everything is known, we do all the same read in Job that God spoke with the Devil, and in the gospel that the dead Abraham spoke at length with a dead rich man.[10] These things could not have been reported to us if Scripture did not express in bodily speech things that are incorporeal.[11] I will say the same of the key, which is attributed to Peter as something indicative of his power. It was only by a bodily simile[12] that his power could be shown to the monk who was to be raised again, and the story could not otherwise have been narrated by another, or otherwise understood by those who heard it.

6. Let us then proceed to the rest,[13] and let our hearts have impressed upon them the unwearying recollection of the holy Mother of God. Her wishes are never without effect on her son: and never without effect just because they are never ill-considered. Far be it from a good mother to ask of her son anything but what she knows that *He* justly wishes. Now that Christ wishes all men to be saved is witnessed to by the apostle.[14] The mercy of the mother, then, goes hand in hand with the justice of the offspring. What she understands He justly wishes, she in her mercy asks Him to fulfil, as it were forcing Him to do what He himself wishes.

---

[7] Not in HM, though it is implied.

[8] Cf. *Comm. Lam.* I, 202 (further parallels are supplied on p. 331).

[9] For the tongue as (like) the quill used to pluck a lyre, cf. e.g. Cicero, *De nat. deorum* 2. 149. *organum uocis* is a common phrase, though it is not clear exactly how it is to be taken here.

[10] Iob 1: 6–12; Luc. 16: 24–31.

[11] Cf. *Comm. Lam.* I, 3000–2 (again concerning the rich man), and above, 10. 6 n. The same point is already made in HM.

[12] I.e. by something visible and tangible standing in for something incorporeal (Peter's power).

[13] Apparently to the second of the pair of stories (see §1).

[14] 1 Tim. 1: 15.

18. Vision of Wettin[1]

1. I shall now add the second incident, similar to the last, which I said[2] took place in Germany. It is long-winded,[3] but I shall abbreviate it in my own words without impairment to the sense, and in much the same order(?).[4] The events can by these means be more easily imprinted on the memory than if I spin out a long narrative. But anyone eager to learn the complete story may read the account from which I took my excerpt, and it is far from inelegant or foolish.

2. Wettin was a monk of a monastery in Germany, who was given a potion to cure an ailment. He could not keep it down on the first day, but felt better until the evening of the fourth day. Then the problem recurred, and his life was endangered. Scarcely had he lain down in bed to gain relief from his discomfort and closed his eyes when lo and behold! he saw that what looked like black manikins had filled the house. Deploying some kind of weapon, they leapt on him as he lay there, and seemed to intend to shut him up in an iron structure.[5] He was scared stiff.[6] Some handsome-looking[7] men were sitting on benches near the sick man, and came to his help. One of them said (to quote the exact Latin words): 'It's not right for such worthless types to act like this. The man is already in his death throes. Tell them to go away.'[8] This routed the black men, and bright light bathed the building.

3. Next, an angel clad in purple appeared at his feet, so brilliant that he dazzled the eyes of beholders and made it difficult for them to look at him. 'I come to you, beloved soul,' he said. Wettin replied: 'If the Lord wishes to forgive my sins, let Him show His mercy. If not, I am in His hand. Let Him do what He will.' Springing out of bed, with fear roaming within him, he prostrated himself

---

[1] Poncelet 1656. The source, which William sometimes quotes verbatim, is Heito of Reichenau, *Visio Wettini*, written soon after Nov. 824 (*PL* 105. 771–80; critical edn E. Dümmler, *MGH Poetae Lat. Aev. Carol.* 2. 267–75; new edn by R. M. Powell in preparation). William implies that copies were easy to find, but in England this can hardly have been so. Fifty-nine extant copies are listed by R. M. Powell, 'Nonantola and Reichenau: a new manuscript of Heito's *Visio Wettini* and the foundations for a new critical edition', *RB* 120 (2010), 243–94, at pp. 283–94. Only three are English: BL Cotton Otho A. XIII, ff. 88–93 (s. xi), London, Lambeth Palace Libr. 173, ff. 202v–211v (s. xi–xii, ?Lanthony), and Dublin, Trinity Coll. 370, ff. 81–8 (s. xiii–xiv). Oxford, Bodl. Libr. Laud. misc. 410 (c.1100) is German and only reached England in 1636–38. Heito does not refer to the Virgin Mary.
[2] 17. 1.
[3] I.e. in William's source.
[4] A strange phrase. One expects rather: 'not much changing the order.'
[5] 'machina fabrilis' (lit. 'something made by a smith') is William's attempted interpretation of his source's 'aedificium ... in modum armariorum Italicorum praefiguratum' (*PL* 772C = *MGH* p. 268; apparently 'book cupboards').
[6] Cf. perhaps *GP* 219. 4: 'compassus ad animam'.
[7] *habitus* is ambiguous between their clothing and their appearance; cf. *Visio* (*PL* 772C = *MGH* p. 268): 'uiri magnifici et uultu honorabiles'.
[8] *Visio* (*PL* 772D = *MGH* p. 269).

in his distress and asked those present to make a request of God on his behalf. And he had seven psalms sung in front of him, and part of the *Dialogues* read.[9]

4. When that was over, anxious not to be tiresome to them or make them work too hard, he let them pass the rest of the night undisturbed. But he had not yet gone quite to sleep when he saw the same angel as before, shining more brilliantly (if possible) than ever, saying something like this: 'You did very well to try to soothe your worries by prayer and reading; this is a practice which gives pleasure to me and which pleases God, so long as it is followed sincerely and without pretence.' Then he said much in complaint about bishops, how they turned their preferments into tyrannies, with no concern for the dangers run by souls; much about counts, how they are rapacious and give crooked judgements, with tongues out to hire, battening on the fortunes of the wretched locals; much about monks and nuns, how they make light of their professions and love displays,[10] eat too much, and pine for showy clothing. 5. 'God is offended by all sins,' he said, 'but especially by the sin that goes against nature and distresses shame: the sin in which the headlong search for pleasure forgets <distinctions of> sex is especially to be avoided. All other are venial, but that one is abominable to God and accursed in the eyes of men. I am the angel who once kept the mighty Samson[11] safe from losing his chastity, but who forsook him when he fell in love with a harlot[12] and was enslaved by the charms of Delilah.[13] You, similarly, did please God in the pure innocence of your boyhood; but when you broke free of the reins in your youthful escapades, you displeased Him not a little. Now, however, by facing up to God in His anger with the remedies of penitence, you have called Him back to grant you grace for a second time.[14] Tomorrow you will die, but meanwhile let us strive for mercy.'

6. With these words he seemed to lead Wettin to heaven.[15] As their journey went on, they came to a conclave of holy confessors. On the angel's advice, they both supplicated them, and asked for[16] intercessors to plead for the monk's fault. Then they approached the throne briskly, and, prostrated before God in His majesty, requested mercy. At once an oracular judgement thundered out from the inmost

---

[9] I.e. the seven penitential Psalms, and the *Dialogues* of Gregory the Great.

[10] Neither William nor the *Visio* enables us to guess what these were; perhaps elaborate liturgy.

[11] The relevance of Samson is hard to see (he was heterosexual and had lost his virginity well before he met Delilah!), but the reference is in William's source.

[12] Cf. *GR* 404. 1: 'illicitis ardoribus defeneratus'.

[13] Iud. 16: 4–31.

[14] The sense seems to be that the man had been recipient of God's grace when 'in the pure innocence of ... boyhood'. Then he lost it by sinning. Now he wishes to access it a second time through penitence.

[15] In the *Visio* the angel's admonition *follows* the visit to Heaven.

[16] Cf. *Visio* (PL 776D-777A = MGH p. 272): 'quos inter intercessores pro indulgentia peccatorum tuorum quaerere debemus', 'among whom we should look for intercessors for your sins'.

sanctuary:[17] he could only obtain forgiveness for his sins if he corrected those whom he had caused to err by his bad example. Wherefore all who had strayed from the path of good because of anything he had said or done must be brought together and adjured as he lay prostrate both to repent themselves and to aid him in *his* repentance by their prayers. The martyrs too were brought to bear as intercessors; they did the same and received the same reply.

7. The gracious Lord Jesus did not allow His blessed mother to prostrate herself before him with her fellow virgins, but when they begged for a long life <for the monk> He cheered them with this reply: 'Let him go back to the body, correct his accomplices in sin, and rejoice that his wrongdoings have been forgiven.'

I pass over much regarding the vision, for to relate what he saw that concerned the emperors, bishops, and abbots of that period is not my concern. I do not aspire to let my pen run free, only to touch on what is relevant to my topic.

8. Wettin came to himself, and, just as the dawn chorus was ushering in the arrival of day, he ordered all he had seen to be recorded on wax to avoid it being forgotten. Soon afterwards, he gave it to the father of the monastery to read when he came to see him, commending his imminent death to him and to the others with great sighs. They in their turn confidently encouraged him, for all his despair, to hope for life, since they could see he was neither deathly pale nor feeble of pulse. But he held to the word of the angel, and the whole of that day and the following one till dusk he did what he had been told, communicating with those present orally, with the absent in writing. He was of course hesitant and in suspense because of the prayer that the holy virgins had uttered for his life to be lengthened. Next day, as the sun was going down, his limbs failed; he heaved deep sighs, and summoning all the monks personally set them to sing all the psalms. Then he took the viaticum and bade farewell to this life for ever.

---

[17] Cf. *Visio* (*PL* 777A): 'a throno uox' ('uox de throno' *MGH* p. 272). William talks as though an ancient oracle is being consulted.

19. St Odo and the thief monk[1]

1. In the Life of St Odo,[2] first abbot of Cluny, unless my memory fails me,[3] I have read that someone who had turned away from the world and become a monk of the place saw as he was breathing his last a woman of incomparable beauty. She inquired kindly about the course of his illness, and asked if he knew her. When he confessed that he did not, she said: 'I am the Mother of Mercy. So do not be afraid. At that hour[4] I will come to you and receive you into the joy of my Son.' Happy the soul that had such a last sacrament to nourish it, and that cheerful and in haste broke free of the bonds of the body and departed full of joy!

2. This is why the monks of that place to this day venerate their common Mistress with unparalleled honour.[5] For example, in all their communities, which are spread very widely over the Latin world, they are not content with each monk paying his respects to her in private, but they extol her in their assemblies with a public saying of the Hours.[6] They have persuaded themselves that she appeared quite clearly in person to one of their number, and taught him the Compline that all who profess particular devotion to her now think should not be neglected.[7] I do not say this to insult, rather to exult, for every occasion should be taken for a man to be attached more intimately to her service. I may borrow the saying of the apostle: on whatever occasion *Mary* is praised, 'I rejoice, yea, and will rejoice'.[8] Hence, I think, the fact that the Cluniacs inwardly remain fixed in their resolve, and outwardly have no lack of the necessities of life, which all as it were fall into their hands unsought.[9]

---

[1] Poncelet 14 (890), found in many versions, compared by Carter, pp. 435–7. Summarised by William from Dominic 6 (ed. Canal, pp. 28–30). William omits to say that the monk had been a notorious thief, who asked Odo to grant him entry into the monastery, and says nothing of his subsequent virtuous life.

[2] John of Salerno, *Vita S. Odonis*, 2. 20 (*PL* 133. 71–2). William has lifted this reference from Dominic, but may also have consulted John (*contra* Carter, p. 435), who also uses the expressions 'in extremo uitae', 'mater misericordiae', and 'cognoscisne' for Dominic's 'ad extrema', 'misericordiae mater', and 'agnoscisne'.

[3] It did; Odo was second abbot, the first was Berno, as John of Salerno makes clear (*PL* 133. 58B, 60A). Dominic offers no opinion.

[4] Dominic says 'post triduum hac hora'.

[5] For William's admiration for the Cluniacs, see also *GR* 339. 2, *GP* 44. 3 n.

[6] Apparently Cluny only introduced the Hours of the Virgin late and cautiously: Bishop, *Liturgica Historica*, p. 228. It was still not part of the community's daily devotion in the reign of Abbot Peter the Venerable (1122–56). The practice does however appear, though not prescribed daily, in the customary written by Ulrich c.1065 (*PL* 149. 758).

[7] A possible reference to TS 10 (Dexter, p. 15) which, however, does not specify the monk as Cluniac.

[8] Philipp. 1: 18. The adaptation is the substitution of Mary for Christ.

[9] From 'I do not say ...' William's train of thought is difficult to follow. Why did he think his remarks could be misunderstood as insulting the Cluniacs, and is his concluding comment implied reproof?

20. The pilgrim of St James[1]

1. There was a monk of the same house called Gerard, as Abbot Hugh of venerable memory used to recount. While still a layman, of such a status that he neither crept along the ground[2] nor had any high pretensions, he had made a vow to go to St James in Spain. He got ready what was needed for the journey and packed his bags. The morning the journey was to start he said goodbye to his girlfriend with a kiss. As he went on kissing her, a fire came over the man, and with the woman's eager consent he embraced her and sinned in the flesh. That over, as his companions were ready and waiting, he went on his way.

2. He was walking along by himself, apart from the others, shame at the thought of the saint heavy on his conscience, when the Devil, who had made use of that vice to trick him when he was off guard, raised the stakes. He took on the shape of St James, and whispered in his ear: 'You have fallen pitiably, in blackening a holy journey with so foul an act. If you want to be forgiven, cut off the member with which you sinned. Besides, in order to live with less anxiety elsewhere,[3] you must altogether break off a life that serves the Devil and gives scope for sin: kill yourself. It makes no difference if you are killed by your own hand for love of God or by another's, except that the one is voluntary, the other involuntary.' So the sensible man recognised that it would please God more if he obeyed of his own accord rather than acting under coercion.

3. Need I say more? The Devil needed only a few whispers to seduce his brutish mind; it was easy enough to make him cut off his genitals forthwith and draw a knife across his throat. His comrades, seeing him weltering in his blood, hurried away, so as not to be thought to have murdered him out of some long-standing feud or a sudden impulse to steal.

Meanwhile, his soul was taken up by demons and haled off. When they were passing through the forecourt of the church of Rome, the apostles Peter and James ran up, and urgently asked the demons in blunt terms why they were so exultant. They were given the reply: 'He lived in folly and killed himself.' 4. St James riposted: 'No, you unspeakable spirits, he lived an innocent life, and died out of naïveté because you deceived him with your tricks. You are wrong to be punishing someone whose death you caused by your wickedness. If you have a charge to bring, let us go for judgement to the holy Mother of God.'

---

[1] Poncelet 30 (397). A popular story, told by many sources earlier than William (discussed by Carter, pp. 442–53), who got his own account from HM 8 (Dexter, pp. 22–3), which was in turn derived from Alexander of Canterbury, *Dicta Anselmi*, 22 (*Memorials of St Anselm*, pp. 200–7).

[2] Cf. Horace, *Epist.* 2. 1. 251; also echoed in GR 262. 2.

[3] This seems to correspond to HM 8 (Dexter, p. 23): 'et ob hoc habebis a Deo premium sempiternum'. *alias* then = *alibi* as used in 25. 7, 'in the other world'.

So they went. When they appealed to her, the Judge solved the riddle by bringing the man back to life. His soul returned to his body, and he got to his feet. His throat was healed, but all his life he had a scar to show for the wound. He was quite without genitals, though beneath the groin was a small hole for him to direct the burden of his urine. Then he completed the pilgrimage to St James and became a monk at Cluny, exhibiting the by no means trivial traces of the miracle that had been wrought in him.

20a. *Haec profecto ...*

These, surely, are no beggarly or ordinary miracles.[4] These poor few are worth more than ones done without number by any common-or-garden saint. From them we can vividly conceive with what compassion she shows pity to those who deserve it, how kindly she addresses them, how wonderfully she watches over them. She who, on hearing long ago that she was to be Mother of God, boasted rather of being His handmaid,[5] she (I say) is no handmaid in prodigies: she is like a queen, not an ordinary woman, in the miracles she performs. Because, as the well-known proverb goes, all that is rare is dear,[6] because even precious things grow cheap through familiarity, our Lady, though she may be thought to do few miracles, does astonishing ones, does unusual ones. But even in small and everyday ones she is not greedy or sparing, as anyone can see for himself better than he could express in writing. What for her are small and everyday are for others very great and well-considered.

---

[4] Cf. the comment on Aldhelm's miracles at *GP* 270. 7; also 48a below. Similarly, Augustine, *Enarr. in psalm.* 110. 4 (*CCSL* 40, p. 1623).

[5] Luc. 1: 38.

[6] Cf. Walther, *Sprichwörter*, no. 19877.

21. Stained corporal[1]

1. Of this type is the story of a monk of St Michael, Chiusa, whose name I suppress because he is said to be still alive.[2] As a deacon, he was assisting the priest saying mass. After the lesson from the gospel, when as ritual demands he was pouring wine into the chalice, some drops fell on to the corporal.[3] Immediately the absorbent material, stained by the liquid, took on a purple hue, the local wine being exceptionally red. The terrified young man, quite sure he would be severely punished for the offence, brandished the weapons of belief and love for Mary, and with secret groans asked for her help. 2. When mass was over, full of apprehension, he went to inspect the cloth, intending that if his request had been vain *he* would be the one to inform on himself and tell the tale. He went then – but found no trace of dampness. All the liquid had gone, and the wine stain had disappeared. It looked like a miracle to him and to the others, for it is well known that if the wine of that district touches any cloth, not just white but dyed with all skill, it can never be removed by any possible means, so dominant is its redness over every dye; it reigns everywhere, wicked and tyrannical.

[1] Poncelet 287 (1313). Based upon HM 14 (Dexter, pp. 28–9).
[2] This is William's own comment. The monk may have been the Italian Anselm, abbot of Bury 1121–48, probable commissioner or compiler of the HM-TS collection of miracles. Chiusa is in the Italian Tyrol (province of Bolzano).
[3] The corporal was a cloth used to cover the surface of the altar, which could be folded over to cover the chalice, while it stood on the altar during communion: D. Rock, *Church of our Fathers*, ed. G. W. Hart and W. H. Frere (4 vols, London, 1905), I, pp. 32 n. 33, 212–13, IV, pp. 174–5.

22. The prior of St Saviour's[1]

Of the same type is the story of how [Mary] rescued the soul of the prior of the monastery of St Saviour's, Pisa[2] from the pains of hell. He had while alive sung her Hours,[3] though he was in general dull and without foresight. He told the tale to the sacristan of the place, by name Hubert, in a dream. He had called on him by name on two previous occasions while he was awake, once when he was lighting the lamps, and again when he was seated for a natural function.[4] Almost dead with fright, Hubert would not reply. So it was in his sleep (as I say) that the prior told him how he had been rescued by the blessed Mary,[5] foretelling, furthermore, that *he* would die before long. Hubert woke up and said nothing of his vision. Its veracity he made clear by dying soon after.

---

[1] Poncelet 100 (1314). Taken from HM 12 (Dexter, pp. 27–8), but placing the monastery in Pisa instead of Pavia. William presumably made a simple slip; there was no monastery of San Salvatore in Pisa. The one in Pavia was Cluniac, founded not long before 972: Cottineau II, pp. 2237–8.

[2] Literally, and oddly, 'the Pisan prior of the monastery of St Saviour's'.

[3] HM adds 'Et dum eas caneret, semper stabat, nec ullatenus sedere uolebat.'

[4] HM has, more coyly, 'ad mansiones priuatas que erant in domo infirmorum quoniam uiciniores erant monasterio accessit'. A monastic infirmary always had latrines; either such was HM's meaning, or William deduced it, not unreasonably.

[5] HM gives more detail.

23. Monk of Eynsham[1]

1. There is also the story of a monk of Eynsham, who with a young man's energy never neglected anything that related to the service of Lady Mary. When close to his end, he saw the enemies of souls[2] clear before him, though they soon turned tail when holy water was sprinkled. Then, at death's very door, he saw that she had come to him, and declared the fact, with a reverent bow. He sang the responsory 'Rejoice, Virgin Mary',[3] and then, as we rightly believe, she escorted his soul to heaven.

2. It is justly then that all Christians burn to serve her, competing how to please her: not merely those of good character, but also those ill-suited to the good. For she stands by all men, and rewards them according to their deserts: she loves the just, but does not drive off sinners; she directs the former in the good, and stands the latter upright when they have slipped.[4] For instance, even if one of her humbler clients is overcome by sudden death, she is there to help. An example of this took place in a monastery in Burgundy.

---

[1] Poncelet 735. Repeated from William's own story in *GP* 177. 8–9, where the miracle is said to have occurred 'last year', i.e. 1124.

[2] I.e. the demons.

[3] 'Gaude, Maria Virgo, cunctas haereses sola interemisti', responsory for the Annunciation, in existence by the mid-ninth century: Hesbert, no. 6759; L. Brou, 'Marie "destructrice de toutes les hérésies" et la belle légende du répons Gaude Maria Virgo', *Ephemerides Liturgica* 61 (1947), 321–53. In England, it is found in the eleventh-century Winchester Troper (CCCC 473, f. 194), and in the Office for the Virgin in a twelfth-century breviary from Westminster (BnF lat. 10433, f. 232v).

[4] There is play on verbs in *-igo*. For the emendation *iustos diligit* cf. Ps. 145: 8.

24. Sudden death[1]

1. There was once a pious monk, who, as it seemed, was doing no damage to his soul by any kind of offence. Suddenly, at dead of night, he died. The monks, hearing his dreadful screams, hurried up; they each put a hand to his nostrils, and could tell that he had expired. The monks had no hesitation in performing the rest of the rites, but they did raise a dispute about the burial.

2. Those of evil disposition argued like this: 'He must not be buried among the holy. A man whom such a dire judgement of God has marked out as guilty of some major crime, whom God's wrath has shown to be worthy of condemnation by depriving him of confession and the last rites, the only remedies Christians have, such a man, to repeat, cannot be absolved by human judgement.' Others, however, affirmed that the just as well as the unjust come to a sudden death; as Solomon says: 'The just man, with whatever death he is prevented, shall be in rest.'[2] 3. But if a sinner incurs death for a sin, the sin is effaced by death, as is shown by the instance of the prophet who was sent to Samaria and ran into a fierce lion; the lion killed him to punish his disobedience, but even so kept the corpse safe.[3] 'So your view is shaky either way. Either this man did not die because of a sin, as even the just cannot escape this kind of demise (though we don't in fact pronounce him unjust, for we saw him to be good by human standards); or if God did punish him with death for a sin, that sin was wiped out by his death. For He will not judge the same offence twice.'[4]

4. Neither side would give way, everyone holding to their own side of the question; so they left it to God to decide: they must turn to fasting and vigils to merit a pronouncement from on high. And behold, on the following night the dead man appeared to some of the brethren, men who would blush to tell a lie,[5] and in whose heart morality and learning rivalled for supremacy. 'You should know,' he said, 'that I have been released just to bring you an answer to your prayers. I lost my life not as punishment for some specific sin, but because of a sudden onset of illness. At that very hour I was reflecting on the Matins of St Mary, and bewailing my own misdeeds while you were asleep. She gave me a signal reward, by snatching my spirit from the demons. What is more, deigning to call me her beloved son, she placed me at rest, free from punishment, to attain eternal joys when God so wishes.' 5. After this vision, they woke at the call of the morning

[1] William apparently summarises Poncelet 202 (1186), found in Carter's MB collection (Dexter, pp. 57–61).
[2] Wisd. 4: 7.
[3] Cf. III Reg. 13: 21–7; Gregory, *Dial.* 4. 25. 1.
[4] Cf. Nahum 1: 9 (*Vetus Latina*); *Comm. Lam.* III, 967–8.
[5] Cf. *Comm. Lam.* I, 2625–6.

bell, and compared notes on what they had seen; they came to a unanimous view, as though they all had been given the same task or duty to perform.[6]

Such things, brought about by our Lady's mercy, show and continue to show her untiring work to mortal men; no one who seeks her in full faith is ever quite rejected. Other saints cure bodies, but *her* power is praised for her effect on body and soul combined. She always places the souls of her devotees at rest; bodies she cures when she knows it to be to our good.

6. But there are still many things for me to bring to the notice of the faithful listener. If I have said enough of monks, let me go on to another rank of men. [C For this reason, a new turn in the narrative will be marked by the start of a second book.][7]

---

[6] Cf. Cicero, *De leg*. 2. 6 'tamquam id habuerit operis ac muneris ut …', 'as though Nature had had the task and duty to …'. William quoted from this rare work in GR 374. 1. The source (e.g. Dexter, p. 61) makes it clear that the monks proceeded to bury the body; similarly the addition in B cited in the app. crit.

[7] Some such transitional phrase will have stood in P, but the wording of C is not quite happily phrased. See above, Introduction p. xxxviii.

BOOK TWO

Prologue

1. In making a new start to my narration in praise of the Lady, I am influenced by two considerations. I decided to stop writing for an interval in order to remedy a debilitating illness, while at the same time making sure that I do not bore any readers I may have. But the gap has now mitigated both these worries. The love of the Lady is rousing me from my sloth to renew my praises of her, and I am by now pretty convinced that no composition of this type will be found tedious by anyone. As I hope, praise for the matter will suppress any ill will, bringing the writer favour and wiping away any feeling of satiety from the listener. I shall therefore go on with what I began, relying on God's favour, and everywhere making it my first concern that the truth never comes to grief in any respect. Every Christian should think it far from him even to contemplate the wickedness of using lies,[1] however decorative, to press the claims of one who is the Mother of the Truth.[2] Thanks to her merits, she is far ahead of all mortal praise. No one has to contrive or devise some fabrication in order to magnify her.

2. All men have this indelibly imprinted on their consciousness and as it were inborn in them; this is pondered in their breasts, breathed by their hearts, often heard from their lips. Indeed, absolutely all Christians hope that they are freed from any kind of peril if they merely call upon her name. In fact, confident devotees, hastily but piously, pass by the name of her omnipotent Son, so much so that they think He is not needed when His Mother has been invoked, not because she is in herself more powerful than her offspring, but because she is (so to speak) closer than Him[3] and nearer their low level. In the secret recesses of His own godhead, He is not to be reached by our senses; human frailty does not presume to win through and worship His power. 3. It must therefore bring mediators to bear, who, having once upon a time shared in our mortal nature, feel favour towards us and can be won over to intercede with Him. But it can find no saint who can be put in the same class as this potent Empress or found comparable to her in clemency. By her power, she can, thanks to her rights over her son, wrest from Him whatever she pleases by a sweet violence. By her clemency, she pities the pitiable;[4] she is so distinguished for it that she positively glories in being known as the Mother of Mercy. That is absolutely the right name for her; for it was only the clemency of God that brought God to become man,

---

[1] Cf. *GP* 230. 5, on the miracles of Aldhelm.
[2] See above, p. 3 n. 12.
[3] Cf. *Comm. Lam.* III, 1144: 'propinquius aspicit'.
[4] Cf. 20a.

for fear that, driven into guilt by the wiles of the Devil, man might for ever turn the wheel of misery.[5]

4. That is why the psalmist calls God his mercy,[6] so that Scripture can express in our language the sweet feeling He has for us, though deeper understanding makes us aware that these emotions do not affect God.[7] So God, though it is said to be characteristic of Him to pity and to spare,[8] instilled His mother, among the rest of the virtues, with mercy: the mother into whom He carried himself in the fullness of His godhead, into whom He brought all good things *en masse*.[9] We may therefore find the courage to assert that our Lady possesses no virtue more gladly, displays none more readily, than the one with whose name she rejoices to be distinguished.

5. She rejoices, I repeat, she whose joy is the salvation of the living, the raising of the dead. Now such is the force of clemency that even those who harass it by their deeds love and preach it by their words. It shines forth in all persons, but it is praised especially in eminent men who do not misuse power for a whim, and prefer to find the opportunity to forgive, rather than punish. For princes are thought to deserve praise and honour if when they have been wronged they would rather forgive than retaliate. So the mercy of our Lady is the more agreeable, considering that, though she could in a moment destroy all who offend against her and her Son, she is happy to incline and yield to the lighter sentence, and wishes her sinners to return rather than to perish.

6. What is more, though she has never suffered a blot on her gemlike chastity, or even admitted a stain into her thoughts, yet she looks with no harsh eye on sinners of every kind. She suspends judgement on them, so as to lead back to life even those pitiable men who are teetering on the brink of despair. It is an incentive for sinners to return to the good if they see one of their number turned to God and loved by God. But if they were to see some notorious sinner had never returned, they would all slumber in deadly torpor. Hence the correcting of a single sinner is a warning to many.

7. That is why the most blessed Virgin and Mother takes great pains to correct such men; she has long taken this as her province. For she loves and supports the

---

[5] Cf. Virgil, *Aen.* 6. 748, echoed by William elsewhere, e.g. *Comm. Lam.* I, 2838–9.

[6] Ps. 143: 2.

[7] *Comm. Lam.* often, e.g. I, 1823–4: 'nec huiuscemodi affectus in eum cadant'.

[8] Collect used in Masses for the Dead: P. Bruylants, *Les Oraisons du Missel Romain* (Louvain, 1952), nos 207, 208; found e.g. in *The Leofric Missal*, ed. F. E. Warren (Oxford, 1883), p. 195, *The Bec Missal*, ed. A. Hughes (Henry Bradshaw Soc. 94: 1963), p. 267. Prof. N. J. Morgan comments that the latter is the sort of Mass for the Dead that might have been used at Malmesbury in William's day.

[9] For *coagulum* see *ODML* s. v. 2. For instances in William, see below, 28. 10 (with n.); *GP* 46. 8: 'coagulum uitiorum' (clotted vices). In the present passage, it is relevant to note that *coagulum* could be used of sperm: 'de substantia e qua fetus in utero formatur' (*Thesaurus Linguae Latinae* s. v. 1381, 8–9, citing esp. Pliny, *Nat. Hist.* 7. 66; William transcribed 7. 65, 68–9 in his *Polyhist.*, p. 48).

ugly in her sweet bosom, in order to make them beautiful by the arts of her pity. As we have often learned by experience, some who have been changed from bad to good see the good with a clarity corresponding to the stubbornness with which in the past they fostered vice, and come to practise it.

But enough of this proem.

25. Clerk of Chartres[1]

1. Fulbert, as I said,[2] displayed the brand[3] of love for the holy Mary in the city of Chartres, making her sweetness blaze forth and kindling a stimulus <to others to adore her>.[4] He left many pupils just as high-minded, who kept to his sentiments in this respect at least, but did not love the same path(?).[5]

2. One of these was a scholar of (as is said) no small learning. But he disgraced his fine intellect by evil actions, and fell deeper into depraved ways thanks to his wealth.[6] To his wantonness was added the employment of arms, something alien to a clerk's status, and a wicked avarice, which meant that any loot that came the way of his greed was never returned, despite all entreaties. Yet he sang the Hours of holy Mary no less ardently and dutifully, and he would greet her more than casually.[7] But he acted in such a way that men were not aware of this; they saw the evil façade, not the good that lay deep within.

3. I think this was ill-advised, for just as it is full of boastfulness to make your good qualities public, so it is impudent to fail to hide your bad ones. Surely a man will go to rack and ruin if he has no respect for either the hidden judgement of God or the regard of men. So modesty suggests that we should so far as we are concerned hide any good we do, to avoid becoming puffed up; but so far as concerns our neighbours we should let them be seen, so that God may be honoured in them.[8]

4. But this man did not mind causing scandal among men. He behaved with open brutality while praying in secret, with the notion of excusing and mitigating the burden of his outrages by his service to St Mary. And these hopes were not lost on the winds. For when <once>, as was his wont, he was borne into the alarums of war, he was cut off by the enemy and killed. He was not decently gathered up even by his own people, but found an inglorious sod in a lowly spot; a clerk deserved better. This was the doing of the canons, who thought he should be deprived of burial with his ancestors because a pitiable death had put a swift end to his wanton life. There was no funeral procession; the body had scarcely been carried out when clods of earth were thrown on to it in a far corner of the cemetery.

---

[1] Poncelet 339 (668). Based upon HM 3 (Dexter, pp. 18–19), with a good deal of embroidery, e.g. the connection between the clerk and Bishop Fulbert.

[2] 9. 1 above.

[3] Cf. *GP* 82. 1.

[4] The meaning is not certain.

[5] The text is apparently corrupt.

[6] Cf. 5. 2, 40. 2, and *VW* 2. 22. 2 with n. 5. Similar is 5. 2 'pro lasciuia opum suarum'.

[7] So *ODML*, s. v. *intranseunter*, citing only this passage. This exceedingly rare word (ignored altogether by the other dictionaries) is used, as a synonym for 'intransitiue', by Sedulius Scottus, *In Donati artem minorem* (*CCCM* 40C, p. 19).

[8] Cf. I Pet. 4: 11. But the statement hardly makes sense.

5. Mary's bowels <of pity> were troubled over all this, and after thirty days had passed she appeared in a vision to the *primicerius*[9] of the church and asked severely why they had treated her chancellor[10] like this; her voice was harsh, and she was to all appearances far removed from her normal merciful self. He was hesitant in the face of such an unexpected inquiry, and asked the name of the chancellor. She replied: 'My chancellor is the man whom you threw out of your cemetery thirty days back.[11] He was a better man than you, yet in your folly you condemned him without due thought. Go then, bring back the body, and place it in an honourable tomb. You must be made to understand quite clearly how great an insult you are guilty of.'

6. He awoke, and what he had dreamt came to light. Everyone gave their agreement, the ground was dug up and the grave opened. Then indeed might you have seen the wonderful grace of God: the body of the man free of stink and decay, the tongue aquiver, as though ready to perform its usual task in praise of God. From the mouth had grown a most beautiful flower, fit to draw onlookers to grace. The stem was coming out of the tongue, surrounded by playful sprigs of little blooms, trying as if by a valiant effort to break through the stones that had been hastily thrown upon it and so to protect the corpse from the earth injuring it. 7. This was the reward for service rendered:[12] the tongue that had so often hailed holy Mary was found to deserve a crown of flowers. Everyone understood what the Lady had promised,[13] and speculated how glorious a life the soul must be living in another place considering that the body had already been given such an evident pledge of glory. They bewailed their own impudent behaviour, and to lighten their guilt they buried the body with due ceremony. To ensure that posterity was well aware of the miracle, they took care to have it written down.[14]

---

[9] Dean or possibly precentor. William's classicising 'primicerius' is unhelpful. In any case HM has merely 'cuidam clerico' (Dexter, p. 18).

[10] Cf. 11. 2 and n.

[11] Cf. *VD* 1. 1. 2 n. 2 for various meanings of *atrium* in William's works. Here it seems to mean the cemetery, following his source, which has the Virgin ask 'Cur ita egistis circa meum cancellarium, ut poneretis eum *extra cimiterium* uestrum? Cui interroganti quisnam esset ille eius cancellarius, sancta inquit "Ille qui ante dies xxx. a uobis est *extra atrium* tumulatus ..."' (Dexter, p. 18). Yet, in §4 above, William says that the body was buried 'in extremo cimiterii angulo'.

[12] ?Ambrose, *Epigr.* 2165, ed. E. Diehl, *Inscriptiones latinae christianae ueteres* (3 vols, Berlin, 1961[2]), I, p. 424; *CPL* 164; *SK* 16800. William may have found this in a *sylloge inscriptionum*, though it does not appear among the excerpts from one such incorporated in his own version of *Liber pontificalis*: Thomson, *William of Malmesbury*, pp. 125–9.

[13] She had said (§5) that they would come to understand how they had gone wrong; and so they did, when they found the body undecayed.

[14] William's comment.

26. Five *Gaude*s[1]

1. This event was noised about the city, and it struck a spark of good into a canon of the same church, who, besides fulfilling the other observances connected with the service of the Lady Virgin, used to sing every day the antiphon 'Rejoice, Mother of God, Virgin without stain'.[2] 'Every day' is an understatement: he sang it whenever he passed near the altar. His love for her had brought about this practice, and it was virtually becoming second nature. No necessity, no hurry as he went by, ever made him neglect the custom. If he was sent on a journey he used to say this antiphon with only Heaven as witness; and in a crowd he would go over it with his mouth tight shut.[3] Seeing that he never thought the Lady absent, he had persuaded, indeed ordered himself, always to imagine her as present; thus, out of reverence for her, he might avoid exposing himself to temptations, and also hold back from the unlawful.[4]

2. It is the oldest precept of philosophy, and one with no small weight in the attainment of the good life, that you should place some person of honest life before your mind as though he is present, and blush to sin out of regard for him, if not for God's sake.[5] One who does this will sin rarely or never, and will gradually reach a point where the good he had begun out of consideration for repute in men's eyes he practises habitually out of love for God alone, and out of the pleasure he takes in good as such.[6]

3. This is how our canon lived: wherever he might be, he always worshipped Mary with a willing heart. His prayers were accompanied by tears that attracted pity and displayed devotion.[7] But when he had lived his life out and he was gradually growing stiff unto death as his soul took flight, he began to be oppressed by the familiar dread of terrors <to come>, growing anxious and complaining of what was to become of him. When he was in this sad state of mind, Mary, holy Mother of God, appeared to him, and in the manner she knows so well lightened his misery by saying these very words (as we have heard) in a kind voice: 'Why are you so afraid, considering that you have so often spoken to me of joy? Do not

---

[1] Poncelet 69 (697). Apparently taken from HM 4 (Dexter, p. 19), but much embroidered, e.g. HM does not connect the clerk with Chartres. The title refers to the fivefold repetition of *Gaude* in the antiphon, which is given in full in HM, as in its ultimate source, Peter Damian, *De uariis apparitionibus et miraculis* (PL 145. 588D). It originated in the late tenth century, and is first attested in England in a mid-eleventh-century MS from Christ Church, Canterbury: BL, Cotton Tib. E. III, f. 111.

[2] Hesbert, no. 2920. Cf. below, 43. 1.

[3] A somewhat mixed metaphor, perhaps based on Cant. 7: 9: 'labiisque et dentibus illius ad ruminandum'.

[4] Z's *a licitis*, no doubt a conjecture, makes better sense: 'from lawful things.' Cf. pr. 14: 'quomodo enim illicita committeret quae a licitis temperabat?'

[5] Seneca, *Epist.* 11. 8–10.

[6] Similar sentiments and vocabulary at *Comm. Lam.* III, 1109–12.

[7] *illices* and *indices* are also paired at *Comm. Lam.* II, 1084, the former with uncertain meaning, as here.

panic, for you will suffer no evil; from now on you will share with me and my Son in the joy you used to sing of to me.'[8]

4. He had not yet quite cast off love for this life, and, imagining his bodily health had been restored to him, he tried to raise himself on one elbow. But his limbs had lost their strength, and he straightway fell back on the bed. Soon he breathed away his spirit, and found a life other than the one he had in mind. The man's speedy death convinced those present that it was in truth St Mary who had, as he had said, spoken with him, though all the rest had been able to hear was the sound of *his*[9] voice.

[8] Almost verbatim as in HM 4 (Dexter, p. 19).
[9] We presume that this is what is meant ('a voice' Carter).

27. Clerk of Pisa[1]

1. Pisa is a city in Italy, a busy place thanks to its markets, its detachments of soldiers, and (in particular) its experienced sailors. Thus men from the city, while taking the islands of Corsica and Sardinia from the Saracens, even captured the king of Africa and forced him to pay tribute.[2]

At Pisa there is a church of St Cassian, who, as Prudentius says,[3] was handed over by a heathen judge to be tortured by boys whose hatred he had incurred as their teacher. They accordingly made a martyr of him, contriving a most spiteful device; they hurled their pens at him. Their hands were not strong enough to be effective, so he died the more painfully because it took so long.[4]

2. To this church a clerk had been presented by his father for the service of God. He had spent his childhood there, and by now had become a man. As he grew older, his love for St Mary grew too. He always sang private Hours and private Offices for her. And though he was often summoned home to pay a visit to his relations, he obstinately declined, on the plea that St Mary by herself showed him the affection of father, mother and absolutely all kin – and indeed surpassed it. But when his parents had lived their lives out, his more distant relations approached the youth. 3. His father and mother had died, they said, leaving to him, and him only in the absence of any other heir, the ancestral treasures, rich estates, and palatial houses. He must take up his inheritance, which would be ruined if it went any longer with no one to look after it. Back there, he could much more quickly win God's grace by living modestly and distributing his substance to the poor, whereas here he had to be content with a pittance and did not have enough even for himself. The clerk was not much swayed by these arguments. So they took him to law, and, such being the custom of the country, they obtained an injunction and made him take up his inheritance whether he liked it not.

4. At first he raised objections; in the end, though, he gave in, to humour his friends. But when he had tasted and experienced the allurements of the

---

[1] Poncelet 109 (1211). Mostly taken from HM 16 (Dexter, pp. 30–1), with additional historical context.
[2] Cf. *GR* 92: 'In our times, however, [the Saracens] have been forced to abandon … Corsica and Sardinia by the Pisans'. William refers to the famous Mahdia expedition of 1087 and the lead-up to it. Pisa and Genoa drove the Arabs from Sardinia and occupied it in 1015–16. In two separate expeditions of 1014 and c.1050 they captured Corsica. In 1034 they carried the offensive to north Africa and in 1087, in combination with other Italian cities, they captured most of Mahdia (Tunisia), the capital of the Zirid emir al-Tamim ibn al-Mu'izz (d.1108), who surrendered and paid out an immense sum in reparation. K. M. Setton, *A History of the Crusades, I: The First Hundred Years*, ed. M. W. Baldwin (Madison, WI, 1969), pp. 40–53; H. E. J. Cowdrey, 'The Mahdia campaign of 1087', *EHR* 92 (1977), 1–29.
[3] Prudentius, *Peristeph*. 9. The church is presumably Santi Ippolito e Cassiano in the municipality of Cascina, about 13km south-east of Pisa, in existence by the tenth and perhaps the ninth century. The present structure dates from the late twelfth century.
[4] Apart from Prudentius, note William's allusions to the same story in *GR* 122. 6 and *GP* 240. 8 with nn., and his Letter to Peter (*GR*, ed. Stubbs, I, p. cxlvi).

world, which tend to creep like a sweet poison into the minds of the unwary, he gradually began to sicken in the affairs of God and become practised in the way of the world. Pleasure took complete control over him. He now surrendered very willingly, and resolved to take a wife. There was some delay until the girl of his choice should reach marriageable age: for as yet she was still too young for the attentions of a husband. Yet no troublesome business, no clamouring cares could tear away from his mind his love for St Mary. But his shy virginity was tottering, as though on the brink of a precipice, and would have gone plunging over had not the Mother of God come to his aid. He went on singing her Hours, though rather out of habit than with any sincere feeling.

5. By now his madness had gone so far that on the appointed day he started off with high hopes and without a qualm to wed the woman. As he walked along, it occurred to him that he had not yet sung Nones for his Lady.[5] So he asked his companions to be so kind as to bear with him till he had sung it through. He turned aside into a church that chanced to be on the travellers' way, and stood there in a daze, in the thrall of quite other thoughts. Obsessed with foul lusts, he stammered out the Hour with his lips only. 6. Then the holy Mother stood there by him, glaring at the guilty man with threatening countenance and fierce eyes. Her grace and authority were added to by the forcefulness of her look and a severity that she seemed to have sought from elsewhere, leaving her sweet nature unimpaired. After complaining bitterly that he had abandoned her and deprived her of his old love, she added: 'Foolish wretch, do you disdain me as your friend? Has another woman seemed better? Where is a demon driving you with your senses dulled? What madness, to misuse my love and to lust after unchaste embraces? No one can serve two masters,[6] or please two mistresses.'

7. That was all she said. He had nothing to mutter in reply, and she disappeared. The clerk went out <of the church>. He was wounded to the heart, though he hid the clouds of his mind behind a fair front,[7] and persisted in his journey. He went through the whole marriage ceremony, taking part in the jests and the feasting. But at dead of night, when the rest lay buried in wine and sleep[8] (for drink was relentlessly pressing home the drowsiness it had induced so gently), he went off who knows where, telling the secret only to his bride. He never again showed himself in that province. Doubtless, in his devotion to St Mary, he sought out a spot where he could safely live the quiet life to which he was used,[9] and grew old in her service.

---

[5] The Hour is not specified in HM, but is in at least two other variants of the story ('Roman Noble' and 'Brother of the King of Hungary': E. F. Wilson, *The Stella Maris of John of Garland* [The Mediaeval Academy of America, Publ. no. 45, Cambridge, MA, 1946], pp. 162–3). William may therefore have had access to a written source other than HM.

[6] Matt. 6: 24.

[7] Cf. *GR* 398. 7 ('frontis sereno').

[8] Cf. Virgil, *Aen.* 2. 265.

[9] Cf. *GR* 73. 1: 'otio inglorio tutus uictitare'.

28. Love gained by black arts[1]

1. Another clerk experienced the same sweet severity in return for his crimes, though *he* had committed a more heinous offence. His bishop, thinking him worthy of tender and heartfelt affection, gave him the facilities to study every kind of learning. The clerk took this work seriously, but after mastering the permissible arts he turned, out of normal human curiosity, to illicit ones too. Instructed by certain 'characters',[2] as they are called, he had reached such a point of sacrilege that even if she struggled to resist him he could snatch kisses from any woman he pleased, and overcome her chastity. No doubt then: whatever girl he looked upon with that roving eye, he had no trouble in having his way with her.

2. There was only one girl whose beauty entranced him whom he had to work hard to seduce. The hidden wound festered in his breast;[3] he was desperate to win her, and what fed his passion the more was that the girl had set her heart on remaining chaste. So he used the familiar muttered spells to summon the Devil into secret conclave; then he proceeded to prayers, complaining that one silly girl had the impudence to find a weak point in incantations that were powerful over the whole world. 'Then do me homage,' said the Devil, 'and abjure Christ and His mother Mary.' The clerk blenched at these horrific words: 'I would not,' he said, 'for all the world deny my Lady St Mary and her son. But there is nothing I would refuse to do if only I could have the girl I love.' So the Enemy, dropping the idea of his abjuring Christ and Mary, accepted the homage that was being offered unasked. He had two reasons to feel pleased with his plan: the clerk would never come back to his senses while he was taken up with such an outrageous affair, and to do homage to the Devil meant completely abandoning his soul. 3. So the innocent girl, having evaded a man's spells, yielded to pleasure when the Devil pricked her with his goad. It was not enough for her to yield to lechery in silence; she had to cry aloud: 'I want that clerk, show him me, I tell you! Make me his wife, if you want me to go on living!' Disturbed by these cries, her parents and friends were in doubt how to proceed. If what she asked for was denied, they feared for her well-being; if it was conceded, it meant a blot on their family escutcheon, for the man was humbly born as well as a clerk. His clerical status meant offence to God's majesty, his low status damage to their distinguished family. They counted it as a positive marvel that one of the weaker sex should disregard natural modesty and think it proper to persevere in shamelessness.

---

[1] Poncelet 94 (396). Taken from Carter's MB collection. There is both a metrical version (Poncelet 1230), and a verbally very similar prose one (pr. Crane, pp. 47–51). William's account includes some variants and elaboration.

[2] See *ODML* s. v. *character* 1b ('magical character').

[3] Cf. Virgil, *Aen.* 4. 2: 'uulnus alit uenis et caeco carpitur igni' (of Dido). Also echoed at VW 1. 6. 1, HN 2. 22.

4. The bishop was unaware of all this, and found it in him to believe that his clerk was chaste. For his part, the clerk disguised his role of lover behind a cloak of religion, praying openly and often to God and St Mary. And belief in his piety was not altogether unfounded, for he had since boyhood held to the rule of missing not even one of her Hours. Later, Mary, who can plumb mysteries, showed that he had behaved like this in all sincerity. So, as I said, the bishop was taken in by outward appearances, and he had forwarded the man's progress up to his present age in a relaxed spirit of affection. If anyone thought fit to cast aspersions on the clerk in the bishop's presence, he smoothed the matter over, putting the laying of such disagreeable information down to mere ill will. And even now, when the girl's relatives made well-founded assertions, he long shrank from believing them. But he did take the young man aside and try to ascertain the truth. The clerk had no hesitation in bewailing what had happened on the breast of his kind father. He confessed at least to loving the girl, though he concealed his dark arts.

5. The bishop now thought that the rigour of the canonical rules should be somewhat bent, for fear that if he broke up the longed-for union the clerk might go to the dogs. So he agreed to his protégé's marriage. He had a word with the family, and easily brought them round to his view. Then he saw to the engagement, and fixed the date for the wedding. The day dawned, the nuptial mass had begun. The clerk started singing the Hours for Mary, but did not reach the end of Nones, the priest having gone too fast for him. For the moment, he went off in some gloom, but he had more pressing things to think about and put the matter out of his mind. But when the attendants had laid the sumptuous feast amid much hubbub, and were already crying 'Water! Water!',[4] the Hour he had missed came back to him as he was about to start eating. He asked the guests to excuse him, and went into a neighbouring church, where he fell upon the floor, only to be overcome by sleep during his heartfelt prayers.

6. He dreamt a woman stood at his side and asked if he knew her. When he said 'No, not at all', she replied: 'I am Mary, whose Hour you were singing. I once had a friend, but he has now brought in a rival and is trying to mar our old treaty.[5] But if I am the Mother of God, powerful in heaven and queen on earth, I shall see

---

[4] That this is a reference to the washing of the hands before the meal is indicated by the MB version (e.g. Bodl. Libr., Laud. misc. 359, f. 72v): 'dum mense pararentur et manus abluerent'. Presumably William's wording reflects what happened in a large household, the servants calling the guests to table with their cry.

[5] The same play at *GR* 8. 1 ('fedus fedatum').

to it that the treaty-breaker does not rejoice for long: the man who undervalued me when I was patient with him will from now on feel my fury. If I so wish it, prompt punishment will attend this outrage, and the turncoat will receive the due reward for his sacrilege.' The words struck him like a thunderbolt. He was aware they were spoken of him, and in his dream he cried out: 'Lady of ladies, joy of the universe, mercy of the world, though I did think of doing the dreadful thing you accuse me of, I have not yet done it. I *have* committed another crime, and that is what makes me afraid. If you erase that one, I will bid farewell to this. I do not want to abandon you as my bride, or to substitute a base love for my friendship with you. Only stand at my side, Lady, stand by me and show me your favour! I will put the rest to rights, if only you forgive me for my fault in act and thought.'

7. After saying this in his dream, he wept and wailed. Then the Lady, being happy to check offenders with a word and to mitigate the gravest offences by mere speech, was heard to say: 'Enough, stop crying! When you return to yourself, you will show if you love me. Speed of conversion will be proof of love; punishment will attend the insolence of scorn.' With this declaration she was gone. He came to himself, and running straight off to the bishop made him cognisant of the whole matter from the beginning. When he heard what his pupil wished, he set him a penance to match the offence, and dissolved the marriage as easily as he had contrived it: he was a man of persuasive tongue as well as one revered for his qualities. So the clerk from then on avoided evil and was fruitful in good. He spent the rest of his life in such a manner that, thanks to the favour of his preserver, God could by a lovely miracle make his innocence clear. For a dove, a bird that symbolises good, was seen by those present to issue from the mouth of the man as he died and reach clear air[6] through the thick cloud cover.

8. By these works, which move effortlessly beyond the scope of human possibility into the realms above, the happy Virgin is proved to be patron of all that is human and judge of all that is divine. She does not wish that those who love her should hanker after corporeal and corruptible forms of beauty while ranking the eternal forms in second place. It is madness to expend effort on things that will perish and that slip away of themselves, while turning your back on things perpetual and subject to no corruption. What in the world of men is the beauty of the most celebrated body but (as it were) the vulnerability of a flower however pretty? A flower is ruined by lack of sunshine or dried up by heat or shaken off by the wind. In just the same way, the beauty of the flesh is dried up by a slight fever, or shrivelled by lack of food, or impaired by advancing age, or at the last

---

[6] Cf. *Comm. Lam.* I, 2378: 'in liberius caelum euadit' (figurative).

altogether reaped by death. The eternal beauty of the soul is not like that, no indeed it is not. Just when one most thinks it to be departing the dross of this world and taking its leave, it is in fact darting forth rejoicing, happy in its youth, like an eagle shuffling off its old feathers.[7]

9. Everyone can see that these pleasures should be scorned by the wise man, especially as on an improper act follows repentance for it. The very whiteness of skin that catches the eye and unsettles the mind is no more, so to speak, than a whited sepulchre.[8] What a short distance separates things you praise from things that you would shrink from if you looked at them with attention! That vulnerable skin is the deceptive cover for many a deformity, the thin veil for excrement and filth. Everything may be fair inside and out, but it is not eternal. Hence there is particular applause for the saying of a clerk of our time, a man of upright morals. A friend of his advised him to relax his principles and fall in love with some pretty girl. 'I will do that', he said, 'if you show me a woman in whom I could find no just fault.'[9] His friend, who perhaps wanted to test his resolution, set himself to bring along a succession of women, day after day. 10. But for a long time his efforts were wasted: the clerk always found some fault that his friend could not deny. Finally, when he put on display a woman in whom all beauty had flowed in a single mass,[10] the clerk was defeated by this prodigy of beauty and could not take exception to anything. But he at once recovered his shrewdness, and said something that amounted to the same thing as his previous rebuffs: 'All this would be beautiful if it were perpetual. But whatever is not perpetual is not perfectly beautiful. A lack of perpetuity diminishes beauty. So this, though it may seem beautiful, is really frail and fleeting.' He then brought his powerful eloquence to bear on the woman's heart; seeing that her waxlike softness could be turned to a good use, he advised her to dedicate such looks to the God who had given them to her. She did not spurn what the chaste man had said. With the help of his money, she led a holy life first in a nunnery, and later, in her longing for greater strictness, by herself in a cell.

11. This may seem an intrusion into my narrative, but I had no wish to pass over something that chimes so well with the admonitions of Lady Mary. For she does not tolerate those who love her deeply being corrupted by entering on silly love affairs, which delay or prevent them from striving for the eternal. Even a foolish man(?) should not value any pleasure so much that he lays up everlasting punishment for the sake of a moment's satisfaction.

[7] Ps. 102: 5. The renewal of the eagle's feathers is mentioned in the Bestiary, a version of which was doubtless William's source: Clark, *A Medieval Book of Beasts*, 52 (p. 166).
[8] Matt. 23: 27.
[9] Cf. *GR* 154. 4 (where see n.) = *GP* 86. 2.
[10] Cf. *GR* 135. 2: 'omne coagulum pulchritudinis ... confluxerat'; see also above, p. 71 n. 9.

29. The priest who only knew one mass[1]

1. There was once a priest with a countryman's simple-mindedness. He was more or less devoid of any book learning, and dim-witted to boot in that area, for he could not even make out a text syllable by syllable unless it was something he was used to. I am thinking of the mass for St Mary, in the introit to which the Lady is most graciously saluted in a verse by Sedulius.[2] But he was not that uncouth in character, for he spiced the rusticity of his knowledge with the comeliness of his life, preferring to be more skilful in life than tongue, more polished in nature than in assiduity of study: such was his success in scraping off from his soul the rust of vice and avoiding the gulfs into which they might plunge him. His way of life was meagre and slender, but he was very generous-hearted in helping the poor even out of what he received from others.[3] 2. His poverty gave him pleasure; in fact, he was on such good terms with poverty that he was not poor at all.[4] He lived, then, from the offerings of the faithful, and wanted nothing more. The mass he knew he did not miss for a single day. Mere prayers were not enough for him: any words in them that he could understand he furnished forth with pious sighs and tears. He offered to God a sacrifice that was rich, not starveling, an afflicted and contrite spirit.[5]

3. Matters standing thus, something pitiful and detestable took place. There were men who were piqued by the holy man's good life and the favour it brought him, foolish and malevolent persons who hated wisdom and out of envy hurled abuse at the good in him that they could not see in themselves, giving it a malicious twist. Foremost among them were the clerks whose job it is to spy out the misdeeds of parish priests. That type (if the few good ones will excuse me saying so) is well practised in speech and greedy for gifts. They weigh right and good by the standard of advantage, and the canonical rules tip the way the money goes.[6]

4. These people summoned the priest: how could he presume to sing the mass when he was illiterate? He saw that they were not relying on reasons but were interested only in bribes, and he denied them an answer. Piety yielded to venality, simplicity gave way before wickedness.[7] This only provoked them, and

---

[1] Poncelet 40. The source is HM 9 (Dexter, p. 24), embroidered.
[2] Sedulius, *Carm. pasch.* 2. 63–9. HM refers to it by its first line 'Salue sancta parens' (*SK* 14574).
[3] Cf. 36. 1.
[4] Cf. Seneca, *Epist.* 4. 11: 'cui cum paupertate bene conuenit, diues est'.
[5] Cf. Ps. 50: 19.
[6] William presumably refers to archdeacons, whose venality was a matter for widespread contemporary comment: M. Brett, *The English Church under Henry I* (Oxford, 1975), pp. 199–211 (and cf. above, 31. 2 n.). However, one would only expect one of them, not a team acting in concert.
[7] Presumably meaning that the priest could not or would not stand up to his greedy opponents at this interview. They are 'provoked' by his apparent unwillingness to answer.

they accused the man before the bishop, wrapping the truth up in lies: this was someone who mocked God and led the people astray, for he dared to pollute the holy objects by handling them when he was stuffed full of food and hiccupping with drink. This riled the bishop, who had the priest brought before him at once. 5. But when he came he did not allow him to be examined according to canon law; he gave overhasty credence to what the clerks said, and stripped him of his post. All that was proved was his illiteracy; the rest was not scrutinised. In another, this would have been enough to justify his deprivation, but this man should have been completely cleared by his good life and his devoted service to the blessed Mary. What is more, the accusers could make none of their charges stick, and the case had no substance. So[8] this bishop should not have degraded a priest who had been ordained by another; he could after all at least stammer out a single mass. Rather, he ought to have encouraged him in what he did know, and used threats to spur him on to learn more.

6. So the priest went away deprived of the office which was at once his means of living and a cure for his soul. Back home, he turned his complaints heavenwards, and told his special patroness that he had been cast into need. And lo, she appeared to the bishop in a dream on the following night, Mary the couch of piety and the refuge of the wretched. She asked why he had treated her chancellor[9] like this, and told him to soften his sentence and cut back on its rigour. To these orders she joined threats that only a queen could make: he must know that if he did not obey he would die within thirty days, and realise that he should have believed the promptings of his own heart rather than the whispers of clerks. The last thing he wanted was to die, and he sent for the priest with a formal embassy from his own staff. He forthwith restored him to his rank, and enjoined on him a lifelong duty, never to sing any mass except that for St Mary. And to ensure that the priest forgave[10] the injuries that had been inflicted upon him, he clothed and fed him as long as he lived.

---

[8] One expects rather the sense 'in any case'.
[9] Cf. above, 11. 2.
[10] Cf. GP 82. 4.

30. Prayers of a friend[1]

1. This man got his reward for a good life through the Lady Mary; but another escaped eternal perdition by the same means. A scholar by profession, a priest by rank, he was nonetheless a sty for all foulness, a sewer for every manner of filth. He was the sort of man who could never bring himself to abstain from something illicit, despite his holy office. For instance, headlong as he was carried to every misdeed (for shame could not rein him in), he had the effrontery to violate a nun's virginity. A wretched sin indeed, deserving of a thunderbolt! But so limitless is God's mercy that it was not punished – at that point. He kept it hidden from everyone all his life; but when death drew near he tearfully confided it to a loyal friend, himself a priest; for he did not want to take the secret with him to hell. He had lived in this man's company since he was a boy; and their consequent closeness had made him trust him.[2] So he was the only person to whom he could pour out his secrets.

2. Bravo! The perfect man should always live as if he were at God's side, as if he were clearly visible to everybody. But this is given to few, if any; and as every man has things that habit has led him to keep secret, the wise man must have a friend with whom he can share what he has done in the past; one who will lend his help in planning and regulating his future actions; one from whom he can seek remedy in adversity, one with whom he can weigh up how to react to prosperity. He must admit him deep into his whole heart, call him the half of his soul,[3] and treat him as just that. I certainly know many a man who would prefer to go unshriven than to make confession to the sort of person who looks frowningly at him.

3. This would have happened to our hero too if he had had no intimate friend. How remarkable then that, though he always frankly shared all his other secrets with him, he was miserly when it came to divulging this one piece of information! It was, I believe, because his sacrilegious act was so heinous that he shrank from wounding his friend by mentioning it. Even when he did come round to the topic, he employed a good deal of circumlocution. He put it like this: 'You see, my friend, that I am departing this life; my body is breaking up, and abandoning a soul that has sinned. My limbs are failing me, my tongue stammers, my eyes grow dim, my breath is giving out by degrees. I am not casting my life away, or breaking it short: I am losing it to an overpowering disease. So I am being tortured, yes tortured, by being deprived of this pleasant light of day, and of you, my friend, in whom I used to take such pleasure. But in these wretched straits I am flattered and

---

[1] Poncelet 505, source unknown.
[2] Cf. GR 230. 3.
[3] Cf. Horace, *Carm.* 1. 3. 8 (of Virgil).

comforted by the hope I repose in you: for you are surviving me. I shall not wholly die,[4] not wholly depart into ashes, for the moment at least, while a part of me[5] continues to enjoy the upper air. 4. It is now I need friendship, now that I have to draw on reserves of unblemished loyalty. Already I seem to see the demons exacting penalties for my sins: blacker than soot they are, and as threatening in countenance as in voice. Already I experience the terror of eddies of sulphurous smoke, in which – or so I fear – the soul of your friend is destined to be whirled about. All other sinners, I confess it, will find justification in comparison with me, prostitutes from brothels and those who have plotted to violate the marriage-beds of other men. Compared with me, small has been the sin of a tomb-robber who in his arrogant cruelty has disturbed bodies that had long lain untroubled, and exposed them to the light of day. In God's eyes the madness of one who has been lavish with men's blood and lived a life of violent crime will count for less. He killed the body, I the soul. And the less the value the body has than the soul, so much greater the penalty I shall pay. 5. I violated the divine laws of chastity,[6] I broke into the heavenly temple, making of the members of Christ the members of a harlot.[7] My sweet friend and revered lord, you well understand what I wish, or rather do not wish,[8] to say – about a nun. If you have any pity, any memory of our old relationship, any bowels of the brotherly affection you promised me, help, come to my aid, lend assistance: use prayers, masses and fasts to ensure that your soul that is mine, my soul that is yours, does not linger in torment. You must do all you can, with generous alms and continual masses, to have it rescued from its tortures. As for it ever finding a place amid the joy <of heaven>, what hope can I have of that?'

6. As he said this, his voice was interrupted by sobs and drowned by grief. Not much later, he reached his end, leaving his friend a heavy task. He performed the funeral rites, and applied himself in a practical spirit to what was asked of him to free his friend's soul, feeling affection both for him and for Mary, and taking them pleasantly in turns, one day singing mass for her, the next for the repose of his soul. This he did for a whole year, letting no impediment or illness interrupt him. When the year had come circling round again,[9] he was standing at the holy altar on the anniversary of the burial when, in the very midst of the mystery of the mass,[10] he raised his eyes and saw the blessed Mother of the Lord standing on the altar, and heard her say: (7) 'I have come after long being wearied by your

---

[4] Cf. Horace, *Carm.* 3. 30. 6.

[5] I.e. the friend (*dimidium animae meae*).

[6] Cf. Juvencus, 1. 534 ('casti iura pudoris'), and Aldhelm, *Carm. de virg.* 368, 1472, 2124.

[7] Cf. I Cor. 6: 15.

[8] Cf. GR 380. 4.

[9] Cf. II Chron. 36: 10: 'cumque anni circulus uolueretur'.

[10] 'in secreto missae'. Here 'mystery', as against the probably more restricted meaning at 4. 3 above.

prayers, under the pressure of your pious importunity. I have done something great: I have won forgiveness for him from my son, even though he had snatched away from Him what is rightly judged more precious than the whole world. For virginity is of such weight in the eyes of God that it is worth more than anything on earth and outshines even the stars.[11] In fact', she said, 'in case you doubt my words, look, here is your friend by your side, now absolved, his knee bent in his longing for communion.'

He turned a kindly gaze on his friend, and at the Lady's orders let him participate in the holy mystery. She lowered[12] her hand in a gracious gesture, and was seen to lead from the church the man who had offended her, a slave no longer. The priest joyfully completed the mass, and spent the rest of his life in a manner pious and pleasing to God.

8. It should not shake the belief of the faithful to hear it said that a spirit took the last rites. That bread may be bodily, but the sacrament which we see in it with the eyes of faith is spiritual. It was to strengthen the faith and increase the joy of the priest that the dead man was seen to take communion. It was not that a spirit ate bread, rather that by the power and truth of that mystery it escaped from its punishment. Nor is it to be supposed that the body of the Lord, which a living man distributed and a dead man took, perished. Rather, it was at once received by an obedient angel and taken up into the secret recesses of godhead, of which we can have no knowledge.

---

[11] Cf. *GR* 163. 1: 'etiam ipsa prestringit sidera' (of a group of nuns).
[12] Presumably to take hold of the man's hand.

31. Two brothers at Rome[1]

1. Two items come up here that I am anxious to include. They deserve belief for their intrinsic importance, especially as they have been brought to our notice by ancient writings and as the cities in which they took place are the foremost in Christendom. The lofty status of the cities, then, argues for these stories being recorded, and the age of the documents excludes[2] all shadow of doubt.

2. The first story I am promising, which my informant[3] heard from the lips of the blessed archbishop Anselm, goes like this.[4]

Rome is a city whose martial endeavours once made it lord of the world.[5] Now it is famous for the trophies won by the apostles, and lays down the law to the entire Christian world. Here in the time of Pope Leo, fifth of that name,[6] lived two brothers, Peter and Stephen, men of distinguished ancestry whose own industry had taken them to great heights and whose probity brought lustre to their families. Peter became archdeacon of the apostolic see, reaching a rank only to be achieved in those days[7] by a man of acute intellect and proven godliness. Stephen held censorial power and was urban praetor.[8]

3. The archdeacon was a devotee of truth and chastity, who rigorously enforced canon law both on himself and on everyone else. But he was somewhat mean, and less affable to the poor than his person and wealth demanded: the Romans being born and bred to be very greedy indeed, as one may read in ancient histories and prove for oneself today.[9]

Stephen was a layman and a partisan, who took no notice of equity unless it had its cash value clearly displayed. He weighed justice by price alone, and brought a

[1] Poncelet 386 (1183). The sources are Alexander of Canterbury, *Dicta Anselmi*, c. 46 (*Memorials of St Anselm*, pp. 249–53), HM 10 (Dexter, pp. 24–6), which used Alexander but for the first time introduced the Virgin Mary, and one of the *Vitae S. Praeiecti*, probably the earliest version (*BHL* 6916) ed. *MGH Script. Rer. Meroving.* 5. 225–48.

[2] Lit. 'excuses', oddly. For *dubietatis nubilum* cf. Gregory the Great, *Moralia in Iob* 33. 35 (*CCSL* 143B, p. 1726).

[3] Presumably Alexander of Canterbury.

[4] William tells a similar story in *GR* 237, but without identifying the protagonists (see n. ad loc.).

[5] Cf. *GR* 351. 1.

[6] Not Leo V (?July–Sept. 903), but Leo IX (1048–54). The mistake probably arose through mistranscription of William's roman numerals.

[7] Note this hit at modern archdeacons (cf. above, p. 83 n. 6).

[8] Peter, more correctly deacon but also *bibliothecarius et cancellarius sanctae apostolicae sedis*, occ. 1046 (Bonizo, *Liber ad Amicum*; *MGH Libelli de Lite*, 1. 584–5), 7 Sept. 1050, and was succeeded later that year: *PL* 143. 653, 655, 665; R. L. Poole, *Lectures on the Papal Chancery up to the Time of Innocent III* (Cambridge, 1915), pp. 62–5; Stephen, *sacri palatii iudex Romanus* or *iudex Romanae sedis*, occ. 1053 and 1056: E. Steindorff, *Jahrbücher des deutschen Reichs unter Heinrich III* (2 vols, Leipzig, 1874, 1881), II, pp. 235 n., 350 n.; P. Jaffé, S. Loewenfeld *et al.*, *Regesta Pontificum Romanorum ... ad annum 1198* (2 vols, Leipzig, 1885–88), no. 4348.

[9] A subject William had adverted to from time to time: e.g. *GR* 351. 1, *GP* 23. 3, 42. 6β2, 74. 15, 101. 2, 173. 2.

malicious charge or repelled an injury according to the amount of gold on offer. His was a character diseased by corruption; his tongue was for sale in any quarter to which he was drawn by the prospect of coin. 4. As judge of so great city, he twisted right judgement into evil courses, unless there was someone to pay a high price to swell his cheeks.[10] So, wherever he had heard mountains of cash were stored away, he was already looking forward to gobbling it up, so greedy was he for gain beyond all satisfying.[11] What would a man not dare to do, considering that he cleaned the servants of the excellent martyr Laurence out of the profits of three houses whose rents went to pay the incomes of churchmen? What is more, he pilfered the funds of the glorious Agnes's servants by appropriating a single[12] garden. These victims thought that a man who was currently so powerful had better be soothed rather than provoked, so they did not open their mouths to complain. Instead, they prayed to their patrons to avenge them. Money taken from a poor man is a great loss to him, even though it may appear to have added little to the loot of a rich man.

5. This was the way the two brothers led their lives, Peter making small contributions to the needs of the poor, Stephen robbing them of all that he could grab. One erred through meanness, the other through rapacity. But the archdeacon's fault was more covert, and did not quite shipwreck his reputation. The praetor, however, set ablaze by the accursed torch of his cupidity, went on his wicked way quite openly. There was only one remedy for his villainy: he was devoted to Saint Praeiectus.[13]

6. This Praeiectus had been bishop of Clermont, the city in the Auvergne of which I spoke in the previous book.[14] He had aroused the ire of the great men of his province by his active religious zeal[15] and his biting sermons. Because he thought no sinner should be spared out of consideration for his wealth, they conceived a deep hatred for him, and when he left the city they went after him. A few days previously he had gone up to an estate beyond the city bounds, for the sake of his soul,[16] taking with him an abbot called Marinus.[17] He was enjoying a pious vacation there, away from the tumults of the city, when the magnates laid

---

[10] Cf. *GP* 74. 12: 'inflatis buccis' (of pupils spouting dialectic), again signifying tumid eloquence.

[11] Lit. 'in his greed for insatiable profit'. The reading is not certain. Cf. *GR* 347. 7: 'quod reliquum est spe deuorant'; 121. 4: 'magni exercitus ingluuiem exsaturare'; 202. 6: 'pro auiditatis ingluuie'.

[12] Contrasted with the three houses mentioned above (cf. HM 10: 'unum ortum').

[13] Praeiectus, bp. of Clermont 666–76; *BHL* 6915–17; *Oxford Dictionary of Saints*, p. 443. His feast was widely celebrated in medieval England (Carter, pp. 509–10).

[14] 6. 1.

[15] Cf. *GR* 34. 1 (of Cædwalla): 'cum iam dudum efficatioribus studiis bilem principum suae patriae irritasset.' Also *VW* 1. 2. 1: 'deuotione simplici et studio efficaci proposito [of turning to a religious life] exsecuti'.

[16] Cf. below 'sancto ... otio'.

[17] Called Amarinus in the *Vita* (*MGH Script. Rer. Meroving.* 5. 242–3).

siege to his house with hostile intent. Marinus grew pale when he heard the din of the enraged men outside, and was anxious to flee. But Praeiectus emboldened him. 7. It was, he said, base and pitiable for them to try to avoid something[18] that God had offered them without their asking, though no man would venture to promise it to them if they did ask. Death would mean immortality for them: they would be dying for the truth and in all innocence. With these few words,[19] there being no time or need for more, he so emboldened Marinus that he went to the door; he was instantly met by more than one blow, and was the first of the pair to claim a martyr's crown. The butchers thought of going away, imagining in the grim darkness of the night[20] that they had done their job and killed the bishop. But Praeiectus could not bear to be kept away from Christ a moment longer. In his urgent desire for heaven, he shouted from his study: 'I am the bishop. Come back if you want to and sate your anger with my blood.' They did not waste time in fulfilling his noble wish, so pitiless was their cruelty.

8. So this martyr is especially easy to win over and comes speedily to answer prayers. Stephen accordingly loved him dearly, and every year on his feast day fed a crowd of clerks and paupers in his house, showing himself a courteous and cheerful host. His brother died first, and Stephen soon followed him, his life over. His brother was despatched to the pains of purgatory. Stephen's spirit, released from the body, found an opponent in blessed Laurence, whom he had offended. When he saw him face to face, the saint took his arm in a tight grip[21] and damaged it beyond curing. The blessed Agnes, too, denied the wretched man the sweetness of her regard, and glared at him as he went off. 9. There followed a terrifying pronouncement from the high throne of God: 'Because this man, like the traitor Judas, sold the truth for money, it is only right that he be cast into the tortures that afflict the man he took as his model.' Quite right too! Indeed, if it is proper to say so, Judas was the lesser sinner, for he sold the Word of God in ignorance, whereas it was in full knowledge that Peter put up for sale the word of the truth.[22] Hearing the order, the holy martyrs who stood nearby put pressure on the good-natured St Praeiectus not to forget his poor[23] friend and allow him to be cast for ever[24] into hell. Praeiectus, inspired by the urgings of his fellow-saints, first reconciled those who looked askance on Stephen's soul, Laurence and Agnes, so that he could more easily win forgiveness once they had been soothed.

---

[18] I.e. eternal life through martyrdom.

[19] Cf. e.g. Virgil, *Aen.* 7. 599; also above, 27. 7: 'nec plura locuta'.

[20] See above, 1. 3 and n.

[21] An odd use of *compaginare* (normally 'join together'). Contrast HM 10: 'brachium eius artius strinxit' (later 'constrinxerat').

[22] Matt. 27: 3–10.

[23] *pauperis* perhaps means just *miseri*.

[24] For 'perpetuae ... Gehennae' cf. 39. 3: 'gehennalis ignis, et perpetuus et importabilis'.

10. When they had received his prayers with a swift access of favour, Praeiectus knelt before the blessed Lady Mother, and asked her Majesty to deign to obtain from her Son the grant of salvation to Stephen. She, urged on by her pity to speed her business, went to her son, accompanied by the saint. Her prayers met with success, and He ordered the soul to be brought back <to life>, so that Stephen could die only after he had done thirty days' penance on earth. His soul had already been plunged in a whirlpool of burning pitch, and nails had been driven into him from all angles: if he thought of turning in any direction, he would run into danger just when he rejoiced to have got away.[25] 11. But when the command thundered forth from on high, his soul was led out, and saw his brother afar off, breathing out the fires of purgatory.[26] Going nearer, he asked what this prodigious sight might mean, that one reckoned so holy should be in such a plight. 'Only,' Peter answered, 'because of the meanness I revelled in, unbeknown to you, as I brooded like a miser over the wealth I had amassed in my greed.' Asked if he had any hope of release <from punishment>, Peter replied that his escape was imminent, if the Lord Pope would deign, together with his cardinals, to sing masses for him.

So Lady Mary ordered Stephen, on his return, to sing the psalm 'Blessed are the undefiled'[27] every day until his death. Quite soon, he reappeared on earth, and gave the pope, and all who cared to listen, the benefit of his true story. They could hardly venture to disbelieve it, considering that the bruising on his arms backed it up.

12. It may seem passing strange, and to some perhaps incredible, that a spirit's maltreatment should be transferred to the body for the purposes of guaranteeing that he spoke the truth about something for which he had so obvious a mark to show. But I can tell you that there is no room for doubt: I am prompted by a loftier precedent, for St Jerome says in his book to Eustochium *On Preserving Virginity* that he was once rapt in a trance and was ordered a beating for persisting in reading the philosophers to the neglect of holy writ; when he came round, he for a long time carried about livid stripes on his shoulder blades.[28]

So after thirty days Stephen, his penance done on the pope's instructions, died a second time. No room now for fear; hope of good ruled that out.

---

[25] Cf. *Comm. Lam.* I, 980–2.
[26] Cf. Virgil, *Aen.* 7. 785–6.
[27] Ps. 118.
[28] Jerome, *Epist.* 22. 30 (*CSEL* 54, pp. 189–91); also alluded to in VW 1. 8. 5, in *Polyhist.*, p. 87, and in a note by William to his collection of Cicero's works (Cambridge Univ. Libr., MS Dd. 13. 2, f. 111v): Thomson, *William of Malmesbury*, p. 52.

32. Jew lends to Christian[1]

1. But as I have briefly dealt with the miracle that took place in the first of all cities anywhere on earth, I shall now proceed to tell of the one witnessed by Constantinople, which for Christians is second in prestige only to Rome.

2. Of this city Theodorus was a citizen, a layman of praiseworthy modesty, though he made his living by a means that especially seduces men into sullying the truth. He was in fact a trader: you can see almost no one in this line who is afraid to expose his sworn word to perjury if he can turn a penny or two. What is more, when open cheating does not serve, they take advantage of the unwary by craft. Theodorus was not like that at all. He knew nothing whatever about cunning, for he chose to know nothing; and he regarded lying as morally wrong. He did not try to beat down a price or wipe out a buyer's profit. If he gave, he did so gladly and liberally, from a full hand. If he made a promise, he fulfilled it duly and swiftly: to a tender conscience it is a kind of lie to be tardy in doing what one has promised.

3. So, as the children of this world are wiser in their generation than the children of light,[2] his neighbours, noticing that he was straight rather than duplicitous, brought many a trick to bear on this innocent. He was aware of their wiles, but just laughed at them. Finally, it being his fate to be put to the test so that his long-suffering might be of benefit to posterity, he grew so poor that he went short even of his daily bread. But that did not weaken his resolve; out of love for God he went on patiently putting up with chance (or was it divine judgement?), always setting his hopes on heaven. But he didn't think that only prayer was called for – God wants us to supplement His grace by our efforts.[3] So he talked it over with his wife, and began to look for a way out of his troubles.

4. After much pondering they decided to test out the friendship of a certain Jew of the same city by trying to borrow money from him, for he had loved them in the past. Other friends, especially Christian ones, had swung with fortune and refused to recognise them in their need; it had been their former riches, not their friendship, they had cultivated.[4] The Jew was called Abraham. To him came Theodorus, making his woes known: he had no choice. Necessity lent him eloquence, and he shed abundant tears to accompany it. The Jew was moved

---

[1] Poncelet 1748; Ihnat, *Mary and the Jews*, pp. 167–70. This is an amalgam of different stories based on the Antiphonetes legend, for which see B. N. Nelson and J. Starr, 'The Divine Surety and the Jewish Moneylender', *Annuaire de l'Institut de Philologie et d'Histoire Orientales et Sclaves* 7 (1939–44), 289–338 (western versions pp. 313–22, 326–38). It is not in Dominic or HM-TS.

[2] Luc. 16: 8.

[3] I.e. 'God helps those who help themselves', an ancient proverb: F. R. Adrados, *A History of the Graeco-Latin Fable* (English version 3 vols, Leiden, 2003), III, p. 43. Cf. 43. 3 and n.

[4] Cf. below, §15; *Comm. Lam.* I, 150–1, 1193–4.

at the plight of a friend so cruelly impoverished, and went so far as to weep himself. But he would not lend money to a man of a different persuasion on no security. 5. The other gave him his word, and offered to mortgage his house, in the attempt to soften Abraham's hard heart, but all in vain. In the end, having no other recourse, Theodorus recollected St Mary, and murmured her name under his breath.[5] Without much confidence he burst out: 'I will give you St Mary as my guarantor, mother of my Lord Jesus Christ, to be our go-between[6] and stand pledge for your gold. If I break my oath by her, I shall stake my own life, in the presence of witnesses.'

6. The Jew was happy to accept this arrangement; I believe his heart was softened by God. 'What you say', he said, 'is wildly against my principles; but because, my friend, I see you are at your wits' end, I shall not refuse this lady as your guarantor.' So they went along to Hagia Sophia. The church of this name, built by the emperor Justinian in honour of the Wisdom of God, surpasses any building on earth in its wonderfully grand architecture.[7] Here is kept an image of the holy Mother of God, not sculpted, as is our custom, but painted on wood.[8]

7. 'This Lady,' said Theodorus, 'whose image this is, I give you, Abraham my friend, as guarantor that I will repay your money on the due day, with no delay or cheating. As I said before, you need have no fear I want to deceive you; I should rather die keeping my word than be branded as a perjurer. But please let there be one clause of exception: "unless I either die or am held up by obstacles that I cannot surmount." But to be sure I shall not look around for excuses. If the day goes by out of necessity, it is a matter for indulgence; if any fraud is put in hand, it is sacrilege.'

8. The Jew gave his assent to this solemn compact, and, satisfied with the pledge, paid over to the Christian all the money he asked. Theodorus, putting his hope in St Mary, committed himself to the mercy of the unquiet sea just as if it were completely calm, and sailed away to Alexandria with the fair fortune his faith deserved. There he remained quietly for a year; and it was remarkable how quickly he rebuilt his lost fortunes. He congratulated himself with secret joy:

---

[5] Cf. Persius 2. 9: 'sub lingua murmurat'.

[6] *mediatrix* was often used of the Virgin Mary in her role as intercessor, e.g. Alexander of Canterbury, *Miracula*, 52 (*Memorials of St Anselm*, p. 267); other examples are given in ODML s. v. 4b. See M. V. Gripkey, *The Blessed Virgin Mary as Mediatrix in the Latin and Old French Legend prior to the Fourteenth Century* (Washington DC, 1938).

[7] Not that William had seen it; cf. GR 356. 1. His wording echoes Paul the Deacon, *De gestis Langobard.* 1. 25 (PL 95. 468A).

[8] Cf. 49. 2: 'in ligno sculpta' (see n. ad loc.). There were only two icons of Mary in S. Sophia, which never became a major Marian shrine: R. Cormack, 'The Mother of God in the mosaics of Hagia Sophia at Constantinople', in *Mother of God. Representations of the Virgin in Byzantine Art*, ed. M. Vassiliki (Milan and Athens, 2000), pp. 107–23, at 107–8.

everything was going his way! To make it the more extraordinary, he plotted no evil, as traders normally do, but conducted all his business on the level.

9. Gradually the day for repayment approached. In the generosity of his heart he even blamed the year for passing so slowly. Remembering how speedily his friend had shown his good will, he got the boat ready to sail, so that he could pay up early and thus win the more favour with the Jew. But he, back in Constantinople, despaired of the debtor's return, and let his resentment boil over into insulting complaints[9] to Theodorus's wife. Creditors are so ill-disposed to poor friends that he did not imagine that Theodorus was unable to put to sea – supposing he did not wish to come to land by shipwreck.[10] For all this time a violent storm was clouding the sky and disturbing the sea;[11] indeed the world seemed to have it in mind to return to the primeval chaos.[12] Theodorus, at Alexandria, could see all this. But it made him anxious, and fearful for the credit of our faith: Abraham, in his rage, might not merely feel that the bonds of their relationship had been violated, but even weaken the belief of Christians by his abuse.

10. So he made a box out of withies, bound up with iron plates and pitch, and placed in it the amount of gold he had received from the Jew, not leaving him short of bezants but adding more for good measure.[13] And he also wrote a message, sealed with his personal ring: 'Here, friend Abraham, is the money you lent me.' Then, on the night before the set day he entrusted it to the sea, after many a request to St Mary not to let the fierce waves batter the innocent box(?) and break it open, but in person to guide it ashore at Constantinople.

11. She listened to his prayers, and bore the container, with its contents, all that way from Alexandria to harbour in Constantinople in a single night. The Jew had got up earlier than usual, and was strolling on the strand hoping to catch sight of the ship afar off, coming with its freight of joy to satisfy his greedy desires. And behold! he saw waves and sand heaping themselves up and as it were toying with a little vessel, moving it gently hither and thither.[14] Wondering what it might be, he came nearer and read the inscription. Snatching it up greedily, he ran off home, and hid it beneath all his treasures in his private safe, not letting even his wife into the secret.[15]

---

[9] An odd phrase (lit. 'with puffing bubbles of insults').

[10] For the idea, cf. Hyginus, *Fabulae* 190. 2: 'naufragio in terram Cariam uenit.'

[11] Cf. Virgil, *Aen.* 1. 280 (of Juno): 'mare nunc terrasque metu caelumque fatigat'.

[12] Cf. e.g. Lucan 1. 74.

[13] Bezants are also mentioned at GR 354. 1.

[14] Cf. GR 170. 3: 'stagnum *placidum* aquis crispantibus, ubi dulcibus illisa lapsibus *alludebat unda littoribus*'; GP 50. 1: 'ita in omnibus usus est *placido allusu* fortunae ut uideretur cum eo Deus benefitiis certare ...'; HN 76: 'sicut aspectus maris solet esse gratissimus, cum *placidis* allisa lapsibus *alludit unda littoribus*'.

[15] For this part of the story cf. 38. 4.

12. Soon after, when Theodorus had returned, he took an opportunity to dun him for what he was owed, not acknowledging the perfectly clear miracle that God had sent him. Theodorus was patient with the Jew's importunity. 'If,' he said, 'you do not have the money, which I sent you as God is my witness, swear to that effect before my guarantor. If I see you go unscathed after that oath, I shall know you are guiltless of sacrilege, and shall make no bones about giving you a second time what I have given you already.' The matter was referred to arbitration, and the judges pronounced that his proposal was only fair. The Jew thought it a trivial matter: it would, he imagined, bring him no harm if he stained our rites by perjury. And he at once forswore himself in front of the image, asserting that the money had not been returned.

13. But God, who once made an ass speak when Balaam was riding it,[16] now gave speech to an image. A pretty wonder, that an inanimate object should utter words like a human – and show up an unbeliever! 'You say what is untrue,' it said. 'You have a chest you found on the beach and hid under your shekels without even your wife knowing.' You cannot imagine what a happy outcry there was from bystanders applauding the miracle. Even Abraham could not help bursting into delighted guffaws. He blushed for joy, and went so far as to boast of having been caught out. It helped him not a little to come to believe: a compelling argument to accept faith in the Lord Christ. It crowned the happy outcome that all that money was distributed by him for the benefit of the poor.

14. From that day on in Constantinople the wild fanaticism of the Jews grew cold, though previously it had been rampant against us. Mary was to hand, mercifully angry with pretence, showing up faithlessness, and ensuring that by the judgement of the townspeople traitors were stripped of their properties if they did not think they should avoid sacrilege.[17] Yes, she is so unwearying in distributing her mercies that those who are unwilling to be won by benefits are brought over by blows. Some she raises up by honours in the present, others she brings low, according as she sees it to be expedient; for she is aware of all future events in advance. Injuries inflicted upon her faithful she avenges with high spirit; yet soon she mercifully shows pity even to the injurers, if she sees they are penitent.

15. She does not despise men of low rank or condition, so long as she sees that their minds are warm in venerating her. In this way she shows how far from right is the arrogance of rich men who do not receive services from the poor gratefully but extort them without a word of thanks. For in the eyes of mortals only wealth

---

[16] Num. 22: 28–30.

[17] It is unclear whether William is still referring to the Jews; he does seem to have specific events in mind.

recommends a man; anyone who lacks it is dirt. Religious fervour is measured by the standard of treasure, riches are thought to tip the balance in oratory: rare (or rather non-existent) is eloquence that is clothed in rags.[18] Once a man thrived on knowing something; now the real mark of the uncouth is to possess nothing. For instance, only money is nowadays thought to relieve human cares and soothe men's minds with an appearance of tranquillity. An ugly and false state of affairs! The superior mind should not be judged according to the whim of fortune: even a great man does not seem cheaper in his people's eyes if he has found himself lodging in some beggar's hovel.[19]

16. But this can wait for another time. Now I shall take up my thread, by subjoining examples of all that I have said above.[20] First, then, to the miracle concerning a Jewish man I shall link one concerning a boy of the same sect, as a convincing proof of how assiduously Mary works to convert the race she belonged to.

[18] Cf. Juvenal 7. 145.
[19] Fortune is irrelevant to prestige; a great man will not lose face if he finds himself spending a night in a hut.
[20] See above, p. xxxix, n. 68.

33. Jewish boy[1]

1. Pisa, of which I spoke earlier,[2] is the only city that maintains to this day the antique Roman custom of having annual magistracies;[3] it is undefeated in battle abroad, restrained and well-ordered at home. It was here that the event I shall now relate took place; an informant[4] whose trustworthiness is beyond question vouches for its truth.

2. A little Jewish boy had some Christian playmates. He had gone into church with them on Easter Day, and when the others went up to the altar for communion he had gone too. The priest, who lacked second sight, gave him the Eucharist without hesitation. The boy shot outside with his troop of friends, and they went on with their games till mealtime. Then he felt hungry, and ran off home, where he found both his parents at table. When they asked him playfully where he had been, he didn't think there was anything to hide, such was his childish innocence; indeed what could a child of that age imagine he had done wrong? So he said he had been in church, and taken unleavened bread from the hand of someone in religious garb, and eaten it.

3. The father, a rampant unbeliever like all Jews, flew into a rage, grabbed his son, and threw him in to the oven that was being heated up to roast grain. But the Jewess, moved by maternal affection, began to cry: 'Woe is me!' The woman's laments brought in the neighbours, and the house filled up with Christians hurrying from every direction. The father was told how hard-hearted he was, and he was driven out with the abuse he deserved. The boy was rescued from the oven safe and sound, though a pile of wood was feeding the flames and encouraging

---

[1] Poncelet 95 (833). The story appears in very many versions, described by E. Wolter, *Der Judenknabe* (Halle, 1879), Carter, pp. 520–9, Ihnat, *Mary and the Jews*, pp. 160–2, 182–3. William's is based upon his earlier account in *GR* 286. 2. It is also in HM (unnumbered; Dexter, pp. 32–3), and Dominic 1 (ed. Canal, pp. 15–17), which is probably dependent upon it. The *GR* account, however, is closest to the one offered by Honorius Augustodunensis in his *Speculum Ecclesiae* (*PL* 172. 852). Carter thought this work too late to have been known to William, but since his time Honorius' career and writings have been redated, and it is thought that the *Speculum* was composed for the community of Christ Church, Canterbury, c.1110–20, or even 1103–08: R. W. Southern, *St Anselm and his Biographer* (Cambridge, 1962), p. 212; M.-O. Garrigues, 'L'oeuvre d'Honorius Augustodunensis: Inventaire critique', *Abhandlungen der Braunschweigischen Wissenschaftlichen Gesellschaft* 38 (1986), 108; V. I. J. Flint, *Honorius Augustodunensis of Regensburg* (Aldershot, 1995), pp. 104, 136–8. The location of the miracle in Pisa (rather than Bourges) is unique to William, and is inexplicable. Shaw, 'The Dating', pp. 393–8, suggests that William made use of a sermon by Herbert, bishop of Norwich (d.1119): ed. E. M. Goulburn and H. Symonds, *The Letters and Sermons of Herbertus Losinga* (2 vols, Oxford and London, 1878), II, pp. 30–1. But his argument, based upon small differences in wording between the various texts available to William, though attractive is hardly conclusive.
[2] 27. 1.
[3] Pisa's government first took the form of a consulate c.1085, the earliest of any Italian city. William was wrong, however, to say 'alone today', for Milan was a commune governed by consuls by 1097, Genoa the same from 1099.
[4] Doubtless Honorius (see n. 1).

the blaze. The fire in the oven had retreated before the queen of heaven, present in person there, and forgot its nature out of reverence for her. The Christian folk rejoiced at the miracle. Over and over again they kissed the child who had been through this ordeal,[5] asking him how he had escaped the fire. He, still the innocent, said: 'The lovely lady I saw sitting on a throne, whose son was divided among the people, came to me as I was roasting in the oven. It was she who used her robe to disperse the eddies of flame and smoke, and presented me to you unharmed, as you see.'

4. So they realised that it was St Mary who, by calling the boy to grace, had allowed the eyes of the body to see what is <normally> only imparted to us covertly; first she revealed the mysteries to open view, then she drove off the hostile flames.

---

[5] A remarkable use of *martirium*.

34. Bread offered to the Christ-child[1]

1. Bordering on this, and very like it, is something I have recently read about.[2] A boy of good birth was running through the church in the same city[3] when his career took him to behind the altar. He saw there an image of our Lord,[4] temporarily lying on the ground, awaiting a higher and more distinguished station. Thinking it was a boy of his own age, he offered it a bit of bread he had been given by his nurse to stop him crying, and in a child's wheedling voice invited it to eat with him. When the wooden object made no reply, the boy, upset and in tears, invited it a second and third time to eat. 2. Before long, God's mercy vouchsafing a remarkable miracle (for He did not spurn a child's kindly act), the image replied: 'I shall not eat with you now, but in three days' time *you* will eat with *me*.' A sacristan who was busy in front of the altar seeing to the cloths heard the words, and ran up. The boy, asked who had answered him when no one was around, pointed to the image. 'This friend of mine,' he said.

The wise man found it easy enough to understand the bearing of what the image had said and what it portended: after three days the innocent who had been so generous with earthly food would be refreshed with a heavenly feast. The boy's parents were told what had happened, and it made them the more open to the good when they saw the actual outcome supporting the truth of the words: for the boy died two days later.

---

[1] Poncelet 219 (1253). This story exists in 'a bewildering number of variants' (Carter, p. 532), dating from the late eleventh century on. William's source seems to have been the common text *Spiris locus est famosus* (Poncelet 10 [1671]; ed. F. Fita, 'Cincuenta leyendas por Gil de Zamora', *Boletin de la Real Academia de la Historia* 7 (1885), 129–30. William or his immediate source has transmuted Speyer into Pisa (perhaps the result of mere textual corruption; so Carter, p. 532 and n. 6).

[2] Or: 'I have read to have happened recently.'

[3] C makes this Constantinople!

[4] But for the story to have any relevance the statue must be of Mary and Child.

35. Dying rich man[1]

1. Nor should what I shall go on to relate be thought of no consequence, especially as it is taken from writings of our forebears, writings too of high trustworthiness and authority.

2. A man of great wealth, which is more or less always accompanied by the excess that leads to unrestrained vice, was dying. He shed floods of tears as he urged the relatives who stood by his bed to try to safeguard his soul, listing all his dire faults. They ought to have cheered his mind with soft replies and encouraged him to hope he would be found deserving of mercy. Instead, as though furies had sworn a pact together, they said they were horrified at the enormity of his misdeeds. They were men who thought only of worldly matters, and did not know how powerful penitence can be.

3. But the sick man pulled himself together, and recognising the wiles of the Enemy, who was trying through the mouths of his attendants to snare him in the poisonous coils of despair, he exclaimed with all the breath that remained to him: 'All of you only add to my burdens by your consolations. *I* know how compassionate is the Lord to whom I am hastening.' His words were taken up by a voice from on high: 'You called me compassionate, and compassionate you will find me.' That the voice came from God the common people who had assembled were convinced by the swift departure of the sick man and a scent of nard.

---

[1] Poncelet 1779, source unknown. Its presence is puzzling, as it has nothing to do with Mary.

36. Charitable almsman[1]

1. Also: A needy man who had to beg his daily bread spent only so much as he had to out of the alms he was given; from the rest, indeed almost the whole, he gave generously to other poor men.[2] His cheap and tiny gifts were adorned and augmented by his good nature and by his cheerful expression when he announced that he was giving out of love for St Mary.

2. When disease was fast bringing him to his death, he began to call on the name of the Mother of Mercy, asking her with many a groan to remember the poor man who loved her, and to support him in his last need. His repeated prayers called forth her mercy, and the voice of our Lady was heard from the air: 'Come, my beloved, and rest with me and my Son in eternal joy.' So he surrendered his blessed life with two benefits to rejoice in: that he was escaping the burden of poverty, and that he knew he was being rewarded with the grant of eternal life by her who loved him.

[1] Poncelet 311 (393). Taken from HM 5 (Dexter, pp. 19–20).
[2] Cf. 29. 1.

37. Ebbo the thief[1]

1. Especially among laymen the story of Ebbo the thief is told and retold with zest. No man was ever bolder in breaking into rich men's stables or burgling their houses. If his eye was caught by a steed of unusual speed or size, he rustled it by night. If some gold-embroidered garment or purple cloth[2] took his fancy, he stole it without anyone noticing. If anything valuable was rumoured to be hidden in a chamber, he crept right into the room however many bolts protected it, slithering like a slippery snake through the tiniest crevices. Not only strangers were the victims of his obsession: he was unfeeling enough to take plunder even from relatives: his nearest and dearest were scarcely immune[3] from his wicked hunger for possession. To crown his constancy of mind went physical strength and violence: no one, unless the most choice, tried to attack Ebbo, even with companions, let alone by himself. If he *was* attacked, he would often[4] make good his escape, rushing through the hail of weapons like a lion and bursting through all obstacles as though they were no more than threads of flax.[5]

2. Despite all this, he deeply loved our Lady Mary, so far as that kind of man could. He commended himself to her in every situation, and sometimes wept at the thought of her, even though he did not abstain from sacrilege and was driven on by an innate love of sweet greed. Even when he had determined on a robbery, he would call upon her name, begging not to be caught. Similarly, when he had pounced upon the prey he sought and had satisfied his greed, he would make over a tenth of what he had stolen to be used by her servants, especially in a house where he heard that religion was flourishing.

3. By now his hair was growing white, and old age threatened; yet he did not falter in his bold career. But the Lady in her mercy had the foresight to take thought for him who loved her even though he knew not how to take thought for himself. She allowed the man to be captured when he was embarking on a night exploit without taking proper precautions or looking out for ambushes with enough wariness. Sentence on the captor was delayed for more careful investigation. In the morning, judges took their seats and the charge was brought forward; witnesses against Ebbo were produced to state what they had seen. His defence was disgraceful enough, and he was sentenced to the gibbet. For the moment the Lady pretended not to notice and delayed helping him, so that the

---

[1] Poncelet 163. Taken from HM 6 (Dexter, pp. 20–1), with much imaginative expansion.
[2] Cf. Sidonius, *Epist*. 1. 2. 6: 'conchyliata … supellex'. 'Hanging' is O. M. Dalton's translation of Sidonius; in fact, *supellex* could cover any kind of household furniture, including cloth.
[3] Cf. *Comm. Lam.* II, 1422, with p. 333.
[4] 'Always' Carter, not without reason.
[5] Cf. *VW* 2. 5. 1, in this case of a madman.

severity of the peril might be matched by the joy of the remedy she brought. But when he was strung up, and the executioners' hand tried to tighten the unlucky knot that breaks the neck of the condemned, Mary slipped *her* hand to lucky effect between halter and throat, though only Ebbo saw her, and clearly too. They went back home, but Mary did not disdain to show him the same kindness all that day and the next one, and did not allow him to suffer or to die as he hung there.

4. But on the third day his tormentors came back. Finding him still alive, they flew into a passion and tried to slit his throat. But steel could do nothing: the sword blades sprang back, the spear points were blunted. Then he, speaking with no impediment, said: 'You are wasting your time; you will not be able to do me harm. Don't you see St Mary standing here and helping me?' At these words, the executioners grew pale; they slackened the noose and lowered Ebbo to the ground. They cross-questioned him, and he was not afraid to tell the truth, pointing to the Lady standing there. Their eyes were blinded by the mass of their sins, and they could see nothing; but because the futility of their weapons had shown the truth of his words, they let him go unharmed, out of reverence for the Mother of God. For the moment, he went straight home. But as time passed, when his full health and strength came back, he became a monk, a robber turned religious, and slimmed down his excessive bulk by fasts and vigils.

5. This is typical of the Lady's cunning,[6] to spur on those weighed down by much sin to a better course and lead them through to win the prize. Nature helps too by the way she forms character: we often see it come about that the reward is more lazily sought by those who have little on their consciences. Rather, those who are not troubled by serious sins are happy to grow feeble through inactivity, and nod off amid their virtues. If they do some good act, it is not the result of mental energy but of their customary somnolence. On the other hand, when a man has turned away from great evils, fear often calls him back from sinning, and the grief caused him by his past actions sharpens and shapes him to aim for what is good, so that from his habit of boldness he is the more daring to carry through what he embarks on – and the more cautious because he remembers what has befallen him in the past.

---

[6] *artifitium*; cf. *Comm. Lam.* I, 816 (God's), 2704 (Christ's).

38. Rustic church enlarged[1]

1. Here is another story I think it wrong to omit; it is often told, but I have only recently heard it myself. In the lands of St Edmund was a country church, small and ancient.[2] Past this there chanced to travel a rustic on horseback, journeying by night. He was a man too straightforward to make anything up, and incapable of telling a lie. Something had irked him, and he had gone out to let his chagrin simmer down and his irritation lose itself on the wind. Stopping for a little to pray to God, he was astonished to hear a mysterious murmur inside the church. Though he listened carefully, he could make out nothing for sure: the words could be heard but not distinguished. 2. At this point a girl of startling beauty suddenly came out. Her face and clothing were so bright that they sent the thick darkness of the night into retreat. She came up to the man, and said: 'Go to the lady.' 'What lady?', he said. '*My* lady,' she answered, 'and your Lady and the Lady of all men.' He made the excuse that he could not leave his horse. It was a proud, wild and unpredictable beast, only recently separated from the other horses and broken in. It was still reluctant to obey even his orders, and so he was afraid to let it go and risk losing a mount he was used to. But the girl replied: '*I* will hold it.'

3. So he went inside, and saw a group of girls sitting around in due order. On a raised seat by the altar, marked out by the brilliance of her jewellery, sat the Lady, loftier in majesty, more joyful in countenance, more dignified in gesture then the rest. Calling for silence with a nod and a movement of her gracious hand, she ordered the rustic to be brought in. As he stood there, she deigned to treat him as a man of proved experience, and honoured him by entrusting him with a mission. 'Go,' she said, 'to the priest, and tell him from me that he must build this church on a bigger scale. I am Mary, Mother of the Lord.' 4. With these words, she went outside and measured out with her staff the circuit she desired. And to make sure the workman should not be in any doubt, she put in their due place stones to mark the boundary of the building, while repeating her command. He was bashful enough, and said he was a worthless fellow, who would inspire a contempt that would prevent listeners believing him. But she said: 'Tell him a sign: the day before yesterday he put three shillings in a secret box, tied up in a cloth, and placed the box itself in a corner of a bigger chest. He did this without

---

[1] Poncelet 736, source unknown. Perhaps information found by William when visiting Bury, as he is known to have done: Thomson, *William of Malmesbury*, p. 73.
[2] The church cannot be identified, and there is no reason to suppose that it was in Bury itself (*pace* Carter, pp. 544–5).

telling his wife and all the household. If he does what I command, let him know that he will become rich; if he curls his lip and laughs my words to scorn,[3] he will be punished straightaway, and suffer agonies till he repents.'

5. The countryman, charged with this message, went back to the girl, who had been faithfully guarding his horse. She gave the beast back to him safe and sound, and, when he asked who she was, said she was called Margaret, not the least of the blessed Mary's attendants. As they spoke, it began to get light: dawn was thinking of breaking. He went to the priest, and carried out his mission as a freeman would, with a frank countenance. The priest was a little at a loss, thinking the messenger too fickle for such an important role. But the other mentioned the sign, and the threats too. The priest was so struck by this marvel that he soon came round to acquiescing: indeed he could make no objection. But he referred the matter to the woman he took his pleasure with. 6. She, as the sharer of his bed,[4] often gave even a priest the rough side of her tongue. She flew off the handle on this occasion too, and began to shout. This is an affliction common to women of this type: they are all too ready to turn to abuse. 'I will not allow my little substance to be wasted like this. That man has always been a chatterbox, and could easily have learned what you thought to be a secret from someone in the household gossiping.' She was still going on about it when she slipped and fell, breaking her leg; so she found to her cost that the man had spoken the truth and that what the Lady had threatened was all too serious. The priest, however, seeing his housekeeper was having a bad time of it, vowed that he would do all he had been told if she recovered. So he put into a drink of water a little dust from the soil under the stones laid out by the Lady, and also attached to the patient's breast a poultice made from the same earth. She got better directly.

7. This went the rounds, carried by favouring rumour,[5] and evoked pious emulation, as neighbours brought along more than could be believed possible to help pay for the work. The church was extended as Mary had ordered; what was needed was spent on the building work, and the balance went to pay the running costs of the enlarged church. And the miracle also causes happy laughter, when people see a man, once of no importance, now become a master mason.

[3] Cf. Persius 3. 85: 'ingeminat tremulos naso crispante cachinnos'.
[4] Who was this woman? We presume (a) that she was the priest's housekeeper, who also slept with him when the opportunity presented itself; (b) that she knew about the money because the priest kept it to spend on her – hence a secret from his wife; (c) that she assumed that the news brought by the rustic implied that it would be spent on enlarging the church.
[5] Cf. e.g. Virgil, *Aen.* 8. 90 (where it is taken to mean 'with approving cries').

39. The three knights[1]

1. But because many proofs of <Mary's> pity have been brought forward, I shall now introduce a single instance of her severity, which will come in as it were by stealth, when different business is to hand.[2]

A knight had by his obstinate pursuits[3] earned the anger of three neighbours, who plotted against him with hate in their hearts. One day they suddenly attacked him, put him to flight, and followed hard on his heels. Fear spurred his feet to put on a spurt, and though death was near he tried to delay it as best he could. As he ran, a church of St Mary happened to offer him an open door. So he went inside, no longer afraid, and feeling sure of finding refuge. At the altar he flung himself down full-length on the floor: what else could he do?

2. In the heat of their rage, his pursuers were blind to reason, and they competed to slaughter him as he lay there. While he was gasping out his last difficult breath, he murmured a prayer for revenge to the Lady whose aid he had sought. His enemies had in their insolence broken all law, all justice, all reverence indeed in the sight of God and man. But they were to suffer for it. As well as the pangs of a bad conscience that harry all who feel guilt, 'sacred fire' forthwith attacked the criminals' bodies;[4] their wretched limbs were consumed by a hungry blaze, and as they slowly but surely wasted away they seemed to see the underworld already before them.[5] The punishment recalled the brute beasts to the good, bringing them back into line, and the enormity of their suffering they made into material for amendment.[6]

3. So it was that the penalty for their crime was required of them; they were prompted by this temporal fire to try to flee from the other fire that would burn them up for ever. Suffering in this life is either light and can be borne, or grievous, in which case the soul is quickly torn away, and relief is brought by a swift death.[7] But hell fire is both everlasting and unbearable. It tortures for ever without ever consuming. It burns so continuously that it offers no hope of an end. It goes on tormenting souls damned beyond reach of hope, and its very eternity rules out the succour that an end would bring.

4. So one must labour unremittingly to escape hell fire: a modest and good mind can succeed in this if torments like these are patiently borne. The men I am

[1] Poncelet 289 (1074). Probably from TS 12 (Dexter, pp. 33–4), with some embroidery and the details of the knights' penance curtailed.
[2] Cf. below, §5.
[3] Not a very clear motivation. William draws on Sulpicius Severus, *Dial.* 3. 11. 8: 'pertinacioribus studiis (quae non est temporis explicare) iram uictoris emeriti'.
[4] Ergotism or St Elmo's Fire: G. Barger, *Ergot and Ergotism* (London, 1931).
[5] Cf. *Comm. Lam.* I, 301–4.
[6] Cf. ibid. I, 202–3: 'transeat … in materiam laudis comminatio potestatis', with parallels (including 17. 4 above) listed in the Appendix, p. 331.
[7] Cf. Cicero, *De fin.* 1. 49 (also 2. 22 and 95), with Reid's note ad loc.

talking about achieved this by daily struggles(?),[8] and, their minds now steeled by evil,[9] they prayed to St Mary with daily groans. The enormity of their crime had denied them hope of a cure in the flesh, and they strove only for the salvation of their souls, with no thought for the recovery of their bodies. Yet <Mary> looked on them from heaven propitiously, looked on in clemency and serenity, and gave the wretches more than they dared hope. Their old vigour poured back into them,[10] the harmful fire was extinguished; everything was quiet now, everything healthy. What is more, there could be no doubt that they had saved their souls too, seeing that they had gone through such dire hardships so manfully.

5. As I said,[11] I have brought in this story as it were covertly, because it seems to be very alien to her nature that she should ever in her anger go beyond the bounds of clemency. But if you scrutinise what she did in this case, you will realise that it in fact accords with pity rather than rigour on her part, for she gave an appropriate warning to them that they had sinned beyond measure, and out of pity forgave them when they were penitent. Scarcely ever, scarcely ever, can she be brought to allow her remarkable gentleness of character to lapse into anger; she always feels pity, she is always inclined to mercy, firm and mild in her unmoving tranquillity, like the stars that roll on unshaken in their courses.[12]

---

[8] The text is uncertain; one expects some kind of penance.
[9] Lucan 5. 798; i.e. their hearts became hard enough to endure the required suffering.
[10] Cf. VW 1. 15. 4 (as emended), GP 109. 6.
[11] Above, §1.
[12] Lucan 2. 268, also cited in Comm. Lam. I, 1768–9.

40. St Mary of Egypt[1]

1. I have to my mind written enough of miracles performed on the superior sex; now I must speak of the inferior. The door to this group of stories will be opened by the tale of the blessed Mary of Egypt, which deserves respect for its antiquity and its evident truth,[2] as well as being an outstanding instance of sweet forgiveness: a woman who had in the past so readily made herself available to the common people afterwards reached a peak of unlimited perfection.

2. Her native land was Egypt, her place of residence from her twelfth year Alexandria. That city, annals relate, is full of wealth, and overflows with merchandise from every land. The people are gay and wanton, and, thanks to their riches, not disinclined to luxury. There this girl lost her virginity, thanks to the debauchery of the city and the temptations of youth, and went on to become a prostitute. She was a glutton, making herself sick by overeating and overdrinking.[3] She entangled young men, and could make even the reluctant fall into filthy ways. Her singing, her affected sibilance of voice and her captivating blandishments attracted everyone, netting even old men past such things. 3. She danced on stage, and sang comic songs at home. She didn't ask money from her partners in shame; not even when they offered it to her unasked would she take cash or food, for she could make a living by the skill of her hands, spinning flax or weaving. She misbehaved for free, luring men by the very fact that she wanted their attentions, not their money; by clever and shameless practices, and unconcerned with profit, she could allure on a large scale by being so complaisant. For it is a fact that there are many men who avoid involvement with call-girls for fear of wasting money; pleasure drives from in front, but meanness pulls back from behind.

4. In the slippery course of this manner of life not a few years went by, while she ran along the ways of the world from her twelfth (as I said) to her twenty-ninth year. After that, she grew tired of living in Alexandria, and sailed to Jerusalem, on an impulse of folly, not chastity. A young crew took her on board with them free of charge: the moment she saw them, she won them over to do what she wanted by her provoking expression and flirtatious conversation. Even in that perilous situation, when only a slim plank kept death at bay, the itch of pleasure did not

[1] Not in Poncelet. The gist is from Dominic 11 (ed. Canal, pp. 35–7). But William also made independent use of Dominic's source, the *Vita* written in Greek by Sophronius, patriarch of Jerusalem (634–38), as transl. by Paul the Deacon (*BHL* 5415; *PL* 73. 671–90): ed. and transl. J. Stevenson, 'The holy sinner: the Life of Mary of Egypt', in *The Legend of Mary of Egypt in Medieval Insular Hagiography*, ed. E. Poppe and B. Ross (Blackrock, 1996), pp. 19–98, text from 51. The *Vita* was known in England from at least the tenth century, and is transmitted in Passionals of the late eleventh century from William's region (the 'Cotton-Corpus Legendary'): BL, Cotton Nero E. I (Worcester), ff. 179v–184v, and Salisbury Cath. 221 (Salisbury), ff. 195v–205v.
[2] Cf. epil. 8: 'quae et sanxit antiquitas et rerum commendat ueritas'.
[3] Cf. *GR* 245. 5; *VD* 2. 9. 3.

cool but raised just as bright a torch. I should imagine the watery element would have groaned, if it could, at being diverted to such foul and unnatural purposes.

5. Once over the sea and arrived in Jerusalem, she did not alter her ways even now; unrestrained by respect for the holy place, she went on making light of her chastity and did not let pleasure grow infirm in its headlong course. A year went round, and the day came for the feast of the Exaltation of the Holy Cross, filling the peoples with great exultation. Crowds poured into the church, and she went along too, out of sheer curiosity,[4] not religious observance. The others had their prayers answered: they got into the place easily, and came out again happy. 6. *She* tried three times and more to gain entrance, but to no avail. Long did she pause, pondering what strange thing it could be that kept her out of the church, but she could not tell, so thoroughly was the darkness of filth playing havoc with the light of her understanding, so grossly had her sins fattened her reason. Making yet another attempt, under the impression that the problem was womanly weakness amid such a crowd, she mingled with a bunch of men. But their pushing and shoving weakened her feeble limbs. She made no progress, and gave up trying.

7. In the end, without fully understanding why, she raised her eyes to the image of Mary, holy Mother of God, painted in the courtyard into which the violence of the jostling crowd had thrust her, and repenting her misdeeds she bewailed her evil past and promised to do better. As guarantee for her reform she gave to her Son the Lady herself: 'I am not worthy that the brightness of eternal light and the mirror of God's majesty should attend me,[5] when I am guilty of such crimes. But I have heard from those who know better that the Wisdom of God was made body in your unsullied womb precisely to call not the just, but sinners to repentance.[6] Christ Himself is merciful, and in His eyes it is not the penitent but the despairing sinner who is at risk. Let Him therefore judge me worthy of forgiveness, that with her as mediator I may be emptied of crime and cease from guilt. It will be sign enough that I have obtained pity if I gain free entrance.'

8. Her prayer complete, she went up to the door, and rejoiced to find herself granted entry; with the rest she worshipped the holy symbol.[7] She went back to the image in better spirits; such an easy winning of grace had drained off from her heart all the impurities of her desires. 'I am here, Lady,' she said, 'after having my prayer granted beyond my deserts, thanks to you. I will go back on none of my promises, but will go to it in future,[8] adding my own efforts to what you have granted me. It is for you to direct me if I slip, for you to show me the

[4] Cf. Peter Damian, *Epist.* 123 (ed. Reindel, III, p. 405): 'sollicitus curiositatis indagine ferarum lustra perquirit'.
[5] Cf. Sap. 7: 26: 'candor est enim lucis aeternae et speculum sine macula Dei maiestatis'.
[6] Luc. 5: 32.
[7] I.e. the Cross ('sanctae crucis lignum' Dominic).
[8] Apparently = 'try to fulfil them in the future'. Cf. 43. 3 (*adorire*).

way to salvation.' 9. So at once, to prove God's favour, a voice was heard as from afar: 'If you cross Jordan, you will find good peace.'[9] She snatched at the words, understanding them to be spoken of herself, and looked anew to the image of her guarantor;[10] weeping, she asked leave to depart, and walked out of the church. She bought three loaves for threepence, travelled to the Jordan, and spent the night in the church of St John the Baptist. In the morning she took communion there, and crossing the river soon found a place suited to her wishes, a wood empty of wild animals and indeed of all living creatures, but abounding in the harmless plants on which hermits support life.

10. If at this point I recount, in order and in detail,[11] her bodily travails, I shall prove a bore. So I shall summarise them all. Other writings will inform you at great length of the full range of what went on.[12]

11. For fourteen years,[13] from her twenty-ninth to her forty-third, she consumed hardly two and a half loaves, by now flint-hard. The rest of her life she passed content with such plants as did not disagree with her, or, preferably, with the Word of God alone. The clothes she had brought with her yielded to time, and fell to pieces. Naked herself, she put on the new man created according to God.[14] For seventeen years she underwent the trials of hunger, desire and extreme weather. Her hunger was made worse by the memory of the fleshpots of Egypt, the wine and the fish; for that part of the world is said to be especially fertile in things whose pleasant taste invites greed. To rouse her desire there was the madness of her past lapses, and the memory of secular songs that she had not yet lost despite leaving the world. 12. Inclement weather and intolerable sunshine affected her bare body, so that she either grew numb with cold or baked in the burning heat. *That* kind of affliction was cured swiftly by God, who soon raised her from illness just when she might have been thought to be dead and gone. The rest, with God's grace, she cured for herself, beating her breast and shedding tears, to rid herself of the pain of her heart within. Nor did she give up before the clear skies of chastity and temperance drove the darkness of filth far from her mind. With the holy craft customary to her she contrived to keep the holy Mother of God always before her eyes,[15] to praise her when she did well or threaten her if she did not. Safe in the protection of her guarantor and fearful at the very thought of her, she avoided the Charybdis of

---

[9] Cf. Hildebert, *Vita beate Marie Egiptiace*, 543 (*CCCM* 209, p. 270).

[10] Later this icon was transferred to Justinian's church of St Sophia in Constantinople: Cormack in *Mother of God*, p. 108.

[11] *enucleatim* is also used at *GP* 14. 2 and *GR* 5 pr. 1. In addition William employs the less choice *enucleate*.

[12] The *aliae ... litterae* can hardly refer to Dominic, whose account is briefer and adds nothing at this point. Nor is there much in Hildebert, *op. cit.*, 571–689, or Sophronius, 19 (*PL* 73. 684–5; ed. Stevenson, pp. 69–72).

[13] Seventeen according to Dominic, Sophronius (19; *PL* 684A), and William immediately below.

[14] Cf. *Comm. Lam.* III, 285–6 (based on Col. 3: 9–10).

[15] She imagines Mary to be present in the way recommended by ancient philosophy (see 26. 2).

vices for those seventeen years, even though she was often tempted; for the thirty-one that remained to her she did not feel even a stirring of sin.

13. So in the seventy-sixth year of her life, the forty-seventh since her conversion, there came to that solitary spot, which no one had visited before, a monk called Zosimas. This was obviously planned by God, so that in the shame of confession she should purge away any remains of her old faults, and that a woman of such virtue should now be made known to encourage others to penitence. The monk, after gently coaxing from her the whole story of her life, met with signs of wonderful sanctity. So free was she of the stains of vice that while she was with extended hands sending to heaven the perfumes of her prayers, her body became light and she hung poised in the empty air: in her loathing for her sojourn on earth she was drawn towards heaven in the spirit.

14. As[16] the monk watched, he began to have doubts: perhaps she was a spirit freed from the body. She had a prophet's acumen to read his thoughts; she contradicted his error and told him the truth: she was no unclothed spirit, but had a body made of clay, given life by a spirit. And to help him believe she made the sign of the cross over her whole body, the usual method of driving away any phantasm. She was so inspired by the spirit of prophecy that she gave the name of the monk and his abbot, though she had never heard them, <specified> the rule of the monastery he came from, and knew and censured the covert sins of some of the monks. Of course, the wisdom of God had poured into her a deep draught of knowledge, enabling her to spy on all worldly secrets even though she was far removed from the world. Thus a woman always concentrating on other matters, who had never had the slightest education, could readily produce the testimony of the Scriptures, unhesitatingly reciting texts with perfect accuracy. That was as far as their first conversation went, and they said goodbye to each other.

15. The following year, on the Thursday before Easter, as they had arranged, he took his position this side of the Jordan; he had brought with him the Body of the Lord. When the holy woman was slow in coming, the monk began to weep, and with an old man's impatient hastiness started to accuse her of delaying her arrival. But in the end she did come, and stood on the further bank gazing intently

---

[16] 'As ... phantasm' is not in Dominic.

at Zosimas. She made the sign of the Cross on the waters, then walked over them briskly as though on dry land. He was astonished and tried to worship her, but she quelled him by shouting beforehand to remind him that he was a priest bearing the mysteries of Christ. She took communion, and with hands raised to heaven asked permission to die, saying: 'Now thou dost dismiss thy servant, O Lord, according to thy word in peace.'[17] So she went away, striding firmly over the water, but not before giving the monk instructions: he must know that next year he was to come to look for her at the place in the desert where they had met.

16. He did not fail the holy woman, but journeying manfully arrived at the stated time. Casting his eyes swiftly around, he saw a place glowing with a particularly strong light, and ran over to it. There he saw to his grief a body on the ground, and written in the dust the words: 'Abbot Zosimas, bury the frail body of poor Mary.' This was very welcome information, for on the earlier occasion it had not occurred to him to ask the lady's name. Aware of his ignorance thanks to her prophetic insight, she used the written message I have mentioned to remove his doubts and pour into him the light of knowledge.

17. There remained the labour of making a grave. The monk's aged limbs, worn out with fasting and fatigue, were not up to it. So he prayed to Heaven. His prayer brought a helper in the shape of an enormous lion. His unexpected arrival and gigantic frame quite terrified the monk, and at first he grew pale. But when the beast's eyes proved not to threaten trouble, he realised why he had come and asked him to excavate a hole big enough to hold the body. The lion set to at once, digging out a good deal of earth with his paws and claws. The hollow he made was crude enough, but Zosimas gave it the shape of a grave. The holy body was laid to rest, and given to the angels to watch over. The monk returned home.

18. These exploits of the blessed woman surely redound to the pride and glory of the Lady Mother of the Lord: she *did* when she helped the doer. The Egyptian woman would have been wasting her trouble, especially when she had been for so long bound in the inextricable toils of habit, had the Lady of the world not broken the knot which bound her and upheld the liberty she had been granted. It was a sign of her unique grace that she did not allow her to be wrapped in the mockery of continuing misfortune. It was a sign of her imperious powers that she gave her invincible help when the woman made her effort, so that she might nobly press forward the good work she had once begun,[18] and foster it for ever.

[17] Cf. Luc. 2: 29.
[18] Cf. pr. 13: 'perseuerantia, quae bene inchoatum stabiliter urget'.

19. As for us who have much sinned, it is right now to lift up our hearts, and raise the standards of our great-hearted predecessors. We have Mary of Egypt as standard bearer for penitence. We have Mary, the most sublime of Maries, to grant us forgiveness. Let us emulate her audacity as she fights in battle, if we wish to obtain the palm from the Empress.[19]

---

[19] C adds: 'These two things are closely connected together by an invisible bond: there cannot be penitence without a prize, or prize without penitence. When one is present, the other will follow. When one lies low, the other will be missing(?)'. William could have written these words; the 'two things', penitence and prize, pick up 'penitence' and 'palm' from what precedes.

41. Musa[1]

1. This is the place to insert the famous tale that the blessed Pope Gregory tells of our Lady in his book of dialogues.[2] And I shall use his own words: I do not wish to extend this brief work in praise of the Mother of the Lord beyond its due point, and would not want the need to recast the style to hold me up as I approach the close of my little work.[3]

2. He says: 'I must not suppress what Probus, servant of God, used to tell about his little sister Musa. One night the holy Mother of God, the Virgin Mary, appeared to her in a dream, and pointed out to her girls of the same age dressed in white raiment. When Musa wanted to be of their number, but did not venture to join them, she was asked by the blessed Mary, ever-virgin, if she wished to be with them and live in her service. The girl said "Yes", and was at once told to do nothing any more that was trivial and girlish, and to cease from laughter and jesting, knowing for sure that thirty days later she would come to serve her among the virgins she had seen.

3. 'After this vision, the girl's behaviour completely changed, and with the hand of gravity she wiped away from herself all girlish levity. Her parents marvelled at the change, and asked her about it. She related what the blessed Mother of God had told her, and specified the day on which she would go to serve her. After the twenty-fifth day she was taken by a fever, and on the thirtieth, when her end had drawn nigh, she saw the blessed Mother of God coming to her with the girls she had seen in the vision. Mary called her, and in reply she cried aloud, with eyes reverently lowered: "Look, Lady, I come! Look, Lady, I come!" With these words she yielded up her spirit, and departed from her virgin body to heaven.'

---

[1] Poncelet 137 (1031). Taken from TS 3 (Dexter, pp. 41–2), even though William gives the impression that he is directly citing its source, Gregory's *Dialogues*. This is unnamed in most copies of TS, but in two cases (BnF, lat. 5657 and 5268) it is mentioned, so that one does not know whether William was led to Gregory by TS or by his own knowledge of the pope's work, which was certainly extensive: his *Defloratio Gregorii* is extant in Cambridge, Univ. Libr. Ii. 3. 20 (D. H. Farmer, 'William of Malmesbury's Commentary on Lamentations', *Studia Monastica* 14 [1962], 283–311, at pp. 308–11; Thomson, *William of Malmesbury*, pp. 42, 93–4). The text of TS follows Gregory closely, but collation suggests that William may have relied upon TS rather than Gregory.
[2] 4. 18. 1–3.
[3] Freely translated; for the idea, cf. *GR* 54. 6: 'ipsius [*sc.* Bedae] uerba lector recognoscat licebit, ne meis sermonibus uel plus uel minus ipsa nouae formae procudat necessitas.' See above, p. xxxvii.

42. Abbess delivered[1]

1. There was once an abbess who was overstrict in enforcing the rules of the order, and for that reason was hated by all the nuns subject to her. Moderation is a good thing everywhere and in everything. For, as is said: 'All that is excessive turns into vice',[2] and in Ecclesiastes we find written: 'Do not be too just; there is one who perisheth in his justice.'[3] For if, as the apostle says, 'the angel of Satan transformeth himself into an angel of light',[4] he deceives the unwary the more easily that he shows some signs of a kind of virtue. This happened to this poor woman too; later on, she was tricked by the Devil's wiles and conceived a child.

2. Having, as has been said, become an object of dislike to all the sisters, she had no one to whom she dared tell her secret. Full of sadness and beset by anxieties on all sides, she had no idea at all what to do. However, she thought of a plan that would be of prime use in her present plight, if anyone can be safely trusted.[5] She summoned one of the sisters, befriended her, and within a few days appointed her prioress of the house. Eventually she revealed all her inmost secrets to her. But the old hatred had not yet been quite obliterated in the woman's heart, and what she should have kept hidden she afterwards revealed not only to the sisterhood but even to lay persons. The matter became known to the archdeacon and through him to the bishop. Everyone spoke ill of the abbess, and it was judged that she should be deposed from her pastoral role. Nowhere could the poor woman find solace or remedy for such a misfortune.

3. So the months passed, and her time was fast approaching. On the day of the birth, the bishop, accompanied by the clergy, was led into the chapter house by the sisters. The sisters stood up to confront the abbess. This is how they worded their complaint: 'This unhappy woman, who has hitherto been our abbess, is now not worthy even of the name. She has given an example not of continence but of complete impurity. In her all law, all right, all ceremony, all holy living is set at naught. While *we* keep to the rule, she has not ceased to give herself over to her lust and gluttony. What is your will?[6] In her right and wrong[7] are as one. The proof is clear: look, she is about to give birth, now!'

---

[1] Poncelet 4 (605). The source is Dominic 12 (ed. Canal, pp. 37–8), to which William made some minor 'improvements'.
[2] Walther, *Sprichwörter* 19859.
[3] In fact Eccles. 7: 16–17, rendered freely.
[4] II Cor. 11: 14, but not the Vulg. wording. Other twelfth-century writers used this version, e.g. Godfrey of Admont, *Hom. fest.* 31 (PL 174. 771D).
[5] Cf. Virgil, *Aen.* 4. 373.
[6] Or 'What more do you want?'
[7] Cf. e.g. Ovid, *Met.* 6. 585–6: 'fasque nefasque / confusura ruit'.

4. While this was going on in chapter, the most merciful Virgin, flanked by a company of angels, appeared to the abbess as she prayed in private. For having no mortal to console her she had recourse with all her heart to divine help; and the Mother of Mercy stood by the poor woman. Full of pain, and in extreme distress and fatigue, she was overcome by sleep; and in the absence of a midwife she enjoyed the services of the blessed Virgin. Who ever heard of a miracle of the kind? It is quite unparalleled that a woman should give birth while dreaming. But this abbess, after first being reprimanded in her sleep by the blessed Virgin, proceeded to give birth to a son, with no pain. The new-born child was sent by the blessed Virgin, by means of an angel, to a faithful servant of hers to foster.

5. Everyone would find these events incredible if the blessed Virgin Mary were subject to natural law. But because she gave birth to the Saviour of mankind, she has come to surpass human nature in every respect, and cannot be prevented by natural law from doing in full all that conduces to our salvation. Here I ought to say more in praise of the blessed Virgin, but I must pass over mysteries and return to the course of my story.

6. The bishop sent clergy, he sent laymen, he sent nuns, he sent men and women. The abbess was ordered to be brought in and examined in the presence of them all. An extraordinary thing happened: she had been pregnant shortly before, yet now she was found quite free of any sign of such a burden, no trace of childbirth was found on her. In the end the bishop felt the abbess's belly. As the charge against the abbess had been shown up as a falsehood, he ordered the accusers to be put to torture. A fire was commissioned for their burning, men and women alike. But the abbess, mindful of our Lord's command,[8] flung herself at the bishop's feet, told the full story, and begged for her enemies to be spared. The bishop sent messengers, and the child who had been carried off by the angel was found. He was fostered for seven years, and then brought to the bishop's palace to be given a liberal education; his religious fervour shone the older he grew, and on the bishop's death he was appointed bishop of the same city.

7. In all this the supreme virtue of the glorious Virgin Mary is proclaimed. So let no one, however tainted with some sin, fear to invoke the blessed Virgin. Let us not be held back by a guilty conscience, but with all our heart say 'Hail' to her as the archangel Gabriel did.[9] She will be there to help us, she who bore Jesus Christ, to whom with the Father and Holy Spirit is honour and glory world without end.

[8] Presumably Matt. 5: 44 (Luc. 6: 27, 35) or 6: 12.
[9] Luc. 1: 28.

116

43. Nun's penance incomplete[1]

1. A nun had shipwrecked her chastity,[2] and not content with a single lapse had increased the sin by making a habit of it. But, as I have said of many others, she was devoted to the service of St Mary, and sang her Hours each day with no stumbling or omission.[3] She also poured out prayers of her own, and summoned up tears at the altar. She would offer Mary greetings and the angel's Ave,[4] announcing and reiterating the familiar joy. In memory of the five wounds of Christ she genuflected five times, repeating the number of joys: 'Rejoice, Mother of God, immaculate virgin. Rejoice, you who received joy from the angel. Rejoice, you who gave birth to the brightness of eternal light. Rejoice, mother. Rejoice, holy Mother of God, virgin', and the rest.[5]
2. What is more, she competed with those of her own age in dutifulness, with the young in obedience, and won them over by her zeal; she was obedient to all, so that since she could not show chastity like the others she might equal their grace by serving. She did nothing to bear hard on anyone, said nothing to harm anyone, but put in a good word for them all with the mother of the monastery, to whom she was related by blood. By these means she made all love her, and in public and in private great honour was paid her. The abbess loved her more than every other, and everybody loved her more than anyone else except the abbess. This honour summoned her back from her outrageous behaviour: she pondered on the long-suffering of God, who allowed to be honoured one who did not deserve <even> to go on living.

3. By employing her reason, then, she beat back the shamelessness of her sin, and hastened to confess to the abbess what she had done. She in her turn did not scorn her or frown upon her, but took her into her peaceful embrace and calmed her down. Prescribing a penance, she said: 'Daughter, go to it, and rise to your correction. God himself helps the daring.[6] You can easily repair a lapse of the body by the devotion of the heart. And, as I hope, the Mother of the Lord will not fail you; after all, you serve her with entire diligence and revere her with sincere love. I too will accompany my daughter with my prayers, with a mother's close concern and the assiduity of an old woman.' The girl did what she was told, and showed herself keen. But the penance she had begun with great spirit was brought to a halt by her swift demise.

[1] Poncelet 515 (1620). Based upon the metrical version in Carter's MB collection, pr. G. Duplessis, *Le livre des miracles de Notre-Dame de Chartres* (Chartres, 1855), pp. xxi–xiv. The prose version, pr. Crane, pp. 75–8 (from Heiligenkreuz, Stiftsbibl. 11), varies much from William's.
[2] Cf. *Comm. Lam.* I, 551 and IV, 157–8; *VW* 1. 1. 6. The ultimate source may be Jerome, *Adv. Iovinianum* 1. 36 (*PL* 23. 271).
[3] Cf. [Adam of Eynsham], *Magna Vita S. Hugonis*, ed. and tr. D. Douie and H. Farmer (2 vols, London &c, 1961–62), I, p. 11: 'inpretermisse et inoffense' (of giving their due to God and neighbours).
[4] Luc. 1: 28.
[5] C and L give a fuller version of the antiphon. See also above, 26. 1. On the Five (later Seven) Joys, see A. Ball, 'Seven Joys of Mary', *Encyclopedia of Catholic Devotions and Practices* (Huntington, IN, 2003), p. 522.
[6] Cf. Virgil, *Aen.* 10. 284 (Otto, *Sprichwörter*, s. v. *fortuna* 9), and 32. 3 above.

4. The abbess was shocked that a young woman who repented of her sin should leave this world before it became known to what such devotion was aspiring. So she summoned the whole community, and divided among them the dead woman's penance, so that their concerted prayers should form a shield to guard their sister's soul and ward off danger from it. Thirty days later the girl stood before the sleeping abbess in a dream. She asked her without a shudder what she was doing and why she had come. 'I shall benefit from your prayers, mother,' she said, 'but my torments are still going on. I have good hope, instilled in me by the Mother of my Lord, who softens even the direst agonies. For the day after my death I looked from afar and saw her come down to the fires in which we burn.

5. "Why have you come here," I said, "slipping down from the heights of heaven?[7] How filthy this place is, how unworthy of your exalted status! Is it true, then, Lady, that the salutations I so often uttered to you, the tears I shed so profusely at your altar, will do no good? You see how wretchedly I am tortured, yet you are silent?[8] I am punished, yet you put up with it?" She consoled me in my downcast state, and said: "I have not forgotten, and the reward for the services you mention has not slipped my mind. But first you must be purged of your sins. A dangerous wound needs a long treatment; a grave offence demands a harsh punishment. And what crime is worse than your sin? You violated the temple of my son, and dishonoured me, the standard bearer of virginity, the patroness of chastity, the leader of modesty. 6. You destroyed the seal of godhead, broke the bond of my love. Go on taking your punishment, then, until you are rescued by the tears of your sisters. Believe me, the remedy is not far off, for the diligence which you once brought to honouring me will lighten your penalty and hasten your pardon. I will not delay my coming; I will snatch you from these agonies and place you before my son." This the Mother of God told *me*, this I tell *you*; and I ask *you* to tell the others. Let there be no room for laziness; great energy must be brought to bear, to make the fires of hell grow cool.'

7. The abbess woke up and told the whole sisterhood the details of the dream. They, with such prophetic words to inspire them, naturally took greater pains from then on to look to their own welfare and to liberate the dead woman.

Well then, sinner, go ahead and doubt[9] that St Mary is merciful! – she who can reform even those guilty of the most heinous crimes so that they may be forgiven, if only she can find even a slight opportunity!

---

[7] Cf. Boethius, *Phil. Cons.* 1. 3. pr. 3: 'quid ... tu [*sc.* Philosophia] in has exilii nostri solitudines ... supero cardine delapsa uenisti?'
[8] Cf. Aug. *Confess.* 1. 18. 28: 'uides haec, Domine, et taces?' The parallel suggests that these two sentences should be punctuated as questions (the manuscripts vary).
[9] Cf. Ovid, *Ars amat.* 2. 222, Juvenal 6. 306, Martial 8. 63. 3.

44. Childbirth in the sea[1]

1. At a sea-girt spot called Tumba,[2] there is a church dedicated to St Michael the archangel. At this place the tide, the one the Greeks call *rheuma*, comes in and goes out twice a day, terrifying all visitors to the holy place.[3] The locals call the incoming tide *malina*, the outgoing *ledo*. The tide ebbs and flows not gradually as elsewhere, but very fast, with a terrible roar. Hence the place is called 'Sea-Peril'. Many people come here to ask for the merciful aid of the blessed Michael the archangel.

2. One feast day, then, crowds were hurrying there, among them a poor pregnant woman near her time. And here comes the terrible roar of the advancing waves. Terrified at the sound, everybody doubted for their safety. The able-bodied could get away by running fast. But (poor thing!) no one helped the unhappy, or I should more properly say the happy, woman. For happy indeed she was, as the outcome showed.

3. She was enveloped in the waves, grim death was upon her, no one was helping. Let everyone who hears this search the depths of his own conscience, and judge, if he can, with what sobs she assailed Heaven; for I cannot put into words what the woman felt in such straits. But because she had absolutely no help from man, the Virgin Mary came with help from Heaven; she protected her with her sleeve, and kept her safe from all danger. In the midst of the waves there formed an agreeable place for her to give birth: the Virgin's sleeve made a chamber scented more sweetly than balsam.

4. Those on the shore were concerned for the woman who had been left behind, and knocked at heaven's gates with groans and devout prayers. They waited at the edge bewailing the woman's fate, hoping at least to bury the drowned body when the ebb tide drew the waves back. But quite the contrary: when the water receded she returned to the people alive, not alone either but with her new-born son, whom a little while before she had been carrying in her womb. Everyone was struck dumb with wonder at such a miracle. Everyone listened while the woman related how the holy Mother of God had taken pity on her; and everyone alike praised the Creator.

5. O Virgin, so beautiful, descended from the seed of King David, how near at hand you are to all people, how quick to help in all our straits! You receive our prayers, take them to your Son, and at once bring back the desired result. In accordance with what suppliants ask, you provide the due remedy for our

[1] Poncelet 25 (499). From, and closely following, Dominic 3 (ed. Canal, pp. 23–5).
[2] Mont St Michel (Manche), off the coast of Normandy.
[3] There is a similar account in 49. 1 below. Cf. GR 179. 3 n. for the tides. For *reuma* see now *ODML* s. v. *rheuma* 1c, with helpful parallels.

wounds. How much we need the help of your mercy! The unhappy woman had no human aid, and prayed for yours instead. You performed a miracle that is now spoken of all over the world.

Therefore, Lady, commend us to your Son, who with Father and Spirit is glorified, world without end. Amen.

44a. *Multa quidem ...*[4]

1. Many, and beyond telling, are the miracles that are performed every day throughout the world by the glorious and unstained Virgin, Mary Mother of God. Even did Tully wish to decorate them with his rhetorical colours, oratory hides away, eloquence gives out, all power of speech is entirely despised. For in them is disproved the memorable dictum of Sallust: 'the virtue of those who have done virtuous actions[5] is as great as first-rate intellects have been able to extol it.'[6] The Virgin Mary's miracles are not commended by words, or extolled by first-rate intellects, or decorated by eloquence, or given authority by the elegant urbanity of any good speaker, but rely on their own virtue. 2. For the eloquence of orators normally finds scope for exercise in narrations where the sense seems obscure or void of utility; and such accounts are welcomed the more enthusiastically the more elegantly and charmingly they are written.[7] But the miracles of the Virgin Mary, read as they are by many, expounded by the learned, and listened to with emotion by everyone, are commended by their own virtue, and it is by their own worth that they attract the minds of listeners.

3. Up to this point I have given as it were an introduction to all the miracles of the Virgin Mary. From now on I shall try to give, not with pompous words or oratorical gloss, but in a straightforward style,[8] a special miracle not heard of before, essential reading equally for the just and for the sinner.

---

[4] This chapter is apparently misplaced. See Introduction, pp. xxxiv, xliii.
[5] William makes use of the non-classical meaning of *uirtutes*, 'miracles'.
[6] Sallust, *Cat.* 8. 4 (also cited by Augustine and Jerome).
[7] *amplectuntur* is apparently used passively.
[8] Cf. Ennodius, *Dictio* 7. 9 (ed. Vogel p. 7): 'non *faleratus sermo*, non inlecebrosa tantum et depicta *fucis* narratio [cf. §2] delectet. quaerite apud me non blanda sed *necessaria*, non deliciosa sed fortia.'

45. Mead[1]

1. The author of the Life of the blessed Dunstan relates that there was once a married lady[2] at Glastonbury who was devoted to St Mary. Glastonbury is a town in England, distinguished more for its monastery than for a favourable position or the attractions of the place.[3] This woman was related to the royal family, and was nurse to the royal children; but she was not seduced by prosperity and good fortune, but rather encouraged to be more pious. For example, she had given all her substance for the poor, and she had also assembled there a group of clerks to serve the Lady. She gave them the victuals they needed every day, and (as I said) spent all that was left over on the needy. She herself was content with simple fare, living a good life and praying constantly; and she had so won the friendship of the queen of the world that she got from her whatever she thought she should have as though by order rather than on request.[4] I shall give you an instance.

2. King Æthelstan, without an equal in England for devotion and good fortune,[5] was attracted by the sanctity of the place, and had came there to pray. After his devotions, he was asked by the woman to honour his nurse's home by coming to feast there.[6] He was for long in a quandary of well-bred embarrassment: should he burden a woman of slender means with the noisy company of his great household, or go off with his head in the air and chagrin her despite her pressing request. He was in a dilemma, for he was no lover of moderation, and was accustomed only to jolly and extravagant banquets. 3. In the end, under the woman's pressure, he yielded to her urgency. But he sent ahead staff to check that all was in good supply. They reported that everything was there in abundance, except for a shortage of the drink they call mead. She was given courage by her faith, and said: '*That* will not be lacking: on the contrary. Take your seats, gentlemen.' It needed one visit to the church for her to come back with her prayer fully answered. And indeed the whole day they drank from a small vessel that was late on in the evening found to be still running over. This was the more miraculous because there were so many drinking: everyone,

[1] Poncelet 120 (121). From William's own *VD* 1. 12, rather than the much vaguer TS 14 (Dexter, pp. 38–9), which he set out to correct.
[2] Æthelflæd, for whom see *VD* 1. 11. She was the king's niece. William presumably refers to the account in the *Vita S. Dunstani* by B., 10 (*Early Lives*, pp. 34–7), though it also appears in Osbern, *Vita Dunstani*, 15. However, the information that she was Æthelstan's nurse (hardly likely if she was his niece) is stated here for the first time. William may be confusing her with the king's aunt of the same name, whom in *GR* 133. 2 he says took part in his upbringing.
[3] Cf. *GP* 91. 1 (where Glastonbury is only a *uilla*; *uicus* is also used in TS 14).
[4] Cf. *VD* 1. 11. 2.
[5] I.e. among kings (cf. *VD* 1. 12. 1: 'nullus umquam regum').
[6] *VD* 1. 12. 1–2, more sensibly, has the invitation made well beforehand, and the messengers ride a long way to inspect the provisions.

not just the royal retinue but those of lower degree too, quite understandably went away with a smile on his face and in the best of cheer.

4. You might well think this too small and even paltry a story to boost the blessed Lady's merits; but one may say that it was a wonderful and praiseworthy thing that her sublime Majesty, through whom the whole globe stands in its due position, condescends to give these more humble gifts to her servants: she who reigns on the grandest scale as it were relaxes in the tiniest matters.[7] She grants favours to all who love her, permitting no one to go away sad if they live a good life and offer her their loyal prayers.

[7] Varying *VD* 1. 11. 2; cf. also *GP* 270. 7.

46. Various minor miracles

1. The following stories also are trifling, and too cold to spark men to love her. They can be found in writing elsewhere, and I shall only summarise them here.

Wife and mistress[1]

2. That she restrained by means of a vision a woman who out of contentious hatred cursed a rival[2] and asked for revenge from the Lady. 'I do not wish her to die,' Mary said, 'though she has strayed from the good and is unchaste. For every day she makes me a hundred genuflections and greets me a hundred times. Sin may be succeeded by reform; death cannot be repaired.' To make her gracious vision the more beautiful, she brought her secret influence to bear to make it up between the two women when they met by chance next morning: one abandoned her quarrel, the other her affair.[3]

47. Woman cured of an evil spirit[4]

That another woman, who had lost her wits but had not been found worthy of being cured at Fécamp, was freed from the harmful spirit in the course of a single night spent in a church of the blessed Mary, and was restored to health.

48. Foot cut off[5]

That she healed a man sorely afflicted with the sacred (or rather accursed) fire.[6] He had cut off his own foot, to prevent the mischief creeping further up. After meeting rebuffs over a long period, he complained to her in a church. Sleep came over him when he grew tired of his cries, as happens in cases of mental anguish. Mary stood over him when he was unconscious, and with a gentle hand seemed to touch his leg and to reattach the foot to it, smearing it with a healing

---

[1] Not in Poncelet. Summarised from the MB version in e.g. Bodl. Libr., Laud. misc. 359, ff. 74–6. In turn, the source for this was Guibert of Nogent, *De laude S. Mariae*, 11 (*PL* 156. 572–4).
[2] I.e. to her husband's affections. The aggrieved woman wishes to go to law (*litigio* below), and that might result in the execution of the rival (*exitio*).
[3] B has a further sentence: the women founded a nunnery.
[4] Poncelet 1525. A drastic summary of HM 17 (Dexter, pp. 31–2), where the woman is named Murieldis.
[5] Not in Poncelet. From TS 2 (Dexter, pp. 40–1), which situates the miracle in the city of Viviers (dioc. Grenoble). This is independent of the story first told by Guibert of Nogent, *De laude S. Mariae*, 11 (*PL* 156. 568–70), according to which the problem was not ergotism but gangrene caused by physical injury. The considerable detail he provides yields outside dates of 1111–15 for the sequence of events.
[6] See above, p. 106 n. 4.

ointment.[7] Starting from his sleep, he caused the onlookers to sing out in praise,[8] for all were amazed equally by the direness of the original affliction and the novelty of the succeeding miracle.

48a. *Talibus dicendis* ...

1. I resolutely[9] refrain from telling stories of this kind,[10] for fear that their being judged worthless might tend to lower rather than heighten praise for our Lady. This point will surely be taken by those who are well aware that any saint you like performs the same miracles.[11] So whatever is said of Mary must be so great that it needs no eloquence to help it shine forth, for the material will surpass the manner of its expression;[12] it gleams of its own accord, and does not need words to proclaim it.

What is more, because we know that it was precisely for the saving of souls that her holy son slipped into her virgin's womb and was brought to birth, we take especial pleasure in relating things that look to the curing of souls. 2. She too, after all, is more eager to concentrate on miracles of that sort, while neglecting or only rarely performing the other kinds. She knows that often bodily health and other kinds of worldly prosperity stimulate sin and prick a man on to misdeeds. But when someone with faith comes up against the pleasures of things of this world and then they do not go the way he wishes, his own onrush makes him (as it were) rebound; he recoils because his prayer has not been answered, and from then on loves this world less and less ardently. Therefore if the Mother of the Lord allows those who love her to be stripped of worldly joys, I hereby assert in terms that this is cause not for surprise but for praise. For she is doing what is in her own interest, and keeping to her custom: preferring to have her servants free from 'wrappings'[13] rather than entangled in them, so that she may truly say: 'Such as I love, I rebuke and chastise.'[14] In fact, everything she does is with a view to its expediency to souls.

---

[7] TS does not mention the cloth soaked with ointment.

[8] Cf. *GP* 276. 4: 'quae miraculi certitudo ciuium ... in laudem Dei ... ora laxauit', and esp. *VW* 2. 10. 2: 'quae res in laudem Dei ... ora resoluit' (Virgil, *Aen.* 3. 457).

[9] The rather unexpected *obstinate* is chosen for its likeness to *abstineo*.

[10] That is, stories like those told in 46–8, for whose 'trifling' nature see 46. 1.

[11] Parallels in *GP* 270. 7, and above, 20a.

[12] Cf. Ovid, *Met.* 2. 5 (*GR* 169. 2 n., to which perhaps add *GP* 43. 5).

[13] I.e. earthly possessions. Cf. below, epil. 1; *GP* 73. 21; *Comm. Lam.* I, 1719; *ODML* s. v. *involucrum* 1b.

[14] Apoc. 3: 19, here cited with *redarguo*, as e.g. by Cassiodorus and Gregory, as against Vulg. *arguo* (thus cited in *Comm. Lam.* I, 1940).

49. Fire at Mont St Michel[1]

1. For example, because of the sins of those who dwell there, some churches are burned up by voracious flames or taken over by some other misfortune. Mary often allows the images of her in those churches to share in such dangers; but more often she protects them from all damage, as happened one year[2] in Normandy at Mont St Michel. The place is surrounded by sea, in such a way that every day the incoming and outgoing tide prevents or allows access to it, turn by turn, on and on.[3] Here the church of the holy archangel, whether because God was angry or naturally (for as someone says 'Lightning smites the tops of mountains'),[4] was struck and completely burnt out. 2. Everything made of wood was reduced to ashes, and only the image of the holy Mary, beautifully sculpted in wood,[5] escaped, so unscathed that even the linen veil[6] on her head was not singed by fire or discoloured by soot. Indeed, a fan of peacock feathers leaning against the image, employed to drive tiresome flies away from those officiating, remained untouched too.[7] It is no surprise that lightning fire was no match for the image of one to whom the fire of lust never brought sorrow or concern.

[1] Poncelet 1340. Taken from HM 15 (Dexter, pp. 29–30).
[2] Lit. 'in a (?the) past year'. But the fire in question was presumably that which occurred on 25 Apr. 1112: see the local sources cited by Canal, p. 164 n. 69, e.g. Robert of Torigni, *Chron.*, ed. L. Delisle (Rouen, 1872–73), 1. 142. HM says 'quodam tempore'.
[3] See above, 44. 1.
[4] Horace, *Carm.* 2. 10. 11–12.
[5] '*ex ligno*' HM, surely correctly, i.e. we have to do with a statue, not some sort of icon (cf. what William says of the difference between Byzantine and Western practice in 32. 6).
[6] See ODML s. v. *peplum* 3a. HM has 'in modum mitre uelamen ... uelamen candidum.'
[7] For the 'flabellum' and its use in Western liturgies, see Rock, *Church of our Fathers*, IV, pp. 228–33; A. A. King, *Liturgies of the Religious Orders* (London, 1955), Appendix pp. 321–2.

50. Saracens cannot deface Mary-image[1]

1. It is quite a few years since the Saracens, sent by the king of Babylon, besieged Baldwin king of Jerusalem at Ramlah, defeated him, and put him to flight. Made more bold and haughty by their success, they ranged the entire region around Ascalon, profaning church buildings or levelling them to the ground. My informant saw what I am telling you. They went into a church of St Mary and launched their spears at the pictures of all the saints painted on the wall, gouging out an eye here, cutting off a nose or foot there, and scoring marks over absolutely all of them with the points. 2. But their madness faltered and came to a halt at the image of St Mary. They could make no impression on her, often though they tried, and for all their efforts they wasted their strength;[2] their hands either trembled too much to have any effect, or slipped to one side. When they got back to Ascalon the infidels were chagrined to tell this tale, in the hearing of our people in prison there. *They* shed pious tears of joy on that occasion, and later, after escaping their captors, returned and told the story at home.

[1] Poncelet 1199; told to William by an eyewitness, and not known from any other source. The events took place shortly after the second battle of Ramlah in May 1102, recounted in *GR* 384. 1–3.

[2] Cf. *GR* 35. 2: 'mox omnibus temptatis et uiribus in uentum effusis' (based on Virgil, *Aen.* 5. 446).

51. The Virgin's image insulted[1]

1. A Jew living at Constantinople was led by his fanaticism to steal an image of the holy Virgin, beautifully painted on a panel in the church called Blacherna,[2] and to throw it into a pit designed for human excrement; and sitting there he disturbed the air,[3] intending to bring disgrace to our faith by emptying his bowels on the image. Worthy punishment followed the sacrilegious man, for his innards went down into the pit in a horrid stream. The sacred image, brought up from the filth, poured forth a long stream of oil (what a wonder!).

2. Men whose word we can trust affirm that this same image, shrouded in a silk veil, is endowed with divine powers. Every Friday, when the sun is sinking into the sea, the veil is spontaneously raised; up to the ninth hour of the Saturday it hangs (as it were) in the air, and reveals the image clearly to all who wish to see it. During this period it is open to view, but on all other days it is hidden. The veil is spontaneously lowered after the ninth hour on the Saturday, just as it had previously gone up of its own accord.[4]

---

[1] Poncelet 20 (916); Ihnat, *Mary and the Jews*, pp. 162–3. The first part (§1), normally treated separately in the tradition, is from TS 7 (Dexter, pp. 45–6), curtailed towards the end. Both TS and its source, Adamnan, *De locis sanctis* 3. 5. 1–9 (ed. D. Meehan [Dublin, 1958], p. 118), locate the image 'in pariete cuiusdam domus' in Constantinople. The second part (§2) is from TS 16 (Dexter, p. 51), which refers to an image of Mary with Child, kept in the church at Blachernai. One does not know what warrant William had for linking the two stories by treating the images as one and the same. Certainly the church at Blachernai possessed many icons and other relics of the Virgin: I. Ševčenko, 'Virgin Blachernitissa', in *Oxford Dictionary of Byzantium* (Oxford, 1991), III, pp. 2170–1; M. Vassiliki and N. Tsironis, 'Representations of the Virgin and their association with the Passion of Christ', in *Mother of God*, pp. 453–63, at 462 n. 26.

[2] St Mary at Blachernai (*lucenna* TS 16, Dexter, p. 51), built by Justin I (518–27) and Justinian (527–65), renovated by Justin II and Sophia; it and the church of the Chalkoprateia were the two major Marian shrines in the city: C. Mango, 'The origins of the Blachernae shrine at Constantinople', in *Acta XIII Congressus Internationalis Archaeologicae Christianae* (3 vols, Vatican City and Split, 1998), II, pp. 61–76; D. Krausmüller, 'Making the Most of Mary', in *The Cult of the Mother of God in Byzantium*, ed. L. Brubaker and M. B. Cunningham (Farnham, 2011), pp. 219–45.

[3] Cf. *GR* 248. 1.

[4] The wonder-working veil or robe (*maphorion*), brought to Constantinople from a village near Nazareth and at first housed in a reliquary chapel built shortly before 475, prior to the building of Justin's basilica: Mango, ut supra, pp. 65–6; id., 'Constantinople as Theotokoupolis', and A. Weyl Carr, 'The Mother of God in public', in *Mother of God*, pp. 17–25, 325–37, at 19 and 327. Also N. Baynes, 'The supernatural defenders of Constantinople', *AB* 67 (1949), 165–77; A. Cameron, 'The Virgin's robe: an episode in the history of early seventh-century Constantinople', *Byzantion* 49 (1979), 42–56; H. Maguire, 'Body, Clothing, Metaphor: The Virgin in Early Byzantine Art', in *Mother of God*, pp. 43–7; R. Janin, 'Notre-Dame de Blachernes', in *La Geographie ecclésiastique de l'Empire Byzantin* 1/3 (Paris, 1953), pp. 169–79. On this particular miracle, see V. Grumel, 'Le "miracle habituel" de Notre-Dame de Blachernes à Constantinople', *Échos d'Orient* 30 (1931), 129–46; B. V. Pentcheva, *Icons and Power: The Mother of God in Byzantium* (University Park, PA, 2006), pp. 154–61. A detailed eyewitness account of the 'habitual miracle' was given by a western visitor in the twelfth century: K. Ciggaar, 'Une description de Constantinople dans le Tarragonensis 55', *Revue des études byzantines* 53 (1995), 117–40, at pp. 121–2. The church was completely destroyed by fire in 1070 and 1434, but the 'perpetual miracle' seems to have ceased by 1204.

3. So there are two images of the Mother of God at Constantinople, both marked out by signs from Heaven: one in Hagia Sophia, mentioned above,[5] spoke up for the innocence of Theodorus, bringing opportune aid to the truth when it was in trouble thanks to Jewish disbelief, and this second one in the church of Blacherna, the inspired work (they say) of Nicodemus,[6] who brought remarkable artistry to the portrayal of the height and gracious form of the Mother of God, thereby not allowing posterity to be deprived of something so impressive.

4. Thanks be to you, Nicodemus! We congratulate you on the knowledge of your mind and the industry of your hands! Thanks to you, mortal men can see before their eyes a representation of the shape whose miraculous beauty[7] angels look up to and adore. There are indeed in that city so many bodies of such excellent saints that each by itself could make a whole province brilliant by its sanctity and by the miracles it brings about.[8] But the minds of the citizens are overtaken, their praises outstripped, by love for the image which is older in the historical record and the more attractive by reason of the novelty of its miracles.[9] The locals yield place to the holy Mother of the Lord, and rejoice that she regards them with pre-eminent favour. They run to her image in all crises, and come back with their prayers answered. The fervour of the Greeks has encouraged and inflamed our people to love the Lady; and, like many other things, this example of veneration has spread from the Greeks to the soil of Latium.[10]

5. She herself has since olden days raised to extraordinary heights the city that loves her, and she now guards and protects it from its enemies.

---

[5] 32. 6.

[6] Nicodemus is not mentioned in TS nor, apparently, in any of the relevant Byzantine texts.

[7] See n. on 15. 3.

[8] William listed the tombs of some of the saints in Constantinople at GR 356. 4 (and see n. ad loc.).

[9] It is not clear whether William refers to the image in Hagia Sophia or that in the church at Blachernai (see above, §3). For the play on *uetustus/uenustus* cf. e.g. Bede, HE 1. 1. 1.

[10] An interesting and, of course, correct perception of William's: Knowles, *The Monastic Order in England*, pp. 510–13, digesting the earlier specialist literature. Malmesbury itself had had an exiled Greek monk (perhaps a bishop) living on site as a hermit in the late eleventh century: GP 260. See also K. N. Ciggaar, 'Une description de Constantinople traduite par un pèlerin anglais', *Revue des études byzantines* 34 (1976), 211–68, on Bodl. Libr., Digby 112 (a late eleventh-century account of a pilgrimage to Constantinople), where we find 'non est maior fides nisi orthodoxorum recta et firma' (Ciggaar, p. 225).

52. Constantinople

1. For instance,[1] in the time of the emperor Arcadius, when Rhoilas chief of the Scyths crossed the Danube and surrounded the city with his clashing arms,[2] Mary, when prevailed upon, secured a thunderbolt and launched it at the enemy, who was burned up together with his army, the furious onrush of his wicked prowess brought to naught.

2. The Saracens too, in the time of Emperor Leo II, besieged the city for three years in their dire quarrel with the Christians. The citizenry cried urgently to Mary. All the enemies' efforts were snatched away on the winds, and the besiegers, more afflicted than the besieged, withdrew in disgust. It was not enough for them to go away baffled for all their strength: they had to pay the price for their rash daring. Some were slaughtered by the neighbouring Bulgars, others were drowned in the waves of a stormy sea.

3. This image the emperor Heraclius took with him on his Persian war,[3] for he thought he could do nothing daring in its absence. As a result he only lost a small number of his soldiers during the long eight-year campaign. Success always attended him, except for a single occasion when his soldiers disobeyed orders and recklessly attacked the enemy, in breach of military discipline. But he soon restored the situation, renewed the war, repelled the Persian columns, and was victorious. The image was at his side, and the enemy prince was killed. A miracle was to be seen that day: a single man fighting a whole battle-line after all his troops had defected and turned tail. He won spoils beyond price, and brought the Cross triumphantly into Jerusalem. He himself wished all this to be put down to the Mother of God's anger at her Son's trophy being purloined by a pagan brigand.

---

[1] The first story is from Cassiodorus, *Historia Tripartita* 10. 27 (*CSEL* 71, p. 620), except that there the miracle is attributed to 'maiestas diuina', not to Mary specifically. William is wrong in believing that the invasion took place in the time of Arcadius (395–408), since the correct date is 434 when the emperor was his son Theodosius II (so Cassiodorus); he might have been led into this error by identifying Rhoilas with 'Radagaisus Scytha' in Jordanes, *Romana* 321 (*MGH Auct. Ant.* 5. 1, p. 41; in his own copy, Bodl. Libr., Arch. Seld. b. 16, f. 131r). The wording of the second story follows Hugh of Fleury, *Historia Ecclesiastica*, for which see A. Wilmart, 'L'histoire ecclésiastique composée par Hugues de Fleury et ses destinataires', *RB* 50 (1938), 293–305. The relevant passage is in William's abbreviated version, Bodl. Libr., Arch. Seld. B. 16, f. 138r, but it does not mention Mary. This detail William could have found in Paul the Deacon, *Historia Miscella* 21 (*PL* 95. 1079). The siege began in 716, was broken off for a time, then resumed through 717–18. The emperor was therefore actually Leo III ('the Isaurian', 717–41). The third miracle is in both of these sources: Hugh of Fleury as in the Selden MS, f. 136rv, and Paul the Deacon, *Historia Miscella*, 18 (*PL* 95. 1033). William follows the former: Paul mentions the Virgin's intercession for the Christian army more than once, but not the presence of her icon. Both he (1032D) and Hugh have a giant Persian warrior not killing large numbers of opponents single-handed but himself killed by the emperor. The last sentence 'He himself wished … brigand' appears to be William's own comment. None of these stories is in Poncelet.

[2] Cf. Virgil, *Aen.* 8. 474, also echoed in *Comm. Lam.* I, 2879–80 and *HN* 501 (p. 108).

[3] So Bodl. Libr., Arch. Seld. B. 16, f. 136r: 'ferens secum imaginem … quae in urbe illa habetur, diuino ut ferunt miraculo picta'.

53. Purification[1]

1. I had almost passed over what should have been placed earlier in this group of stories about Constantinople. It goes like this. Justinian Augustus was ruling the state, the builder, as I said,[2] of Sancta Sophia. At first law-abiding and catholic,[3] he later became cruel and heretical: his favour gave the most staunch support to the heresy according to which there is one operation in the two natures of our Lord Jesus Christ.[4] The imperial mind was poisoned by an evil influence, a heretical wife capable of pushing her husband into any crime. With her encouragement, he dealt severely with two popes who stood up to his lack of faith: Silverius, whom he exiled, and Vigilius, whom he whipped and abused. It is true that the latter was justly punished, for he had given his uncomplaining assent when his predecessor was deposed.[5]

2. On the emperor's sacrilege followed disaster for the world. The earth paid for his sin: the soil dried up and refused the means of life; a scant crop and no harvest confounded the hopes of every district. Amid all this, as famine stalked abroad, a pandemic preyed upon the common people. They fell without limit or number, and each day added to the funerals. Plagues multiplied as the rotting of unburied bodies exhaled its characteristically fell odour and infected the air. The sky grew ever more tainted, corrupting the city as the elements grew sick, and all but emptied it of people. Death supervened swiftly before one felt it coming, and anyone remaining in good health might well have thought he had been whisked off to another world.[6]

3. It was late in the day that a remedy was thought up for these ills, a procession in the city accompanied by the image.[7] It took place, and wherever the image went

[1] Poncelet 920 (1195). Partly from Hugh of Fleury, *Historia Ecclesiastica*, the full text of the second edition of c.1110, pr. from a single MS by B. Rottendorff (Münster in Westfalen, 1638), pp. 138–9. Hardly any of the relevant details are found in William's abbreviated version in Bodl. Libr., Arch. Seld. B. 16, f. 135r.

[2] 32. 6.

[3] Cf. Bodl. Libr., Arch. Seld. B. 16, f. 135r (Paul the Deacon, *De gest. Langobard*. 1. 25) 'erat enim … fide catholicus'.

[4] William describes Monothelitism (actually named as such by Hugh of Fleury), but the heresy with which Justinian was involved was Miaphysitism (a variant of Monophysitism), which held that Christ had a single 'nature' which was a synthesis of human and divine. In fact Justinian always maintained the orthodox (Chalcedonian) position but was outmanoeuvred by his wife Theodora.

[5] Silverius (536–37), deposed in March 537 by Justinian's general Belisarius and sent into exile, replaced by Vigilius (537–55), ordered by the emperor back to Constantinople 545. Both fell foul of Justinian and Theodora because of their opposition to Monophysitism and condemnation of Anthimus, Monophysite patriarch of Constantinople. Cf. Paul the Deacon, *Hist. Misc.*, in the Selden MS, f. 113r.

[6] There is an important parallel to this plague scene in *GP* 76. 7 (of the Danes), with much overlap of wording.

[7] Once again, it is unclear whether William refers to the image kept in Hagia Sophia or that in the church at Blachernai (see above, 51. 3.)

all illness fled away. People on their deathbeds leapt up to meet the procession when they heard the noise of its coming. And on the third day of the lustration, full clemency was to hand, scattering the noxious mists, strengthening bodies, and soon bringing back a year that was prosperous and fruitful. The emperor and patriarch, with an eye to rewarding our Lady by a lavish return, ordained the holding every year of the feast of her Purification, which had never taken place anywhere before.[8] The famous rite remains still, and always will remain; it will live for ever and conquer the ages.[9] And it was from Constantinople that it went forth into the whole world.

---

[8] On the origin of the Feast, probably more complex than William allows, see e.g. E. Michelsen, *Zur Entstehung und Geschichte des Lichtmessfestes* (Kiel, 1922), pp. 149–96; D. De Bruyne, 'L'origine des processions de la Chandaleur et des Rogations', *RB* 34 (1922), 14–26.
[9] Cf. Virgil, *Georg.* 2. 295.

Epilogue

1. More on such lines can be related, nor will there ever be any limit to telling such stories. For with a new informant always on the heels of the last, one always has a new miracle to be lost in wonder at. But I think the stories I have recorded will be enough for someone who knows how to weigh them on their merits rather than just count them up. In the meantime, I deposit with Mary these pledges of my love. Others may build churches in her honour, and pile up gems as presents for her. Some will consecrate scents of innocence, some will give burnt offerings of chastity. If *I* give a libation of worthless words, it ought to be thought a great matter if, by putting up with them, the Lady of heaven shows her judgement that I am not unequal to this task. But she may deal with me as she pleases; what I ask first and foremost is that the old sinner may shed the former crimes that envelop him and burgeon into a new man.

2. So though I shall bring my work to an end, no limit will be allowed to my love. Let her be loved in my inmost heart, thought of by day, dreamed of by night. Readers may judge as they will; *my* conscience is clear: I undertook to say these things to win her love, and have said nothing that shrinks from the truth. But I am sorely afraid on my own account, that I may lose the fruit of my hope;[1] for it much derogates from the reverence owed to the miracles of the Lady Mother of God that I have presumed to praise them when I am no more than an ignorant sinner.

3. But make allowances for my fears, clement Mistress and powerful Empress, and think it proper for me to have praised you. Do not, I beg, make a source for complaint out of what I planned to win the fullest grace. If I deserve punishment for my temerity, remit it in view of my devotion. This task may be great in terms of my labour, but it is small compared with the praise you merit. Who could praise you as you deserve, whose Son created everything and rules and disposes of it by His will? I can well believe that angels are unequal to the role, and are unwilling to profess themselves capable of such a burden. How much more does the loftiness of the task put pressure on *my* narrow ability! But however small my <gift> may be, it will be weighed according to how you receive it, at the value *you* judge it to have. The price will be greater or less in proportion to the regard you accord it.

4. Repay, then, and reward one who has given you his obedient service. My prayer presumes rather more than it should;[2] but any temerity in the asking is surpassed and conquered by your ability and willingness to give. It will cost you

---

[1] Cf. William of Malmesbury, *De antiquitate Glastonie ecclesie*, ed. and trans. J. Scott (Woodbridge, 1981), prol. (p. 42): 'agite ne fructu laboris excidam'; *VW* 3. 20. 3.

[2] It is not clear how to take *maiuscula*. The text may be at fault.

few pains to save a poor man now, considering you once at a single birth brought forth the salvation of all ages.

5. Show then to your exigent hireling what you have always shown to everyone who wishes it. Do not deny me your grace, which is at hand even for the mob. Your love is easily won and (so to speak) popular; it forwards mutual love between all who desire it. Guard my soul amid the toils of its sick body. After it is unbound, do not drive it away as it pants after you, but bear it on high. Meantime, while the last hour is being delayed, and the judgement of Heaven delays to strike down one who deserves it, banish far off him who ambushes from afar.[3] Cast out[4] and drive off Leviathan, the crooked serpent,[5] who with a myriad sinuous coils creeps in where he is least feared and attacks where he is most guarded against. 6. May I never relax into complacency, the sign of a lazy mind negligent towards God, but may my conscious self always be as it were in battle order, harassed by deep fears about past sins, troubled by misgivings about ones to come. May the pains of penitence anticipate the torments of hell.[6] May I do nothing, I beg, to make me grieve for a good reason, desire nothing to make me rejoice for a bad one. May I not be a cause of shame to myself by doing what I regret having done, committing what I repent having committed. But if I do fall, may I not go on wallowing in sin, but rise again swiftly. May I not be arraigned in God's eyes on a true charge, or defamed among men on a false one. Both things must be guarded against by a good man, either to be suspected falsely or to be fund guilty on a true charge.

7. May this material that makes up the body be quiet and untroubled in its movements,[7] let there be no dissonance between the material of heavenly and earthly.[8] May the flesh whose services I enjoy be wounded in no part of itself, miss nothing that it has lost, so that it may hasten above with freer hope. I love a

[3] I.e. the Devil. For 'Guard my soul ... from afar', cf. Ausonius, *Ephemeris* 3. 37–8 'pande [addressing God] uiam, quae me post *uincula corporis aegri* / *in sublime ferat*.' Then (76–8): 'quod [*sc.* iudicium tuum] dum sua *differt* / tempora *cunctatur*que dies, *procul* exige saeuum / insidiatorem blandis erroribus anguem.' For further use of this celebrated poem see below, n. 6.
[4] *exsuffla*: literally 'blow upon', a gesture of exorcism: cf. e.g. Isidore, *Etym.* 6. 19. 56.
[5] See Is. 27: 1. Leviathan was often interpreted by patristic and medieval commentators as representing the Devil.
[6] From 'May my conscious self' cf. Ausonius, *op. cit.* (n. 3) 55–7 (our passage should have been mentioned in the discussion at *Comm. Lam.*, pp. 318–19): 'tacitum si paenitet *altaque sensus* / *formido* excruciat *tormenta*que sera *gehennae* / *anticipat*.' The same poem of Ausonius' is yet further drawn upon in §§6–8 from 'May I do nothing': '(58–61) da, pater, haec nostro fieri *rata* uota precatu. / nil metuam *cupiam*que nihil; satis hoc rear esse, / quod satis est. nil turpe uelim nec *causa pudoris* / *sim mihi*. ... (62–4) nec *uero crimine laedar* / nec maculer dubio; paulum distare uidetur / *suspectus uere*que *reus*. ... (66) sim carus amicis ... (68–70) non animo doleam, non corpore; cuncta *quietis* / fungantur membra officiis; nec *saucius ullis* / *partibus amissum quicquam desideret usus*. ... (72–3) suprema diei cum uenerit hora, nec timeat mortem *bene conscia* uita nec optet. ... (79–80) haec pia, sed maesto *trepidantia uota* reatu, / nate, apud aeternum placabilis *assere* patrem.'
[7] There is a parallel in Chalcidius for this phrase (*In Plat. Tim.* 265, ed. Waszink p. 243: but there of the mind of God). *moribus* (read by Canal; cf. GR 388. 6) is less appropriate.
[8] I.e. body and soul. The Latin as transmitted is ill-expressed.

life shared with others; may I have friends who are loyal to me as I am to them. May no cause for offence in me ever drive them away, but let the affection between us always compete on equal terms. May I attain what is necessary and expedient. May I not strive for what is excessive.[9] May I not be straitened by poverty or enervated by abundance. 8. Lastly, may I live in such a way that at the point of death I have a clear conscience, and do not either fear to die because of my sins or seek to die because some importunate misfortune presses upon me. May I not fear death or blush for my life. This gift from God should not be cut short without an order, but one must not skulk when He does give the order.[10] These pious offerings, these good prayers, though they are timid because I know I have sinned, Lady, kind Lady, bring to your Son, and defend them to our Judge. And so that my prayers may have validity and weight, deck me out with your virtues, granting me the ...[11] of your dignity which antiquity has hallowed and the truth of things commends.

9. Mary, temple of the Holy Spirit, shade me from the seething heat of vice.[12] Mary, perpetual virgin, cleanse me from the stain and corruption of sin. Mary, Mother of Mercy, lead me out of the mire of dregs and the pit of misery.[13] Mary, star of the sea,[14] direct and convey me to the port of salvation. Mary, mother of God, make fruitful the mind of your servant so that it is fertile in virtues. Mary, ladder of God, make me ascend from virtue to virtue,[15] so that as by degrees I grow towards the good I may deserve to come to the highest peak of perfection. Mary, doorkeeper or rather door[16] of the sky, let me in to the joys of paradise. Mary, queen of the angels, make me lie hidden at least in the furthest corner of the kingdom of heaven, so that I may see the God of gods in Sion.[17]

[9] Cf. *GR* 8. 3: 'uitio quodam humani ingenii ut quo plus habeas plus *ambias*'.

[10] Similar is Cicero, *Tusc.* 1. 74: 'uetat enim ... deus iniussu hinc nos suo demigrare; cum uero causam iustam deus ipse dederit, ... uir sapiens laetus ex his tenebris in lucem illam excesserit'.

[11] *recognomina* is not an attested word.

[12] Cf. *Comm. Lam.* IV, 807: 'dum eam [Mary!] ab omni estu uitiorum protectionis suae defendit umbraculo.'

[13] Ps. 39: 3.

[14] Cf. e.g. Isidore, *Etym.* 7. 10. 1: 'Maria inluminatrix, siue stella maris,' Fulbert, *Serm.* 'Approbatae consuetudinis', ed. Canal, pp. 58–9 ll. 77–88 (*PL* 141. 322A-B): 'interpretatur enim maris stella. ... oportet uniuersos Christicolas, inter fluctus huius saeculi remigantes, attendere maris stellam hanc ... Quod qui fecerit non iactabitur uanae gloriae uento ... sed prospere ueniet ad portum quietis aeternae.'

[15] Cf. Ps. 83: 8.

[16] Cf. *Comm. Lam.* I, 2791–2: 'sicut enim ipse in euangelio [John 10: 7 and 9] se uult intelligi hostium, se hostiarium'.

[17] Cf. Ps. 83: 8.

Appendix A

Contents of Marian *miracula* collections known to William

(For those stories actually used by him, *MBVM* numbers are given in brackets.)

HM/TS (see above, p. xvii and n. 16)

HM

1. Ildefonsus (3)
2. Drowned Sacristan (16)
3. Clerk of Chartres (25)
4. Five *Gaudes* (26)
5. Charitable Almsman (36)
6. Ebbo the Thief (37)
7. Monk of Cologne (17)
8. Pilgrim of St James (20)
9. Priest of one Mass (29)
10. Two brothers at Rome (31)
11. Rustic who removed landmarks
12. Prior of St Saviour's (22)
13. Jerome of Pavia (11)
14. Stained Corporal (21)
15. Fire at Mont St Michel (49)
16. Clerk of Pisa (27)
17. Woman cured of an Evil Spirit (47)
     (Jewish Boy) (33)[1]

---

[1] The status of this story is unclear. Southern seems to consider it part of HM but does not give it a number. It is found in most but not all of the MSS containing HM or substantial parts thereof. And yet it is the only HM story which also appears in Dominic, suggesting that he found it circulating separately. His version is much longer, and at first sight it might seem that the HM version was a summary of his. Against that, what appears in Dominic but not in HM is purely rhetorical expansion; and both he and the HM text say that the story was originally told by Peter, monk of St Michael's Chiusa, suggesting a connection with Anselm of Bury.

TS
1. Toledo (4)
2. Foot cut off (48)
3. Musa (41)
4. Sicut iterum/Mater misericordiae
5. Libia
6. Gethsemane
7. Virgin's image insulted (51. 1)
8. Drunken sexton
9. Devil in three Beast-Shapes (15)
10. Compline (?19. 2)
11. Milk: Monk laid out as dead (10)
12. Three Knights (39)
13. Eulalia
14. Mead (45)
15. Elsinus/Abbot Ælfsige (13)
16. Saturday (51. 2)
17. Leofric

Dominic of Evesham (formerly '"Elements" series') (see above, p. xvii)
1. Jewish boy (33)
2. Theophilus (1)
3. Childbirth in the Sea (44)
4. Julian the Apostate (2)
5. Chartres saved by the Virgin's Shift (8)
6. St Odo and the Thief-Monk (19)
7. Nativity (not actually a miracle)
8. Hours (not actually a miracle)
9. Compline (not actually a miracle)
10. Drunken clerk
11. Mary of Egypt (40)
12. Abbess delivered (42)
13. Monks of Jumièges and Evesham

MB (see above, p. xviii)
1. Milk: Monk laid out as dead (10)
2. Sudden Death (24)
3. Nun's Penance incomplete (43)
4. Wife and Mistress (46)
5. Love gained by Black Arts (28)
6. St Bonitus and his Vestment (6)

Appendix B

Handlist of Manuscripts Containing
Miracles of the Virgin in Latin[1]

Aberdeen, University Libr. 137 (Dominic)

Cambridge
    University Libr. Mm. 6. 15
    Corpus Christi Coll.
        42 (HM-TS)
        316 (*Dicta Anselmi*)
        457 (*Dicta Anselmi*)
    Gonville & Caius Coll.
        91/173 (Jewish Boy)
        223/238 (Theophilus)
        384/604 (Elsinus)
    Peterhouse 131 (Elsinus)
    Sidney Sussex Coll.
        47 (a single miracle)
        85 (29 stories)
        95 (500 stories)
    Trinity Coll. 255 (Wm., Prol.)

---

[1] Readers of this list should be aware of its limitations. We have not viewed at first hand or even through reproductions many of these MSS, even within the UK. Consequently a good many of the collections in them are as yet unidentified. Those in England, France and America are listed by Carter, pp. 624–6; those in Italy in the very thorough studies of M. V. Gripkey, in *Mediaeval Studies* 14 (1952) and 15 (1953); for those in Germany the basis is Mussafia; for those in America S. De Ricci and W. J. Wilson, *Census of Medieval and Renaissance Manuscripts in the United States and Canada* (3 vols, New York, 1935–40). Some of Mussafia's MSS now have different shelfmarks; we hope that we have caught most if not all of these. Many of the MSS listed by De Ricci have since changed hands; RMT is grateful to Professor Lisa Fagin Davis and Librarians at Cornell, Duke and Princeton Universities, and St Bonaventure College, NY, for helping trace them.

Dublin, Trinity Coll.
    167 (Dominic)
    277
    667

Durham Cath.
    B. IV. 19
    B. IV. 30, ff. 24–9v

Exeter Cath.
    3504 (1) (Wm., Prol.)
    3505 (Wm., Prol.)

Hereford Cath. P. I. XIII

Ipswich, Public Libr. 4

Lincoln Cath. 35 (extrs. from Vincent of Beauvais)

London
    British Library
        Add. 10050 (1 mir.)
        Add. 11284
        Add. 11579
        Add. 15723
        Add. 16589
        Add. 18344
        Add. 18346
        Add. 18364
        Add. 18365 (1 mir.)
        Add. 18929
        Add. 19909 (Herolt)
        Add. 27336
        Add. 27909
        Add. 32248
        Add. 33956
        Add. 35112
        Add. 38101
        Add. 39996
        Add. 57533 (formerly owned by F. Wormald)
        Arundel 23
        Arundel 346 (HM-TS)

Arundel 406
Arundel 407
Arundel 506
Cotton Nero E. I (1 mir.)
Cotton Tiberius E. VII
Cotton Vesp. D. II
Cotton Vesp. D. XIX (Nigel Whitacre)
Cotton Cleo. C. X (see pp. xviii and xlviii n. 91)
Egerton 1117
Egerton 2947 (HM-TS)
Harl. 268 (excerpts from Vincent of Beauvais)
Harl. 1288
Harl. 2316
Harl. 2385
Harl. 3020 (1 mir.)
Harl. 4719 (1 mir.)
Royal 5 A. VIII (28 mir.)
Royal 6 B. X
Royal 6 B. XIV (28 mir.)
Royal 8 C. IV (John of Garland)
Royal 8 C. XII
Royal 8 F. II (Wm., prol., extracted)
Royal 8 F. VI
Royal 12 E. I
Lambeth Palace Libr.
51 (Peter of Cornwall)
214 (HM-TS)

Maidstone Museum, All Saints A. 13

Manchester, John Rylands Libr. lat. 365

Mirfield, Community of the Resurrection, 2 = York Minster Libr., Add. 300

Newcastle, University Libr. 8, ff. 373v–376v

Oxford
Bodleian Library
Bodley 386 (2 mir.)
Canonici liturg. 226
Canonici liturg. 325 (HM-TS)
Digby 39, ff. 93–9

e Mus. 62 (*Spiris locus est famosus*)
Hatton 26 (Jerome bp. of Pavia)
Laud. lat. 18
Laud. misc. 171
Laud. misc. 359
Laud. misc. 410 (HM-TS)
Laud. misc. 471
All Souls Coll. 22 (89 mir.)
Balliol Coll. 240
Corpus Christi Coll. 42 (115 mir.)

Salisbury Cath.
56
97 (Wm.)

Ushaw, St Cuthbert's College 33

FRANCE AND LOW COUNTRIES

Amiens, Bibl. mun., L'Escalopier 7

Bruges, Bibl. publ. 546 (John of Garland)

Brussels, Bibl. Royale
Phillipps 336
1927–444 (Wm., Prol.)
5519–26
7797–806

Cambrai, Bibl. mun. 739

Charleville, Bibl. de la ville
79
106 (1 mir.; Theoph.)
168

Chartres, Bibl. mun.
178
341
1027

Ghent, Universiteitsbibl. 245 (HM-TS)

Laon, Bibl. mun. 177 (2 mir.)

Lyon, Bibl. mun. 622 (Wm., Prol.)

Marseille, Bibl. mun. 230 (Wm., Prol.)

Metz, Bibl. mun. 612

Montpellier, Bibl. de la Faculté de médicine 146 (HM-TS)

Nîmes, Bibl. mun. 51 (13747)

Paris
    BnF
        lat. 673 (Guibert of Nogent, c. 11)
        lat. 1864 (1 mir.)
        lat. 2333A
        lat. 2445A
        lat. 2628 (1 mir.)
        lat. 2672
        lat. 2769 (Wm.)
        lat. 2873
        lat. 3175
        lat. 3177
        lat. 3338
        lat. 3632
        lat. 5267
        lat. 5268
        lat. 5562
        lat. 5664
        lat. 5665
        lat. 6560
        lat. 10051
        lat. 10522
        lat. 10770
        lat. 11104
        lat. 11750
        lat. 11759
        lat. 12169
        lat. 12593
        lat. 12606
        lat. 13336
        lat. 14363
        lat. 14463
        lat. 14857

lat. 15163
lat. 16056
lat. 16498 (HM-TS)
lat. 16565
lat. 17491
lat. 18134
lat. 18168 (HM-TS)
lat. 18201
lat. 18314
nouv. acq. lat. 357
nouv. acq. lat. 369
nouv. acq. lat. 1154
nouv. acq. lat. 2199
nouv. acq. lat. 2335
Bibl. de l'Arsenal 903

Rouen, Bibl. mun.
A. 535 (1569)
U. 123 (1467)
U. 134 (1403)

St Omer, Bibl. mun. 238

Toulouse, Bibl. de la ville
478
482 (Dominic)
874 (fragm.)

GERMANY, AUSTRIA, SWITZERLAND AND SCANDINAVIA

Admont, Stiftsbibl.
249
638

Bern, Burgerbibl. 137 (HM-TS)

Copenhagen, Kongelige Bibl.
Thott 26 (HM-TS)
Thott 128

Darmstadt, Hessische Landes- u. Hochschulbibl.
> 703
> 2664
> 2777

Einsiedeln, Stiftsbibl.
> 228
> 260

Erfurt, Stadtbibl. Amplon. Q. 44 (Volpert)

Göttweig, Stiftsbibl.
> 83
> 176
> 204

Graz, Universitätsbibl.
> shelfmark unknown (Volpert)
> 1432 (1 mir.)

Heiligenkreuz, Stiftsbibl. 11

Kremsmünster, Stiftsbibl.
> 47
> 114 (5 mir.)

Leipzig, Universitätsbibl.
> 819
> 821

Melk, Stiftsbibl. 280 (E. 81)

Munich, Bayerische Staatsbibl.
> clm 2586
> clm 2617
> clm 2651
> clm 4146 (Volpert)
> clm 4350 (Volpert)
> clm 4620
> clm 13588
> clm 18659
> clm 27330

Reun, Stiftsbibl.
    16
    35

Salzburg, St Peter, Stiftsbibl. a V. 3

Vienna, Österreichische Nationalbibl.
    625 Ad omnipotentis Dei laudem cum sepe recitentur
    3714 (Potho of Prüfening)
    13538 Primo fuit multifariam prefigurata

ITALY

Florence, Bibl. Nazionale Centrale, Conv. Soppr. D. III. 747

Milan, Bibl. Ambros.
    C. 150 inf.
    D. 46 sup., ff. 119v–126v

Vatican City, Bibl. Apostol. Vat.
    Vat. lat. 4318
    Reg. lat. 537
    Reg. lat. 543 (HM-TS)

SPAIN AND PORTUGAL

Madrid, Biblioteca nac. Bb 150

USA

Chicago, IL, University Libr. 147 (HM-TS)

Durham, NC, Duke University Libr., lat. 51

Ithaca, NY, Cornell University Libr. B. 14

Princeton, NJ, University Library 51 (Potho of Prüfening)

Untraced. J. Rosenthal, sale cat. no. 83 1926, lot 75; B. Rosenthal, sale cat. no. 1 1954, lot 68. These were the same book.

Untraced. Formerly Washington, Holy Name College 15, it should have been transferred in the 1970s, along with the rest of the College's MSS and early printed books, to St Bonaventure College, NY. However, it was stolen shortly before the transfer took place and its present whereabouts are unknown.

Index of Sources

This index combines references to a) the sources on which William drew (including some of his own works), or may have drawn, for his information with b) parallels of phraseology in texts he had read.

ALEXANDER OF CANTERBURY
  Dicta Anselmi 88
AMBROSE
  De offic. 2. 25 4
  De virginibus 2. 2 5
  De virginitate 9. 51 6
  Epist. extra coll. 14. 33 8
?AMBROSE
  Epigr. 2165 74
PS.-AMPHILOCHIUS
  Vita Basilii 21
ANSELM
  Cur Deus homo 6
  Orat. 7 ad Mariam 10
  Proslogion 6
ANTIPHONS 75, 117
AUGUSTINE
  Confess. 1. 18. 28 118
  De doctr. Christ. 4. 129 5
  Enarr. în Ps*almos* 46. 10 12
  Serm. 200 12
PS.-AUGUSTINE
  De assumptione Mariae 10
AUSONIUS
  Carm. 16. 58 52
  Ephemeris 3. 37–8 etc. 133

B.
  Vita Dunstani 33, 34, 121
BEDE
  HE 1. 33 33
BESTIARY 82

BIBLE
  Exod. 20: 12 47
  Levit. 12 1
  Num. 22: 28–30 95
  Deut. 7: 14 2
  Ios. 6: 17 18
  Iud. 16: 4–31 60
  II Reg. 11–12 19
  III Reg. 13: 21–7 68
  II Chron. 36: 10 86
  Iob 1: 6–12 58
  Ps.
    7: 10 6
    14: 1–2 57
    18: 6 11
    33: 9 12
    39. 3 45, 134
    44: 8 5
    50 19
    50: 13 19
    50: 19 83
    83: 8 134
    102: 5 82
    113: 3 6
    118 91
    119: 5 12
    143: 2 71
    145: 8 67
  Prov. 12: 23 12
  Eccles. 7: 16–17 115
  Cant.
    2: 1 6
    7: 9 75

General Index

CPSIA information can be obtained
at www.ICGtesting.com
Printed in the USA
BVOW06s2100030417

480211BV00002B/7/P